McCARTHY'S BAR

McCARTHY'S BAR

A Journey of Discovery in Ireland

Pete McCarthy

THOMAS DUNNE BOOKS
ST. MARTIN'S GRIFFIN ⋈ NEW YORK

THOMAS DUNNE BOOKS.
An imprint of St. Martin's Press.

www.stmartins.com

ISBN 0-312-27210-3 (hc)
ISBN 0-312-31133-8 (pbk)

First published in Great Britain by Hodder and Stoughton,
a division of Hodder Headline

20 19 18 17 16 15 14 13

To Irene, Alice, Isabella and Coral
and to Margaret and Ken,
for taking me there

Contents

McCarthy's Bar

Prologue

The harp player had just fallen off the stage and cracked his head on an Italian tourist's pint. There was a big cheer, and Con the barman rang a bell on the counter.

St Patrick's Day, and McCarthy's Bar was heaving.

The Eighth Rule of Travel states: *Never Pass a Bar That Has Your Name On It.* Other rules include: No. 7, *Never Eat in a Restaurant with Laminated Menus*; No. 13, *Never Ask a British Airways Stewardess for Another Glass of Wine Until She's Good and Ready*; and No. 17, *Never Try and Score Dope From Hassidic Jews While Under the Impression They're Rastafarians*, as someone I know once did on a Sunday afternoon in Central Park.

There's an excellent P. McCarthy's at the top of the main street in Westport, County Mayo, where they once made seventeen cheese-and-onion toasties for five of us, all on the same toaster, and never grumbled. I also like Pete's Pub in Boston, Massachusetts, full of second-generation Irish postal workers still arguing about JFK and Nixon; or at least they were the day I spent the afternoon there and the barman gave me his shirt – a very selfless gesture, I thought, especially for such a fat bloke.

But I'd chosen this McCarthy's to spend St Patrick's Day in, even though it was just a plain surname, with no P in front of it. I'd invested £149 in a three-day, two-night St Patrick's Day package from London Gatwick to be here, tempted back by hazy memories of my first visit, when I really had just spotted the sign, obeyed the rule, and walked in off the street.

Turned out Con the barman was from Skibbereen, just eight

miles from where my mother grew up. There was a comprehensive collection of Irish matchboxes from the 1930s and 1940s, and one of Roy Keane's Manchester United shirts in a glass case behind the bar. The grainy old wood and dusty stained glass were full of character, and that was just the harp player's spectacles.

I'd been lured here this time by the dread of spending another St Patrick's night in the Home Counties of England. Each 17 March brings to a head the inability of the English middle classes to deal with the Irish Problem, in the sense that Ireland is a problem because it exists. This is when the radio phone-ins, and the letter columns of local newspapers, are taken over by the Knights of St George, the League of Anti-European Loyalists, and other assorted flag-fetishists and embittered headcases.

The gist of their bile is that, despite a glorious empire, two World Wars, the Falklands, Margaret Thatcher and a Queen Mother who has retained an impressive capacity for gin and Dubonnet well into her nineties, the English refuse to celebrate St George's Day. No one knows when it is; and in any case, St George is also claimed as celestial patron by Alsace. So it's just not fair that we let all these paddies make such a fuss for the Irish saint, who was Welsh anyway; and while we're at it, how come we let Irish people who live over here vote, instead of locking them up? After all, it's not as if the Irish are just Catholic. They're Catholic *and* pagan, and that's just not on.

So some time in February – the worst of all months in England, when the desire to hibernate or flee is almost uncontrollable, and feelings of deepest malice towards Australians and their weather well up whenever the cricket highlights appear on the telly – the thought struck me. Why not get away this year for Paddy's Day? Why spend a feast-day – one that carries echoes of my earliest childhood memories – in an English pub, drinking overpriced Guinness and listening to Van Morrison's *Greatest Hits*, when for just £149, according to the weekend papers, I could do exactly the same thing in an Irish pub, only in more convivial company?

I briefly considered New York, with its green beer and good-natured, ruddy-cheeked, homophobic Irish policemen; or Dublin, with its rich literary heritage, and its scores of English stag parties throwing up on the streets of Temple Bar. But, deep down, I knew it had to be McCarthy's. After all, it had my name on it.

Well, it was a fine evening. At one point the harp player fell off again, only backwards. And what a cosmopolitan crowd we were. As well as the Irish and the English, there were Americans, Italians, French and Scots, some sinister, well-heeled Russians, and even a couple of Hungarians – all agreeing loudly in half a dozen languages that the craic was indeed mighty.

It must have been some time after eleven when I realised that, in a profound and very real way, Con the barman was my best friend, and quite probably a close relative. It was important he should know what I really felt. So I told him I didn't feel English.

'You sound English to me, sorr.'

'But it's what you feel inside that counts, Con. In here! And I . . .'

I knew it was important somehow to convey that this wasn't the drink talking; that I meant it, and what's more, I'd still mean it the next day. So I grabbed him and shouted.

'I . . . inside I feel Irish. I know where I belong!'

To emphasise my sincerity, I knocked a drink over.

'Ah, that's great, sorr. Good luck to ye now.'

Outside, I stood under the green neon shamrock and looked up at the sign. 'McCarthy's,' it said. 'Hungary's Top Irish Pub.'

I turned up my collar. Budapest can still be quite chilly in March.

Sod this, I thought. Next year I'll go to Ireland.

Chapter One

The Whiff

A year later, and I'm on the plane to Cork.

In a cold sweat.

The man across the aisle from me has a menacing aura, and a dog-collar. He may be a priest, but something about him – the way he seems to threaten violence even while asleep, perhaps – makes me suspect him of being a Christian Brother.

From the age of ten, I was taught by the Christian Brothers: the carrot and stick method of education, but without the carrot. My first school report said: 'Peter is an unpleasant and frivolous boy who talks too much and will never make anything of himself, but he does take a punch well.'

At primary school, before the Brothers, it had been the Sisters: six impressionable years trying to work out whether nuns had hair. Curiously, both the convent primary schools I attended have now been turned into pubs. And the Christian Brothers, for their part, have a make of brandy named after them. God moves in mysterious ways, especially after a few drinks.

From an early age it was taken for granted that Jesus was Catholic, God himself was Irish, and I had been born into a wicked, pagan country. On St Patrick's Day you could spot all the kids from Irish families wearing huge bunches of shamrock on their blazers, in a proud display of religious and cultural heritage that also made fights much easier to start. Though my dad was English, half-Irish counted as Irish when the insults were flying.

We lived in the industrial north-west, in Warrington, where the air tasted of detergent from the soap-powder factory, so at least you knew it was clean. The rugby league team was called the Wire, after the town's main product. The Brothers' school was eight miles away, in St Helens; a town so devastated by heavy industry it made Warrington look like an area of outstanding natural beauty.

I went abroad for the first time when I was twelve.

We'd been going to Ireland every year since I'd been born, but Ireland didn't count as abroad. It was much nearer than London, or Bristol or Newcastle or Edinburgh for that matter, and was regarded simply as an extension of home. But in my second year at the Brothers' school we went on a school trip to proper abroad. To our twin town.

To Stuttgart.

I've never really approved of the idea of twinning, because places are invariably matched with other places just like them. So if you live in, say, a stunningly beautiful medieval town with a perfectly preserved castle, or a glamorous seaside resort with a fishing harbour and miles of sandy beach, then you'll be twinned with your exquisite European equivalent. And if you live in Warrington, or St Helens, then you'll be twinned with another industrial casualty.

Like Stuttgart.

So having spent the first dozen years of my life surrounded by wireworks, glass factories and chemical plants, I found myself transported to a place where the high spot of the visit was a trip to a ball-bearing factory. To make matters worse, I contracted hepatitis. I lost a stone in a week and turned yellow, which is quite interesting when you've twelve. So the doctor arrived – a rather severe-looking elderly German gentleman in wire-framed glasses: not the most reassuring sight in the world when you've spent the last term doing a project on Josef Mengele, the Angel of Death.

I'd led a sheltered life till this point, and so far was unaware of the existence of suppositories. The news came as a terrible shock. The doctor explained in schoolboy German what had to be done; when my custard-coloured eyes glazed over in disbelief, he mimed it, but it was still difficult to comprehend.

Surely not? Not with those big tablets? After all, if my parents had wanted me to have foreign objects pushed up my bottom, they could have sent me to public school.

Finally, though, the message got through. The course of medication lasted a week. The first couple of days were the worst. After that, the doctor came back and mimed taking the tinfoil wrapper off, and things got much easier.

It didn't half put me off going abroad, though.

So for the next five years – until I was seventeen, when I went to Stuttgart again, out of force of habit – I gave up on abroad, and stuck with Ireland. West Cork, to be precise. Today, it's a glamorous destination, a haven for upmarket tourists, English expats, and Dutch cannabis importers, but in the 1950s and 1960s it was the arse end of the back of beyond, and that may be talking it up.

We stayed at Butlersgift, the small farm where my mother grew up. One of my earliest childhood memories is of standing near an open gate by a muddy boreen when an enormous sow came through it, grunting and snuffling, the terrifying ring through her nose glinting in the sunlight as she looked down on me. I burst into tears, and ran back towards the farmhouse, screaming for help. The sow trundled along behind, as far as I was concerned, in pursuit, but probably just joining in the fun.

Twenty or thirty yards away my grandfather stood by the back door of the house, roaring with laughter as I approached. I could only have been two or three at the time, because he died when I was four.

I went over with my mum for the funeral. Dad had to stay in England and make wire. After much umming and ahhing between my uncles on the upstairs landing, I was taken in to view the body. To this day the family all deny it happened; but I remember him, laid out in a brown suit and a gold sash, as clearly as I remember not being allowed to go to the funeral itself. I spent that afternoon at an auntie's house near a remote bog, by a lake. I remember hearing the sound of my mother's footsteps on the gravel outside when she returned. Although in your memories your parents are always more or less the same age, I have a vivid picture of her being younger then – younger than I am now – and I know she was attentive to me, though she'd just buried her father.

During the summer holidays we made hay with pitchforks, drew water from the well with an enamel bucket, and went to market by horse and cart. Work stopped in the fields for the angelus. Mass was in Latin. We searched fuchsia hedgerows for leprechauns, with a net and a jar. And although it's statistically impossible in a country as moist as Ireland, I'm certain that the sun always shone.

But these golden childhood memories have become a problem; for now, when I return to Ireland, I feel that I belong, in a way that I have never belonged in the land of my birth. Even though I loved growing up in the north, England leaves me feeling detached: an outsider, an observer, in some way passing through. But as soon as I hit the tarmac or the quayside over there, I feel involved, engaged – as if I've come home, even though I've never actually lived there.

So what I'm wondering is this. Is it possible to have some kind of genetic memory of a place where you've never lived, but your ancestors have? Or am I just a sentimental fool, my judgement fuddled by nostalgia, Guinness, and the romance of the diaspora?

Across the aisle, the Christian Brother is still asleep. I'd wake him and ask him his opinion, if experience hadn't taught me that the clergy can be lethal if riled in a confined space.

I'd briefly considered spending the holiday in Dublin, but I find I like it less since the ruthless redevelopment and marketing of Temple Bar.

Continental café culture has arrived, a forced planting of non-indigenous chrome counters, almond-flavoured latte, and seared yellowfin tuna in balsamic lemongrass and rhubarb jus. Japanese-besuited media ponces sit in windows sipping bottles of over-priced cooking lager, imported from Mexico, and other top brewing spots, to the banks of the Liffey. Plain, unadorned, authentic pubs, previously unchanged for decades, now reek of new wood and paint, as they're gutted and refurbished to conform to the notion of Irishness demanded by the stag nights from Northampton and conference delegates from Frankfurt who fill the streets, interchangeable in their smug fat smiles and Manchester United replica shirts.

Last time I was in Dublin I met a German who actually believed that 'Manchester United' was a place in Ireland. Mind you, in Germany once, in the military garrison town of Erlangen, I had a few drinks with three American GIs who were planning to visit England 'because it would be neat to see where John Lennon and Elvis grew up'. They also wanted to know if they could use dollars, and would the street signs be in English? I tried to tell them about Elvis coming from Tennessee, but it seemed to make them want to kill me. The Twenty-eighth Rule states: *Never Get Drunk with Soldiers* (particularly in countries where the streets are named after dates).

What finally decided me against Dublin was reading that they were bringing some expert over from the States to dye the Liffey green. And anyway, Cork seemed the natural choice. Though it's Ireland's second city, a population of 180,000 compared to Dublin's one million, it's still just a small town; and only forty-five miles to the west is Butlersgift, where my mother grew up, my grandfather died, and my cousin still farms.

As we cross the tarmac at Cork airport and head for the terminal, we are greeted by someone dressed as St Patrick. He has a sidekick who is wearing, and I promise I'm not making this up, a rubber Celtic cross costume. They are lampooning the priests and the religion that held total sway in this country from the seventh century till, oh, about a week last Wednesday. Midgets in leprechaun costumes are running amok in the baggage hall, but luckily I've only brought hand luggage.

I've come for the big parade tonight, but my gracious, silver-haired taxi driver tells me it started at two o'clock, about an hour ago. Never mind. I ask him to take me to the Ambassador's Hotel, if he knows it.

'Ah, yes. Used to be the Hospital for Incurable Diseases. I'm told it's very nice inside. Now, see this now. That no right turn sign. Well, they're very strict on that sorta thing these days.'

Then he asks me to watch out left, because this junction's a bastard, and, like the three cars in front of us, we turn right.

'Very strict, they are.'

We turn into a street with a sign saying: 'This Way To Hospice'. The first building you see is the morgue, which must be a great comfort to people on their way to the hospice. Once inside my comfortably appointed Room with Trouser Press in the former Hospital for Incurable Diseases, there's just time to calculate how many people must have died in here during the hospital's eighty-year lifetime – about 4,000, I reckon – before hitting the streets. As I pass through the lobby I notice, almost subliminally, that lots of overdressed families are sitting round eating salmon, while a priest plays the piano. I pretend this is normal, and smile.

Outside, people are streaming back up the hill from the direction of Patrick's Bridge, carrying tricolour flags and balloons. It only takes me five or ten minutes to twig that the parade's already over. There are lots of cheeky kids with freckles and rosy cheeks, watery eyes and a slightly pinched look, as if they've been standing in a cold breeze. Despite the much-vaunted Celtic Tiger economy, these people dress and look poorer than people where I live.

In the space of 100 yards I pass two newsagents, three antique shops, four restaurants, and more pubs than all of them put together. In the absence of a parade, there's nothing else for it but to observe the First Rule of Travel: *On Arrival, Buy a Local Paper and Go for a Drink.* The court cases, property prices and obituaries will tell you more than any guidebook, and the drink will help you feel you understand things that in reality are beyond your comprehension. The Greyhound, on the north side of Patrick's Bridge, will do for starters. I need to ease myself gently back into the seductive mêlée of Irish pub life, and it's reasonably quiet in here, despite the fact that Cheltenham Races (TV) and Van Morrison (CD) are on simultaneously.

It's quite extraordinary how often Van Morrison is playing when you walk into an Irish pub. Maybe the breweries pipe him in at the entrance, like supermarkets do with the smell of baking bread; or perhaps the government imposes some sort of Morrison Quota, which is rigidly enforced. I order a pint of Guinness and a packet of plain crisps, which in Ireland are cheese and onion flavoured, and once the Irish horse has won the Champions' Hurdle at Cheltenham, I settle down with the paper.

On the front page is a big colour photo of someone I know. All right, vaguely know. Well, at any rate, I interviewed him once. Dan Costello, proprietor of the resort on Beachcomber Island, Fiji. The picture shows him raising a pint of Guinness to the camera, while behind him two languid Fijians unload barrels from a canoe on to a brochure-quality, palm-fringed white sand beach. Dan, whose grandfather was Irish, is bringing St Patrick's Day to the South Pacific for the first time. The global hype about all things Irish shows no sign of burning out yet.

To be Irish today is to be welcome almost anywhere. Grape-pip brandy will be uncorked, daughters unveiled, tables danced upon. People will line up to show you a Portuguese edition of Seamus Heaney or a Romanian Betamax pirate video of *Riverdance*. The Irish are perceived as young, eloquent, romantic, tuneful, mystical, funny, and expert havers-of-a-good-time. And, as a bonus, in the same way that the English abroad are made doubly welcome once people realise they're not German, so the Irish are welcomed for not being English.

As well as St Patrick's Day in Fiji, the paper carries some top local stories. INVALID SPAT IN FACES OF GARDAI, goes the eye-catching headline. 'A man who was wheelchair-bound spat repeatedly in the faces of gardai when he was arrested for creating a city centre disturbance, and he threw himself out of his chair several times when he was brought to the Bridewell garda station . . . Paul O'Mahoney drank from a bottle of Lucozade as his case was brought before Cork District Court.'

Many Irish papers also now seem to have a separate section for sexual abuse cases against the Church. ALTAR BOY ON RAPE CHARGE [of other altar boy] goes this one; and TWO CHRISTIAN BROTHERS WANT DPP TO DROP CHARGES OF SEX ASSAULTS ON BOYS.

I have to say that, whatever their other faults, the Christian Brothers at our school never tried to grope us. There was a fair bit of random brutality, and the occasional show of blood, but nobody was too shocked by that. I think it was on the curriculum. They were hard men, but strangely sexless.

The lurid combination of sex, religion and alcohol is making me feel hungry.

Out on the street, two pints to the good, I look in the window of a traditional 1960s Chinese, the kind of place that people in England used to visit to abuse the staff before the Bengalis and Bangladeshis turned up and got that job. The best gauge as to whether or not a country is expensive is the price of food in its Chinese restaurants. A complex calculation based on the cost of a plate of Singapore noodles will tell you the current rate of economic growth. 'Singapore Noodles,' said the menu, just below an embalmed bluebottle, '£7.80'.

Seven pounds eighty? For a plate of noodles? England's best Chinese restaurant, just off Leicester Square in London, does them for £3.30, and they have to pay London rents, rates and the Triads. There's another one across the street: £7.20. The Thai wine bar wants £8.95 for Pad Thai. This is a countrywide phenomenon in Ireland, and frankly, I'm baffled. Last year, in Galway City, in a poky little place up a stairway above a shop, staffed by one stern Chinese matron and four freckly ginger teenagers in Suzie Wong dresses, a film crew and I were charged £9 for noodles. It's a national scandal. What's going on? Is there an import surcharge on noodles from which we in England are immune? Or a starch tax on all carbohydrates that aren't potatoes?

On a wall up the street a chalked sign outside a pub called An Siol Broin says: 'Traditional Session – 2.30–?'. Fine. A couple more pints, then a Chinese takeaway. Given its price, perhaps I should book Securicor to deliver it to the Hospital for Incurable Diseases.

It's a small, one-room, nicotine-stained place, the bar itself on the wall to the left as you go in. It's packed. Music's playing at a table across to the right. There are kids weaving between the tables, to the sound of authentic-sounding diddly-di.

But the thing that hits you smack between the nostrils as you walk in is the fusty, fungal smell. I've breathed fresher air in a beer tent full of damp dogs at the Glastonbury festival. This is the strong whiff that goes with the tougher end of the hippie spectrum, the ones who regard incense and patchouli and essential oils as hopelessly effete. For years I thought that the earthy odour that emanated from them in tepees and at festivals and street markets was some sort of, well, earthy odour that was applied from a bottle or jar because they find it attractive. Though I have no conclusive proof, the balance of probabilities now suggests it indicates an aversion to showering.

At the heart of the whiff, five musicians on fiddles and guitars are playing a low-octane traditional tune, half-heartedly accompanied by two spaced-out fellow travellers on bodhrans, which is a hard word to spell, especially in smoke this thick.

You often get a diversity of social types, and sexes, at a traditional Irish session. Young players will watch and learn from their elders; but this group seems strangely uniform. The musicians are all men, for a start – thirty-something, dread-locked, bearded with varying degrees of success. At either end of the table, on the fringes of the men, sits a tribe of hennaed, multiply pierced, tattooed women with children in psychedelic face paints teetering on their laps. Other children play between legs and furniture, as is only right and appropriate in an Irish pub. The women are wearing loose-fitting Indian prints, and things with soil on, while the men are in matted jumpers and dead men's waistcoats. One guy has had his beard braided. Everyone, of both sexes, is wearing chunky high-laced industrial boots.

And always, the whiff. Not the BO that surges down the

airline cabin at you when British businessmen take their suit jackets off; not offensive, like that. But distinctive, certainly; as if unusual mushrooms were growing in rich compost in hidden crevices about their persons. It's enhanced by the Samson roll-ups everyone is smoking. Drinks are high octane – Scrumpy Jack, Diamond White, Pils: welcome to the Oblivion Express.

And then, as I listen, I start to catch the accents: Manchester; West Country; south London; Manchester again; West Midlands. Christ, what's going on? They're all *English*.

The women all have pierced noses, but there is only one with dreadlocks. She has a non-English accent that I can't quite identify through the music and the whiff. Maybe she's Irish. Dublin, perhaps; or maybe Belfast? She's in leggings, like the pregnant twenty-year-old in the tie-dyed vest next to her. Leggings. Bloody hell. Imagined by fatties everywhere to create a slimming effect, they make the average body look like a sackful of hammers. The music stops for a moment, and I catch her accent. She's Dutch. Probably brings an old school bus full of Samson over on the ferry every time she goes home.

I notice how kind she and her friend are being to the children, who are having a great time. But I find myself wondering if, in their way, these kids are growing up with just as blinkered a view of reality as we did; and also, whether it isn't a tad dark and smoky in here for them? I have to remind myself that I'm an inveterate, possibly prosecutable, taker of kids into pubs. Suitably chastened, I head for the bar.

Because of the time and care lavished on the pouring of a pint of stout, the trick in Ireland is to order your next one five minutes before the previous one is at an end. That way there'll be no uncomfortable drinking hiatus; but it takes a day or two to become reacclimatised to this. While I wait for the half-poured pint to settle, I get talking to the guy next to me. Mancunian hard knock; two ear studs; powder-blue eyes; feathered hair longer at the back than on top, in the manner of rural New Zealand, or vintage Rod Stewart. A mullet, I believe it's called, which seems hard on the fish.

He tells me he's an ex-roadie for Manchester bands, and asks me do I know the roadies' mantra? No, I don't.

If it's wet, drink it; if it's dry, smoke it;
if it moves, screw it; if it don't move,
sling it in the back of the van.

He's gone before I can ask him how they come to be here. Were they hounded out by Thatcher? By police, after one of the Stonehenge set-tos? Are they just music fanatics? Inheritors of the bucolic English Wordsworthian rural tradition?

Or is it just easier to get the dole over here, as Bridie, the Irish mother of a friend of mine, insists, from her position somewhere to the right of those nuns who keep putting crosses up outside Auschwitz? 'Peter, the lanes behind Dunmanway are full of them! Dirty, filthy creatures, living like tinkers, growing drugs! Sure, the country's being ruined by the English, going over there to collect the dole and get drunk! They should stay in their own country.'

She tugged her beard aggressively, clearly unaware that this was what the English had been saying about her and the rest of the immigrant Irish for the last fifty years. She is an unreconstructed Vatican literalist, with a pinched little mouth like a cat's arsehole, who considers every post-De Valera Irish politician to be a pagan reformer more deserving of hellfire than Boy George, but I can't help liking her.

A few years ago, I'd had cause to visit the lanes at the back of Dunmanway, in West Cork. I was taking gifts from friends of mine in Brighton to their mate Dominic, who had turned Crusty and gone to live in an old gypsy caravan by the side of the road in the middle of nowhere, with a baby son called Merry. We drank poteen from a Tizer bottle hidden in the ditch. I've got some photos, but I haven't shown them to Bridie. I'll wait for the right moment; like when she's pinned to the ground by a heavy object and the emergency services haven't arrived yet.

I drain my pint, and think I might try and spend some time

with the hairy men, and women, of Dunmanway in a few days' time, when I'll be over that way. Perhaps they'll be able to shed some light on why the English Crusties have moved into Ireland in such a big way. Is it cultural homage to the Irish way of life? Or Cromwell's last revenge?

I take one last look round before I go. Perhaps this is what it's like now. Perhaps middle-aged baldie men in tweed jackets don't play traditional music any more. Ireland's modern now. Maybe I'm out of touch. I'm certainly almost out of cash. Only £15 left in my wallet. Just enough to have some prawn crackers with the noodles, if I'm lucky.

As I go through the door, a bloke from Bristol starts singing 'Kevin Barry'.

The Whiff.

It'd be a good name for a band.

Chapter Two

Standing Stones,
Michael Collins, and the
Jimi Hendrix Connection

Ireland's not a cheap country.

In Dingle, County Kerry, in 1993, I was once charged 99p – at that time, more than an English pound – for a single leek. But there are some bargains still to be had. If you shop around, you can hire a car for a week and still get change from a grand. So I've hired one, a bog-standard repmobile with all the up-to-the-minute features, like a radio I can't work, and I'm heading west out of town, past the airport, towards Bandon and Clonakilty. I might visit my family in Drimoleague, but not just yet. And I'd like to spend some time with the Crusties out the back of Dunmanway, but not before I'm bored with hotel showers and clean linen. I have a vague notion of tracking down some obscure stone circles; but mostly I just want to try Ireland on for size, and see if it still fits. Sometimes it's good just to get creatively lost. A sense of purpose occasionally has its place when travelling, but for the most part it's seriously overrated.

I hitch-hiked this road once as a teenager, and got a lift from a farmer in a brand-new Jag. There are no hitchers today, though.

Come to think of it, you hardly ever see people hitching any more, especially in England. Motorway services always used to have about a dozen people queuing for rides, mostly students, or men holding a set of red trade number plates to prove they were truck drivers, and therefore more deserving of a ride than students.

But people stopped hitch-hiking sometime in the 1980s, after somebody in politics or the social services put about the malicious rumour that all hitch-hikers would be chopped up in picnic areas by serial killers. So these days young people get the coach instead; a sly piece of social engineering which prepares them for less eventful and more predictable lives, unless they get the seat next to a serial killer who doesn't own a car.

The farmer, by the way, had taken the back seat out of the Jag, and filled the space with two milk churns, some animal feed, and a small sheep. He'd dropped me in Clonakilty.

Clonakilty today is a picture-book Irish town. A few years ago all the houses and shops on the long, narrow main street were repainted in the reds, greens, yellows and blues that can be seen on the new generation of tourist postcards. These bright colours are the new vernacular in a country where once everything was grey. In Clonakilty they've had time to weather down a bit, and are now just on the vivid side of garish.

It's a delightful place, famous for its black pudding, which is available at many outlets along the street. Let's face it, it's ubiquitous. You can probably get it at the solicitor's, and the Natural Health Centre. No sign of anywhere to get Singapore noodles, though with décor like this, I'd estimate they'd have to sell for at least eight quid. I walk through the town to the West Cork Museum, where I've heard there's some Michael Collins memorabilia. The museum is in a small old schoolroom, and is resolutely shut; so I go for a half of Murphy's in De Barra instead.

De Barra is a bar famous for its traditional Irish music sessions. There are lots of pictures on the wall of the landlord being hugged by men with impressive beards and jumpers. I sit at the bar with the *Examiner*: WHY JAPAN IS GOING GA-GA OVER ALL THINGS GAELIC. ' "I think Irish music closely resembles Oriental music and so people in Japan can identify with it," says Yasui

Takashi, a member of Eiri Na Greine, a Japanese Irish band which gigs in the Shamrock Bar in Shinjuku, Tokyo, twice a month.' I'm reminded of the time I visited Lapland and stayed at the Ice Hotel, where everything – walls, bar, beds, floors, chapel – is made from ice. It melts every spring, and is rebuilt in the autumn. On the Saturday night there was a dance. Huge quantities of beer were brought in, the cans covered in reindeer skins so they wouldn't freeze. The band came on in furs and moon boots, and launched into 'Whiskey in the Jar', in Swedish. They billed themselves as 'Lapland's Top Irish Band'.

I ask the barman if there'll be music tonight.

'Ya, sure. The Noel Redding Band.'

Who?

'Noel Redding. Ya know. The fella out of the Jimi Hendrix Experience.'

That's what I thought he'd said. So what on earth is Jimi Hendrix's bass player doing playing in a pub in Clonakilty, on a Wednesday in March, thirty years after Jimi died?

Poor Jimi. A lot of people say it must be a terrible death, choking on your own vomit; though it strikes me as I watch the guy at the bar next to me eating thick vegetable soup, that it'd be a lot worse to choke on someone else's.

Out on the street I stock up with a smoked chicken sandwich and a bottle of water ('As pure as Our Lady's wimple') at a deli, and head off into the sunshine west out of Clonakilty towards Rosscarbery. West Cork is among the finest of Irish landscapes; not wild and melancholy and majestic, like Connemara and Mayo and Donegal, but undulating and welcoming, lush green fields rolling like waves down to the sea, always just a mile or two to the left off this road. Thanks to EC subsidy, the main roads are excellent and well signposted; but as soon as you turn off it's like going back in time, a maze of conflicting signposts (where there are any), and mileages with all the accuracy of a builder's estimate.

Just before the causeway that carries the road across the estuary at Rosscarbery, I spot a hard-to-spot sign leaning at a drunken angle and pointing to the right, north off the main road: 'Michael

Collins Birthplace – 2 miles'. Well, why not? A sharp U-turn that takes me first on to the grass verge, then nearside wheels down into the ditch, then up over a boulder – after all, it's what hire cars are for – and I'm off into the deserted back lanes that carry no clue that Ireland's biggest industry is now tourism.

Remarkably, I don't get lost, and after a distance that turns out, uniquely in my experience of Ireland, to be indeed two miles, I find Michael Collins's birthplace. As with all Irish historical monuments out of season, there's no one else here. The site looks out on beautiful open countryside, rising towards a nearby hill. Next door, a man is gardening outside a modern house. There are no other buildings. All is silence.

The display is simple and dignified. Go through a gate off the lane and you find the wall bases and floor of the house the Collins family built and moved into at Christmas 1900. It was burned down by the British Black and Tans under Captain A. E. Percival on 7 April 1921. There's a photo of Collins beside the burned-out remains, looking as if he means business.

I found an interview recently with Jack Ryan, a ninety-eight-year-old IRA contemporary of Collins. Percival, it seems, was hated in West Cork. He had a particular fondness for taking early morning drives through the countryside in his open-topped touring car, taking pot shots at farm workers in the fields who, he said, 'had no stake in the country'.

While fleeing from British troops after an abortive arms run, Ryan was confronted in a field, man to man, by the hated Percival.

He describes the scene: 'I always carried two guns, hidden with my arms folded, so I could have my fingers on the triggers, ready. So I pulled out both of them, but one of them didn't go off. The firing pin had broken, so I let him have it with my left-hand gun, and down he went.'

Ryan escaped, but Percival, thanks to a chain-mail vest under his tunic, was simply knocked out.

The ninety-eight-year-old ruefully concludes: 'I wanted to get that bastard so badly, and it's to my eternal regret that I didn't.'

A short way from the ruin is Collins's actual birthplace, a very basic structure which became a farm building after the family moved into the new house, when Michael was ten. Born in 1890, he was the eighth of eleven children. He went to school in Clonakilty, which must have been a bit of a hike. From the age of fifteen he spent nine years in London, working in the British Savings Bank, in stockbroking, and the civil service, before coming home and taking part in the 1916 Easter Rising, for which he was interned in Wales. He went on to lead the volunteers of the IRA, and to negotiate personally the flawed and contentious Home Rule settlement with the British in 1921. He was killed in an ambush in the Civil War in 1922, on a roadside in West Cork. A small information display tells you the bare facts, in English and Irish, before concluding: 'Let the rest remain to the historians.'

It's a tranquil spot, and long may the tour buses remain in Killarney instead of here. There's no traffic, no admission charge, no refreshments available, no headphones or guidebooks or photos of Liam Neeson in the movie; just three or four bare stone benches on which to sit and contemplate, if you wish.

I lean over the wall to chat with the simple Irish countryman next door, who turns out to be English – a Geordie, from Newcastle in the north-east. He says that, apart from a brief flurry of interest in the weeks after the film was released, few people come. He and his wife have been living here for two years. His dad came from nearby, and though he himself had grown up and spent all his life on Tyneside, he's always felt more at home here. He turns and looks at me.

'Do you know what I love about the Irish?'

I shake my head.

'The way they don't seem to be after your money. Everyone else in the world is. But the Irish just don't care. They just want to know everything about you instead. I love it.'

So there we are. Two Englishmen who want to be Irish, standing in the spring sunshine at a shrine to a republican hero. He's bought a house next to it, for God's sake. I ask him did he realise that Collins went to school in the same town where the bass player from the Jimi Hendrix Experience plays in a pub band, and he concedes that he didn't, but agrees that it certainly is a small world. I make a mental note to pop a memo through to the tourist board pointing this out. They could do a pamphlet: Michael Collins – the Hendrix Connection. ('Scuse me while I kiss the Blarney Stone.')

I bid Collins's Geordie neighbour farewell, and set off to look for a stone circle called Bohonagh, described in a scholarly tome I'm reading as 'perhaps the finest circle now standing in West Cork'. Cork is extremely rich in these ancient monuments, with more than 300 of them in the west of the county alone. However, I've been warned that relatively few of them have official public access or are marked on maps; the majority are away out of sight on some farmer's land, and may only be viewed at the landowner's discretion. I have a rough map showing Bohonagh to be somewhere just north of the Ross-carbery road, within a few miles of the Collins house; but if it is, my Geordie friend hasn't heard of it.

I head north up some lanes with grass growing up the middle of them, always a sure sign that you're going the wrong way, whatever it is you're trying to find. I soon reach a crossroads. A woman of about sixty is standing next to her near-mint-condition Austin 1100, which she has parked inconspicuously in the middle of the road. She smiles and walks across as I pull up and get out of the car.

Now, if you're going to go travelling in Ireland, it's important you know the correct way to ask somebody for directions. What you *don't* do is abruptly say, 'Excuse me! Could you tell me the way to . . . ?' This is an English technique, the subtext of which is: 'I'm interrupting you here in a fairly clumsy way in order to elicit a necessary fact, but otherwise this transaction is of no value and will give no pleasure. Go on, tell me then.'

The preferred approach in Ireland is to turn the encounter into a social occasion, on a par with what goes on when two strangers meet and get chatting at a party or wedding reception. A tangential preamble is essential; something along the lines of, 'Ah, that's a great hedge you're trimming', or 'Sure, it's a glorious day', especially if it isn't. Large quantities of personal information will then be exchanged, in the course of which the directions you are seeking may or may not emerge. Some of the best conversations you will have in Ireland may happen in this way.

I was once travelling in County Clare with a wonderful man called John Moriarty, a Christian mystic who is, by the way, convinced that I do carry the genetic memories of my Irish ancestors, and am therefore genuinely at home here. We were on the edge of the wilderness known as the Burren, looking for one of the ancient holy wells of Ireland, St Colman's Well. We had found nothing, and had been lost several times already in one morning, so this was shaping up to be a top travel experience.

On the road ahead of us, a man was walking. No buildings were visible for miles in any direction, so it was difficult to understand where he might be walking from or to. He must have been seventy, and was dressed in a farm labourer's tweed jacket, shiny with ordure and held around his waist with a length of string. He wore an old flat cap that may once have been shot at by Captain A. E. Percival, and the look of a man who had never been pampered. 'Ah, look,' said John. 'A bachelor.'

We pulled over and John walked across to him – none of this wind-your-window-down-and-bark-an-enquiry nonsense. They then embarked on a wide-ranging discussion that took in meteorology, natural history, anatomy, theology and chiropody, before John deftly slipped in the crucial question, for all the world as if it were an afterthought.

'We're looking for St Colman's Well.'

'Ah, yes. Ah, yes.'

'Do you know it then?'

'Sure, I do. I do.'

'Could you tell us how to find it so?'

Pause. 'What country's it in?'

So as the woman approaches the repmobile, I'm aware of the social etiquette. But will I be able to pull it off? She opens brilliantly.

'I'm just waiting for my daughter.'

Of course. So that's why she's parked in the middle of a crossroads. She has a look that is at once both blank and intense, as if perhaps she's spent too many years as a priest's housekeeper. But I don't let it get to me, and come back with details of my own family. We then banter about crops and such like for a while, until I sense that the moment is right. And then – ping! I'm in.

'I was wondering if you might be able to give me some directions.'

'Ah. Well, I'm afraid, you see, that I don't live around here.'

'Oh, I see. Where do you live, then?'

'Over there.'

She points to a white farmhouse across some fields, on a hillside about a mile away.

'Oh. Right. Well, anyway . . .'

I produce the scholarly tome and show her a sketch of the Bohonagh circle, but it's clear she doesn't recognise it, even though she must have lived her whole life within eight or ten miles of it, according to the complex family history she eagerly provides. But the name itself rings a bell, though she says there's also another place that sounds similar, and it might be that. Or not. Eventually she suggests a route.

'Go back a way below there, now. Go right, and right, and I think left. Do you know the Dunmanway road?'

I nod, and smile, and only I know that I mean 'No'.

'Well, you take that. And there's an old tumbledown wreck of a pub there, and you turn away up the hill. It's painted yellow. Or at least it was twenty years ago.'

Clueless, I head off politely, happy simply to put a few country miles between me and the Michael Collins birthplace. After driving for ten minutes, I round a bend, and suddenly find myself at the Michael Collins birthplace. The Geordie waves and smiles.

I immediately implement Plan B, which in this instance is to drive at random until something happens. It's important to have a Plan B, especially when there's no Plan A. After a few minutes, I find myself at a T-junction I don't think I've passed before, though of course I can't be certain. And there's a pub – no name displayed, but almost certainly called McCarthy's. Unfortunately, it's shut. This is a difficult concept to grasp. I've never found a pub closed in Ireland before, and I'm not sure how to cope. Intellectually, I realise that the whole point of travel is to introduce you to the unknown, but emotionally I'm finding it difficult to deal with. I take a swig from my bottle of Virgin Mary mineral water, and consider my situation.

I'm lost, and the pub's shut. It's hard to see how things could get much worse. But I'm determined not to be thwarted by these elusive stones. They have come to represent the moral high ground, and I am determined to attain it. I drive a few more miles round winding lanes, until I find a sign to Rosscarbery ('Michael Collins birthplace – 1 mile'). Then, within sight of the main road I'd left earlier in the day, my eye is caught by a bright yellow sign on a noticeboard at the entrance to a field.

NOTICE IS HEREBY GIVEN THAT THE OCCUPIER
OF THIS PROPERTY EXCLUDES THE DUTY OF CARE
TO ALL VISITORS.
NO UNAUTHORISED ENTRY IS ALLOWED.

Inside the field, only about fifty yards away, but protected from me by a gate, barbed-wire and an electric fence, sits a huge cromlech – a boulder marking an ancient burial site. Above it, on the west of a hill, is the outline of an old ring fort. If I've got my bearings right, the place is called Templefaughnan, and Bohonagh can't be far away. The tome tells me that St Fachtna, who is credited with bringing Christianity to this area in the sixth century, is reputed to have preached the gospel in this very field.

He wouldn't have much joy if he came back today, mind you. Five modern bungalows guard the field in a protective semi-circle, in case the barbed-wire and the electricity aren't enough to put you off. I think of scaling the gate for a closer look, but the thought of some beefy farmer lurking behind the net curtains, with ginger hair growing out of his ears and nostrils, just itching to exclude the duty of care to some trespassing English bastard, persuades me to drive on.

Round the first bend in the lane, opposite a bungalow with crazy-paved gateposts, is a roadside holy grotto. In marked contrast to the rugged, ancient boulder in the field, it looks as pristine as a gilt-framed picture of Daniel O'Donnell on a suburban convent mantelpiece. Either side of an altar-shaped slab stand the Virgin Mary and a chap I take to be St Fachtna himself, but who is a dead ringer for Willie Nelson. Country and western is popular out here, though, so you never know.

Searching for pagan stones in the midst of this Catholic iconography is making me feel like a devil worshipper who's sneaked into St Peter's and can't find his way out. Suddenly, the lane sweeps sharply downhill towards a junction a couple of hundred yards away. As I change down and negotiate the slope, I look up, and there ahead of me, silhouetted against the horizon on the crest of the next hill, dominating the surrounding landscape, is Bohonagh.

But by the time I've descended to the junction, it's gone. I drive along the road in both directions, but the stones can't be seen from anywhere. To find them, you've got to know they're up there, and know where to go. There's no sign or marker, so people must drive within a hundred yards of them all the time and not have a clue that they're there.

But now I know they're uphill, and just two fields away.

My way is barred by a wide ditch full of blackthorn, which is of course a sacred bush, though that isn't much consolation just now. But thirty yards away is a barred gate, and not a yellow placard in sight, so I stride up to it with a spring in my step. Then, more threatening than any official sign, I spot the fragment of ragged brown cardboard tied to the gate with baling twine. A message is printed on it in Biro, in a crabby hand that lacks generosity of spirit:

DANGER!
BULLS!!
DO NOT ENTER

Hmm.

I've never been one to mess with bulls, particularly in a Catholic country. Spain, for example, is a delightful place, but I've always been mystified by the nationwide passion for taking the piss out of bulls. Sometimes it's a prelude to killing them, of course, but often it's just for the crack.

I have a much-prized piece of home video shot a few years ago at the fiesta in Jávea, on the Costa Blanca, where they let the bulls run through the narrow back streets of the town before emerging into the main square. As the first bulls enter the square, a local sex god in tight black trousers and a puffy-sleeved white shirt unbuttoned to the scrotum leaps out in front of the lead bull, grimacing and pouting, waggling his arse, and making what I take to be the Spanish equivalent of the wanker sign.

'Wanker, eh?' enquires the bull, lunging at him and penetrating his ribs with its horns in a fairly matter-of-fact manner. Sexgod is thrown abruptly to the ground as various spectators rush to his aid and shoo the baffled bull away. Two stewards run in. One picks him up, dusts him down, staunches the wound, and asks if he's all right. He nods; at which point the other steward punches him in the face, presumably for taking the piss out of a bull in an unacceptably flamboyant manner. After all, without rules, society will collapse. As, indeed, does Sexgod, before being carried unconscious from the arena.

Now, if I'm gored by a bull here, within horn-tossing distance of the spectacular, but at this moment invisible, stones, no one's going to leap in and punch me; but no one's going to save me either. There isn't a soul to be seen in any direction. So I try to convince myself to be law-abiding, that I did my best, got as close as I could, so I can give up with honour; but I just feel pathetic. I'm scared of dogs, too. And geese.

I walk back up the steep lane I've just driven down until I can once more see the stones on the horizon, calling me to them. I'm now in a position to survey the land all around, and there isn't a bull to be seen.

It's clear that the DANGER! BULLS!! sign is just a ruse, a scam to keep New Agers, Pagans, Crusties and Whiffies from tramping all over the fields to paint each other's faces and drink Scrumpy Jack in a ritualistic manner in the centre of the stones. There isn't a problem here for me. It's just over the gate, up the hill, check out the stones, no bulls, back in the car and find a nice spot to eat my sandwich.

The first thing to catch my eye once I'm over the gate is a freshly spent shotgun cartridge, presumably fired from the gate at the back of the last person who trespassed.

Bullshit.

Not my thought, but the stuff I'm standing in. Masses of the stuff. And in the soft ground all around me, footprints I can only describe as bull-shaped. Nauseous but undeterred, I press on up the field, then surprise myself by going commando-style under an electric fence – a bit panicky, this bit, so I'm left with extensive grass stains, and a minor pulled muscle in the small of my back.

I'm now on a half-obscured path between two fields. Humming to myself in order to ward off total mental collapse, I follow it up the hill at a brisk stride, adding a little semi-cantered hitch-kick every few steps, presumably in the hope that this will render me impossibly elusive to shotguns and bulls. At the top of the hill there's a wall to the right, and beyond it, perfectly positioned to survey the countryside billowing away at 360° below it, the Bohonagh Stone Circle: thirteen slabs of granite, some of them taller than me, standing where they've been for 4,000 years.

But the dry-stone wall is lined with a single-strand electric fence, with a second wire encircling the stones themselves. Bastard farmers. What a vindictive way to treat people who only want to experience the stones at first hand. But then the thought occurs: what if the motivation was something quite different? What if it's just an attempt by a small farmer, earning an honest punt – plus massive EC subsidies, obviously – to protect the country's ancient heritage from animals?

But what animals?

The bellow comes from over my right shoulder. The beast is black and white, barrel-chested, eighty yards or so away, diagonally down the field. The gate, the repmobile, and the rest of my life are somewhere in the middle distance beyond. As is the electric fence, which I'll have to get under to give myself a chance. Anyway, can't bulls jump them? Or if not, surely they're so bloody hard that they can just crash through the flimsy tape as they thunder down on you in the mistaken belief that you're some kind of Spanish exhibitionist.

Heart pounding, back twingeing, bowels suddenly keen to get involved, I turn my back on the stupid bloody stones that have got me into this mess, and begin to edge down the hill, to my left. The bull backs off, head down, in that way that suggests backing off is just a momentum-gathering preliminary to charging forward. I speed up and head for the nearest point of the electric fence, all the while making a pitiful squeaking sound as I run, mentally reliving childhood promises never to do anything wrong ever again if only God will let me off this time.

As I go to throw myself under the electrically charged cable, I stumble in a rutted hoofprint, and catch the wire with my forehead. Nothing. Except relief. The fence is just for show. The current isn't even turned on. All over Europe, animals are being conned by farmers anxious to keep their electricity bills down, though I'll bet they're claiming the full whack from Brussels.

But what if the bull knows that?

The tape is between us, but the brute has now started to execute a distinctly threatening amble in my direction. Sprawled on my back, legs akimbo, I must make an inviting target. I couldn't feel more vulnerable if I were wearing skintight Spanish jeans with red arrows pointing to the crotch, marked 'Insert Horns Here'.

But surely the gate to the lane, and safety, must only be yards away. Keeping my body perfectly still, I begin – slowly, ever so slowly, so as not to alarm the bull – to turn my head.

There's a man at the gate, watching me.

'Have ya fallen and hurt yourself, or are ye just afraid of the cow?'

Up at the farmhouse, surrounded by sixteen or seventeen of his children, it was clear that Mr Goggin hadn't been making fun of me. It had been a concerned enquiry. He seemed devoid of any malice, quiet and painfully shy, with the look of a man who lives in constant dread of being asked if he plans on having any more kids.

Next to the house was a nineteenth-century sheepshed, recently converted into a three-bedroom holiday cottage, with open fires, old wooden furniture, and iron bedsteads painted bright as Clonakilty High Street. Mr Goggin showed me round, blushing every time I asked him anything, even though it must have been clear there was no chance of my asking him to impregnate me. Just not used to strangers, I suppose.

He'd done the conversion himself, with a dozen or so of the older children. The paint had been dry two days. There was a booking next week, but now I was to be the first guest. The children were sniggering, and muttering to each other behind hands. I noticed they all had extraordinarily rosy cheeks, as if they'd inherited their daddy's blushes as a permanent physical feature. The air of impudence, though, definitely came from their mother's side.

She was in the cottage sitting-room as we finished the tour. She'd lit a peat fire, and somehow had produced a loaf of soda bread, still hot from the oven. She smiled and introduced herself, and politely offered me her hand to shake. So I shook it.

'Sure, ye can see ye've never done a hard day's work in your life.'

She was fingering the soft palm of my right hand, with a mischievous, possibly demonic, glint in her green eyes. As an opening conversational gambit to a paying guest, this was breathtakingly original. The conversational ball was now firmly in my court.

I withdrew my hand and looked at the callus-free palm. I caught a glimpse of Mr Goggin edging towards the door, foetal with embarrassment, and decided to lie.

'Well, you know, there's not a lot of manual work involved being a sales rep. Mostly just sit in the car. You know.'

You could see the repmobile through the window. There was a hanger full of clothes dangling by the rear window, which added authenticity to my story.

'I suppose ye spend a lot of time parked in lay-bys, pretending y'ere on appointments.'

Two of the reddest kids were watching through the window now, gurning menacingly.

There was the sound of a latch as Mr Goggin finally cringed through the door, followed by a sigh, or it might have been a whimper, from outside. Then Mrs Goggin was suddenly gone, before reappearing like a genie on the other side of the room.

'Here are the towels and bedlinen.'

'Oh. Right.'

She was all smiles now.

'Would ya like me to make up the bed?'

Too bloody right I would. What did she think I was paying £18 for? Time to let her see who was in charge round here.

'Oh. Yes, please. If it's not too much trouble.'

Just for a moment, she leaned back and narrowed her eyes. Then she said it.

'Lazy, are ya?'

Nothing can prepare you for this kind of thing when all you're doing is booking some accommodation, a transaction that in most countries and circumstances is emotionally neutral. But I don't think there was anything malicious about Mrs Goggin; she was just interested, and not in possession of the mental filter system most of us put our thoughts through before they emerge as words. She just said whatever popped into her head.

'Well, I'll leave ya to it. I'm sure there are *things* ye'll be *wanting to do*,' she said, with what seemed to be a pornographic leer. Then suddenly she was gone, only to return almost immediately with a wild salmon steak, and salad and potatoes, and a bottle of stout, and eight or nine of her small red daughters, who stood giggling in the doorway at the strange man who was paying money to stay in their sheepshed.

'There y'are, now. Ye look as if ye'd be needing a decent meal. If ye like to take a drink, and I'd say ye do, there's a pub below. Beyond the crossroads there. God bless, now.'

An Irish potato is a wonderful thing. Dry, fluffy, bursting with flavour, it bears no relation to its English cousin, which tastes in comparison as if it's been grown in a dark factory and over-watered with too much watered-down water. Yet in England these days we import vegetables from all over the world. 'Air-freighted for freshness', it says on the mangetout from Zimbabwe. 'Specially grown for flavour', claim the supermarket's Dutch tomatoes. Well, what other reason is there for growing tomatoes? Speed? Comfort? An ability to glow in the dark? We import baby corn from Thailand, yams from the Caribbean, choi sum from Korea. We even import potatoes from Egypt – Egypt! – potatoes that taste like old train tickets, and pay £1 a pound for Jersey Royals that seem to grow in unusually large quantities for a place the size of Jersey, and taste suspiciously Egyptian to me. But in the midst of the global foodie culture that has swamped England in recent years, no one has thought to import Irish potatoes, one of the most delicious and distinctive vegetables in the world, and growing right on our doorstep. Bloody supermarkets. We get the tasteless shite we deserve.

To my amazement, I'd said all this to the landlord within ten minutes of walking into the pub at the crossroads. There were only two other customers in there. One of them looked up and said, 'Feckin' Dutch red peppers.'

In Dingle, County Kerry, there's a bicycle shop that's also a pub. You can't miss it. There's a bicycle in the window, and a Guinness sign above the door. And in the wild west of Cork, on the very edge of Europe, is a draper's shop selling lengths of cloth, farm clothes, wellies, stout and spirits. And in that uniquely Irish way, this too was both a pub and a shop. I'd struggled to find it. The lanes outside were pitch black, and I didn't have a torch. I'd been reluctant to borrow one from Mrs Goggin in case she said, 'Scared, are ya?' or told me I must be a great disappointment to my mother.

It was arranged as a traditional grocer's shop, with displays of tins, pyramids of cereal packets, rows of sweets and some tired oranges, and a large open sack of spuds that were giving off a tremendous earthy smell that permeated the whole room, as if the whiffy musicians from Cork were hiding behind the counter. There was a plain wooden counter with an open drawer for the cash, and two beer taps, one Guinness, one Harp. There were four spirits optics, next to the combs and pantyhose.

The barman-shopkeeper was in his sixties, and a cardigan. Two of the four barstools were occupied by a bearded, weather-beaten farm labourer and a clean-shaven, red-veined school-teacher, both old enough to remember pounds, shillings and pence. They went quiet when I walked in; not in that 'who's this stranger walked into the Slaughtered Lamb this cold foggy night, let's deny everything, then take him out the back, skin him, and feed him to the badgers' way, but simply to make room for me in the conversation. Despite the encroachment of the modern world – Premiership football on Sky TV, and micro-waved Cajun chicken wings, and Recently Invented Traditional Creamy Pisspoor Irish Ale – there are still many pubs in Ireland that exist primarily as venues for conversation, and this was one of them. And I don't even know what it was called. I was going to go back and write it down the next morning, but you know how it is. I could give you directions, though. You know the Dunmanway road? Well, halfway up there's a tumbledown old . . .

He half poured my pint of Guinness, then let it stand for three minutes, in the time-honoured way. This lets the stout settle. It also allows the barman to ask you who you are, where you're from, and why you're here. The other customers listen and nod. Then, he fills the pint, smooths off the head with a table knife with a parchment-coloured handle, and waits for you to take the first sip.

And then the conversation continues.

'We were just talking about that Charlie Haughey there. Used to be the Taoiseach. Y'know, the Prime Minister. Would ya know him? Ah, ya do? Well, a real slippery bastard he was.'

'Sure, the man was a terrible gobshite.'

'But he was a clever gobshite. Didn't he buy his own island, now?'

And so it went on. The EC, and the billion pounds we've had from them. Or is it 34 billion? Laughter all round. Then Sinead

O'Connor. *Riverdance*. That Terry Wogan. Adams, Paisley and Blair. The internet. Clinton's sex addiction. Spanish trawlers. And all the time, what did I think? Really, now? Is that so? It was a long time since I'd had a conversation like that. A sharing of opinions, to be digested, rather than differences, to be confronted. No music, no slot machines, no TV, no food, no till. Just three interruptions, two from kids buying sweets, one a woman buying tights and a cabbage. The perfect evening, in the perfect pub. The kind of evening that leaves you with a warm feeling. Especially when accompanied by seven pints of Guinness.

Before I left, I asked where the fragrant local potatoes came from.

'Egypt.'

On the way home, I fell over a wall.

I think Mrs Goggin knows.

Chapter Three

Drimoleague Blues

The next morning, and I'm cruising the back lanes of West Cork in the repmobile, trying to remember whether the bull had any udders, as I look for the beach at Red Strand. I've already tried to find Castlefreke, because it's got an interesting name, and a ruined old Gothic house, and you're meant to be able to walk through the woods to the beach; but it was altogether too elusive for me. I did manage to find Castlefreke post office, mind you, which sits, quite clearly marked 'Castlefreke post office' in the middle of the picturesque village of Rathbarry.

I'm taking it easy on account of the hangover, just plodding along at thirty while I try and find a station on the radio; but the radio refuses to co-operate and stays in constant search mode, as it has been since the day I hired the damn thing. Just relentless static, interrupted every few seconds by a tiny fragment of a phone-in about adultery, or sexually active bishops.

I'm heading up a gentle hill, trying to forget the expression on Mrs Goggin's face when I declined black pudding, white pudding and a third sausage, when suddenly, round the corner at the top of the hill, a car appears. It's airborne, like a rally contestant, nearside wheels in the middle of the road, the rest of the car entirely on my side. It swerves out of my path and thunders past, pinging a stone against the corner of my windscreen, where it makes a tiny crack. I get a clear look at the driver: a slightly batty-looking sixty-something lady, who grins amiably and waves with one finger as she rockets past. She seems untroubled by the realisation that if I'd been going ten miles an hour faster, or had been fifty yards further up the lane, or both, we'd have met head-on, on a blind bend. Not for the first time I have cause to reflect that all the recklessly fast drivers I come across, who in England would usually be men in their twenties, seem to be elderly women with a strange gleam in their eyes.

Yet their driving seems entirely devoid of aggression; they're just, y'know – *fast*. And at least they retain that old-style country habit of raising a finger off the steering wheel in acknowledgement, for all the world as if you're the only person they've driven past all week. At least, I think it's in acknowledgement. If it's, 'Sit on this, ya English fecker,' then I have to say it's done with great charm.

By the time I happen upon Red Strand I'm more than ready for a burst of air. It turns out to be a beautiful expanse of sand between two green headlands, with the ancient fort of Galley Head just visible away to the west. So it's unfortunate that slap in the middle of the green fields that face the sea, behind the beach, is an extremely hard-on-the-eye mobile-home camp of thirty or forty *units*, I think, is the polite word for them. Still, they're not permanent, I suppose, and they allow people with not a lot of money to come and enjoy this beautiful spot, and no one's built an amusement arcade or fun pub, so who am I with my middle-class back-to-nature aesthetics? If the only thing spoiling the place is the mobile homes, and you're sitting in one of them, then I don't suppose you notice.

But Ounahincha, just a couple of miles along the coast, is beyond justification. I know I used to come here as a kid, but I have no memories, other than that it was the seaside, and there was sand. My cousin had a phobia of feathers, so perhaps it was here that I used to conceal feathers carefully under shells, inside buckets, and in other places she was certain to find them. In my defence, I can only say that I would watch her near-hysterical reaction with fascination rather than glee.

Ounahincha is in a beautiful setting, with an expansive beach, dramatic rocks in the water, and splendid sloping lush green landscape all around. Unfortunately, it was comprehensively buggered in the 1960s and 1970s. The Ounahincha Hotel looks as if it has been assembled from the remnants of a previous building that was demolished for being too ugly, and is a strong contender for Most Tawdry Seaside Building in Ireland. Next to it, a sign on what appears to be a terminally damaged shed screams: SOUVENIRS CHIPS BURGERS; in case you're wondering how you'd obtain them, a smaller sign says: SHOP! At the eastern end of the mess, despoiling another hillside with a sea view, is a trailer park so big there's a Bank of Ireland caravan. I find myself feeling sorry for people who voluntarily spend their free time here. Like me, now.

If you turn left off the main road when you've crossed the causeway across the river estuary at Rosscarbery – there's an enormous and hideous new hotel reminiscent of suburban Oslo, so you really can't miss the turning – and if you keep your wits about you, then in ten or fifteen minutes' drive you will come across the Drombeg Stone Circle. I've been there three times now and only seen someone else there once: an American family. The three children were sitting on top of the stones and shouting, though to be fair they were only up there because their parents had made them do it for a photo. Like the Collins birthplace, it's maintained by the reassuringly antiquated-sounding Department of Works, and none the worse for it. Catering, merchandising and Computer-Generated Interactive Interpretative Heritage Experience have all gone missing. No one's trying to sell you expensive jam or chutney. There's just a small parking area, with nothing parked in it, and a path between fields to the stones.

There are seventeen of them. You enter the circle between the two largest, or portal, stones, which are both bigger than you. Directly opposite, on the other side of the circle, is a stone called 'recumbent' or 'axial' by archaeologists; by which they mean it lies sideways rather than upwards. Ancient markings have been carved on its upper surface. It's been suggested that they represent axes, and that this proves that these circles were not places of worship, but the focal points of a Cult of the Axe which existed in western Europe in neolithic times. Or the stones may have enclosed a marketplace, and the axial stone was the counter on which goods were traded.

I have to say, though, that shopping seems an unlikely motive to me. Proponents of this undeniably imaginative theory make comparisons with shopping malls, which might be seen as the new temples. Shoppers are worshippers, McDonald's is the sacrament, Nike provide the vestments; but the theory is of course rampant bollocks, and seems so particularly in a part of the world where there are no malls, but you can still buy a bicycle in a pub. The stone is, quite clearly, an altar stone, and something would have been placed, or celebrated – or sacrificed – on it.

When the site was excavated in 1957, the centre of the circle contained an inverted pottery jar covering the cremated remains of a young man from 3,500 years ago. Today in his honour someone has left six daffodils tied with green ribbon, ten American cents, and a magnetic glow-in-the-dark dashboard Virgin Mary. On 21 December the sun sets in alignment with the altar and the two portal stones, in a tiny cleft in the hills to the south-west, through which you can see the Atlantic. You don't get that at the average shopping mall.

Sixty or seventy yards away, to the south-west, next to the foundations of some sort of stone hut or shelter, is a sunken pool. For all we know, it could have been some kind of neolithic ceremonial sauna; but it is believed to be a *fulacht fiadh*, or ancient cooking place. Stones were heated in a nearby fire, then plunged into the shallow water to cook deer and vegetables. Experiments suggest that seventy gallons could be boiled in this way in eighteen minutes, and that water could be kept hot for three hours, which explains why Irish vegetables have never been served *al dente*.

I walk up a short path to the north, and realise the stones are on a raised natural platform, almost like a stage. Beyond them, where the audience should be, thirty or forty fields roll away to the sea, half a mile distant, and visible in three separate places through dips in the hills. The only sound is a donkey braying, and the chug of a tractor in a clifftop field – the same guy, on the same tractor, as last time I was here, I imagine.

As evening approaches I drive down the hill and around the perimeter of the glorious natural harbour at Glandore, before hitting the main road at Leap (pronounced Lepp) and continuing west into Skibbereen. The town's enjoyed a fame of sorts because of the song, 'The Reasons I Left Auld Skibbereen', and historically there have been many. The potato famine wreaked a dreadful havoc here; and between 1911 and 1961 more than half the population of the area emigrated because of failing crops and lack of employment. Skib today has a no-nonsense bustle to it, caught between the old Ireland and the new, cosmopolitan, moneyed West Cork, as personified by local residents Jeremy Irons and David Puttnam.

A decade ago I came here for an uproarious family wedding. The reception in the West Cork Hotel was a classic of the genre, and would have been dismissed as over the top had it been accurately portrayed on screen. A hundred and twenty of us sat down for a formal meal at two in the afternoon. Suddenly, the wine waiter was at my elbow, offering a choice of three bottles, with a polite enquiry I never expect to hear anywhere again in my life: 'Red, white, or whiskey, sorr?'

When the band started playing at five o'clock there was none of the reticence and bar-hanging that characterise such events in England. Everybody in the room charged at the dance floor and made flamboyant whoopee non-stop until midnight, at which point the newly-weds were hoist skywards on the arms of their friends, laid horizontal in the air, and flown, shrieking, around the room. The crowd engineered elaborate and erotic airborne collisions between bride and groom, pounding them together till they were intertwined like two lusty cherubs on a Vatican chapel ceiling. Afterwards, we went back to the farm and drank whiskey – I suppose the red and the white must have run out – and played Richard Clayderman tapes, for complex reasons that elude me now, until dawn.

All of which means I feel very at home in Skibbereen, as indeed I should, walking past Patrick McCarthy, Solicitor; Charles McCarthy, Estate Agent; P.J. McCarthy, Insurance Broker; and so many others as to make me feel comfortably run-of-the-mill. The pattern is broken by the ever-expanding Hourihan dynasty: Hourihan's Bar, next door to Hourihan's Fast Food, adjacent to the newly opened Hourihan's Launderette. My favourite is Trendy Hair Fashions, a source of continuing joy over the years. This time, its window display consists of an advert for a trip to Lourdes. Come to Lourdes and have your hair cured.

I'm staying at the Eldon Hotel, a nineteenth-century inn on the narrow main street that was derelict for many years, but has now been vigorously refurbished in traditional modern Irish vernacular. Someone told me that this is where Michael Collins spent his last night before riding out to his death, but there's no plaque or themed display cashing in on it, so maybe he did, and maybe he didn't. Next time I drive past the Geordie, I'll ask him.

As night falls, I adjourn across the road to a top-notch bar called Baby Hannah's. Small and unadorned, with a solid fuel range in the corner, a tongue-and-groove ceiling, and sawdust on the floor, possibly left over from when they were fitting the tongue-and-groove ceiling, this is the perfect bridge between past and present. A pair of children, a boy and a girl, prowl the bar looking for mischief, but settle instead for staring at me like a pair of McZombies. At first I think they must have escaped from the Goggins and followed me here, until I realise they are in some way connected with the group of half a dozen adults who are talking and laughing boisterously – let's face it they're shouting – across to my right.

Two of the company are larger-than-life Irish women who look as if they might be blues singers, or bouncers. The conversation is revolving around them, whether it wants to or not, and the air is turning blue, with approximately two fecks, three fucks, and a God Almighty to each sentence. Even for such vigorous turners of an everyday phrase as the Irish, this is an impressive strike rate.

Once in a while when I was younger, my mother would deplore the pagan values of the English, adrift on a sea of sin with no moral compass to guide them. I now realise this must simply have been a subconscious expression of profound regret for having given up the incomparable natural beauty of West Cork for the chemically enhanced wasteland of south-west Lanca-shire. Ironic, really, that my mother – and many other Irish people of our acquaintance – should have chosen to live in Warrington, a town that has as its centrepiece a statue of Cromwell, the most hated man in the history of Ireland. Any-way, on this particular occasion, she had been outraged by the foul language she'd heard being used by a group of young people hanging out on a street corner, in particular an obnoxious ginger-haired kid with glasses.

'Terrible language,' she said. 'You'd never hear swearing like that in Ireland.'

Mum thought the Irish didn't swear; and to be fair, I suppose the ones she knew didn't, which is why they never made it into a Roddy Doyle book. But the vivid use of language that has put the Irish right up there among the greats of English-speaking literature has also made them world-class swearers.

Of course the Australians, as well as being brilliant and colourful users of the English language, are also absolutely top-notch swearers, and I imagine that's all down to the Irish. A large percentage of the first convict settlement of Australia was Irish; some say their deportation was another failed British attempt to solve the Irish Problem. Forced labour in unnatu-rally hot sunshine must have rapidly expanded the average Irishman's vocabulary of profanities beyond its natural limit; with the result that today the Australian sportsmen descended from them are able to defeat English teams simply by swearing at them.

The little boy in Baby Hannah's has just crept closer, still staring, to try and see what I'm writing down. Fair enough.

FECK OFF, SON

That seems to have done the trick.

I've been planning some kind of late-night snack back at the hotel, but as I leave the pub I pass a tiny and dimly lit Chinese restaurant that had escaped my attention earlier. One look in the window, and I'm in. 'Singapore Noodles,' says the menu, '£5.80.' Bargain.

It's not till the bill comes that I realise that was the takeaway price. Inside, sitting down, they're £8.50. Add tax, plus service, drinks, rice, vegetables and a pineapple fritter, and I could have taken a family of four to the Seychelles for Christmas and New Year and still had change for a curry.

Eight miles north of Skibbereen is Drimoleague, the village where my mother grew up and where my grandfather laughed as I was chased by the pig. It's only a short distance, but the countryside gets wilder as soon as you leave Skib. There's a more rugged feel, compounded by the fact that Drimoleague is off the main tourist beat, and consequently devoid of any cosmopolitan fripperies. We're beyond the noodle belt here. It's only another ten miles to the wild mountainsides behind Dunmanway where the English travellers are camped.

I've decided to drop in unannounced on my aunt, who still lives at the farm. As I approach up the tree-lined drive, I get that curious feeling of everything being the same as it always was, only smaller. From the pig's gate to the back door is twenty yards, but at the time it seemed a mile and a half.

As I knock at the back door – which I never remember being closed before – I have a heightened sense of anticipation; so it's a pity my aunt's gone to Dublin for the weekend. Of course, I only find that out later. For now, I hang about for five minutes waiting, trying to conjure up the spirit of those summers.

My earliest memories of travelling to Ireland are of the *Glengarriff*, which sailed from Liverpool Pier Head to Cork. There haven't always been drive-on car ferries with reclining pullman seats and discos and tax-free perfume. This was a cattle boat, with berths for thirty or forty passengers as a sideline. I remember my father taking me below decks to see the animals. They were in a sort of stable, with straw. No nasty crates in those days. It all seemed perfectly natural; it was hard to tell whether the cows were going on holiday, or whether they'd already been and were on their way home.

We'd leave from Pier Head at night, in what now seems like a scene from a period movie playing inside my head: men in hats, fog, customs officers wielding pieces of chalk. The crossing would turn rough in the early hours of the morning, as we rounded the south-east corner of Ireland, and the swell of the Atlantic hit the Irish Sea. The seasickness was spectacular. Today's ferries may be sleek and comfortable, but they deny young people the un-forgettable experience of witnessing at first hand a cow throwing up. I suppose we can't stand in the way of progress, but holiday travel's a duller business without bovine projectile vomit.

The poorly priests and nauseous nuns were good value, too. You didn't usually see the clergy so vulnerable. But by mid-morning the puking would stop, as we entered the calmer waters at the mouth of the magnificent harbour at Cobh, known as Queenstown in the days of the British Empire. This was the last port of call of the *Titanic*; it was also the major point of embarkation for the Irish emigrating to America, more than 3 million of whom left from there in the course of a century, my own uncle among them. The tears of their relatives have left an unmistakable air of melancholy about Cobh today, though it has its lighter side too. A couple of years ago, a local unemployed man won the Irish lottery. One of his first acts was to buy the premises occupied by the dole office, and double their rent. He's planning a *Titanic* theme restaurant on the harbourfront. Disaster is widely predicted once again.

From Cobh, the *Glengarriff* would head up the River Lee into Cork. I recall fields on either side, and people waving to us as we wiped the carrot from our chins. They always lay on a welcome, the Irish, but you can't help noticing they don't seem keen on waving a Union Jack. A lot of English people still can't under-stand that.

A while ago I found myself wondering whether I might have imagined the cattle boat and the nuns; but a few nights ago, in a pub on Winthrop Street in Cork city, where large joints of meat are carved on industrial slicers by homely women in white overalls, many of them with a full complement of fingers – I found corroboration of my memories.

Framed on the wall is a copy of the *Cork Examiner*, dated Thursday, 23 October 1952. On the front page is an advert:

DIRECT SERVICES–PASSENGERS, GOODS, LIVESTOCK
CORK TO LIVERPOOL SATURDAYS, LIVERPOOL–CORK THURSDAYS
CITY OF CORK STEAMPACKET CO (1936) LTD
TELEGRAMS 'PACKET', CORK

I was about to say that those childhood crossings are like looking back on a different era of travel, but of course it *was* a different era of travel. Pre-1960, you only went on holiday in another country if you had money, or relatives to stay with.

We had the relatives.

Down in the village, I visit the graveyard in the grounds of the not over-pretty modern church. I find my grandfather, buried with Great-Aunt Hannah and Uncle Jack. His surname is spelled 'MacCarthy', with an extra 'a'; like many names here, it's a translation from the Irish, so the 'a' is optional, and may appear and disappear with the generations.

A man is tidying up a grave nearby, his car parked next to him with the doors open and the Spice Girls blaring out. I'd been hoping for a spot of transcendental graveside ancestral contact, perhaps a piercing insight into why I should feel I belong out here. Instead, the DJ has just started a phone-in about cat-flaps.

For old times' sake, I go inside the church for a bit of a mooch, and anyway, it's much uglier outside than in. And almost straight away, there on the notice-board, I see it, half A4 size, held up by two old-fashioned drawing-pins. You don't see them as much as you used to, do you?

ST PATRICK'S PURGATORY, LOUGH DERG
Unique Centre of Celtic Spirituality,
Offering Opportunities For Growth and Healing
3 DAY PILGRIMAGE
Must be at least 15, Good Health,
Able To Walk And Kneel Unaided
PLEASE FAST FROM MIDNIGHT PRIOR TO ARRIVAL
BRING WARM AND WATERPROOF CLOTHING
£20 INCLUDES BOAT FARE AND ACCOMMODATION

Then, in small print at the bottom:

ALSO 1 DAY RETREATS WHICH DO NOT REQUIRE FASTING
OR WALKING BARE-FOOTED.

Purgatory?

Walking barefooted?

This could be just the job: a high-octane blend of fundamentalist Catholic flagellation and Celtic New Age whimsy, with no food. If anything can give me an insight into my sensation of metaphysical Irishness, this might be it. And even if it doesn't, at £20, three days' accommodation and a boat trip comes in cheaper than two plates of noodles, once you've added the tax.

I jot down the phone number, and head for the phone box in the village. After twenty, or perhaps even twenty-five rings, the phone is answered by someone who sounds like a priest with grazed knees. I ask him how much barefoot work is involved, and whether it's very rocky out there.

'Ah, now don't you worry about that. We have ladies of seventy, and young boys of fifteen.'

An unpleasant image wells up, which I suppress immediately. But then there's the bad news. 'Retreats don't begin until the first of June.' As he puts the phone down, I fancy I hear his scar tissue creak.

It's only March. My sado-masochistic epiphany will have to wait.

In the meantime, I'll go and visit the dole-scrounging, pot-pushing, soap-dodging, poteen-guzzling New Agers in their caravans on the wild side of Dunmanway.

Chapter Four

Wild Mountain

'And is it true that English people are fearing you will meet many Germans when you are making holidays?'

My questioner is a German who is making holidays. We've had breakfast, and now we're sitting in the lounge. He has just finished playing the accordion, accompanied by his son on trumpet. He's holding a leather-bound pad in which he's taking notes.

'And what are you usually calling us? The Hun? Fritz? Or Krauts?'

Gunter is a professional musician from Bavaria, over here on holiday with his family. In spare moments he's working on a song he's planning to perform in London later in the year. So, instead of having breakfast in the farmhouse where my mother grew up, as I'd been hoping, I'm in a feng-shuied bungalow acting as English Language Consultant on a satirical piece called 'Please be nice to the Germans'. In Ireland, the unexpected happens more often than you expect.

> Please be nice to the Germans
> We are different than you think
> Our favourite colour isn't brown, but pink
> Please don't fun at us poke
> German humour is no joke
> But it is well organised . . .

After drawing a blank in Drimoleague, I headed back towards the coast to find somewhere to stay for the night. I stopped near Ballydehob, at a tiny lino-and-Formica pub with a niche market of dung-encrusted farmers, and dined on the Irish national pub dish, the Toasted Special — a sandwich of ham, cheese, onion, tomato, and anything else that's in the fridge or on the worktop, all served at the temperature of lava. There was a card on the wall advertising 'B + B − Organic Produce', so I phoned ahead and booked.

> We are really very sensitive people
> Since the last war we don't march, only dribble
> Bumptious and presumptuous, stern without a sense of fun
> All this is just a rumour
> You could learn a lot from our humour
> Though in 1939, our gags didn't run . . .

I was expecting an old farmhouse, but instead fetched up some time after eleven outside a large modern bungalow down an eerily dark lane. Doreen, the owner, had waited up to welcome me and to tell me her life story.

One day, five years ago, her husband walked out after twenty-five years of marriage. No warning, just left one afternoon and didn't get in touch for eighteen months. He's living in San Francisco now with a lap dancer. There were crystals and wind chimes and New Agey books around the place, and a small pagan shrine to the Goddess, in the corner where the Sacred Heart or Blessed Virgin should have been.

'This is a non-smoking house,' she said. 'I do smoke myself, mind, but I do it outside. Would ye like to see the garden?'

'Maybe in the morning, when it's light.'

She said there was a German family staying, but they'd all gone to bed very early.

'Lovely people. He's a musician. He was asking me to help him with a song he's writing, in English like, but I wouldn't have an idea. I'd say he might like you to help him in the morning. Now, so, would you like some sandwiches? A piece of cake? I'll be watching *The Late, Late Show*, if you'd like to join me.'

My bed was fitted with one of those vile plastic undersheets, originally designed to make life easier for carers of the terminally incontinent, that are now found in more and more hotels and guest-houses. These things draw sweat from your pores like suction pumps. It's like sleeping in a plastic paddling pool full of horse sweat. My dreams of drowning in lukewarm brine were interrupted at seven thirty a.m. by Teutonic warbling, accompanied by accordion and trumpet.

Two world wars? Three world cups, that's what counts
We'd even eat English food
And afterwards pretend it was very good . . .

Breakfast was a huge plate of free-range eggs, organic bacon, vegetarian sausages, wild mushrooms spiked with garlic, and a dandelion. Gunter and I got talking, and within half an hour we were working on the lyrics. In fact we've just agreed on the final couplet.

The time for humility is over
So thanks for Rolls-Royce and Rover.

I tell him I'm sure it'll play well in London. I give Doreen £18, and she gives me a receipt, and a small crystal. As I set off for Dunmanway she's in the garden doing tai-chi, while Gunter improvises on flute.

Before I can meet the travellers, I have to find Dominic. Since my last visit he's moved out of the caravan into a house with no address. 'It's sort of complicated to explain,' he told me a few months ago in Brighton. 'Best just ask in town.' He'd been visiting his parents, and turned up with them at my birthday party, wearing one of those white neck braces for whiplash injury, and black jumper and jeans. Twelve years in Ireland, and he comes back looking like a pint of Guinness.

I know the eight-mile stretch of road between Drimoleague

and Dunmanway pretty well. When I was a kid there was a cattle fair in Dunmanway, on Tuesdays I think, and I'd go along with Uncle Jack. We'd sit on the flat cart-back behind the horse, and sometimes he'd let me hold the reins, a huge thrill for an eight-year-old townie obsessed with the Lone Ranger. But then he sold the horse and got a tractor, and fantasy died. Mechanisation has made small farmers more prosperous, but now children grow up in a world without horses and carts and haystacks. Where's the romance in silage?

Halfway between the two villages is a small petrol station and shop. As I'm paying for fuel, I notice a cardboard box of still-warm soda bread and fruit scones on the counter. I'm full from breakfast, even though I didn't finish the dandelion, so I just buy a paper and head on my way.

I've gone a way down the road when it strikes me I'm turning up to see Dominic empty-handed. And I've heard he's been ill, a nasty bout of pneumonia caused either by working as a roofer in bad weather, or by passing out and spending the night on the ground in a tepee at a party, he couldn't be sure which. There was a spell in hospital with the nuns in Bantry, who wake you each day for prayers at first light; but apparently he's recovered now, and he's recovered from the pneumonia as well. The least I can do is turn up with something nutritious.

I do a U-turn and go ten minutes back up the road. The same woman is behind the counter. 'Hello again,' she says, wondering how I've managed to use up so much petrol so quickly.

'Hello. I just couldn't resist your bread.'

'Well, it's very good all right. There's a lady out the back there, used to be a confectioner, and she bakes it for us Mondays, Wednesdays and Fridays.'

I ask for a loaf and four scones; then, as she wraps them, I'm surprised to find myself revealing intimate details that aren't strictly necessary for the transaction. Perhaps my Irish genes are coming into the ascendant, and I'm beginning to go native.

'Yeah, I'm just going to visit a friend of mine who's been a bit ill recently, and I thought, what could be nicer for him than the smell of fresh warm bread. So I came back.'

She hands me the bread and scones.

'Well now, you tell your friend the bread's a present from us, and we hope he gets well very soon. Just give me a pound for the scones. Goodbye now.'

As you enter Dunmanway, you pass a sign saying: 'Best Kept Village 1982'. There's no mention of what's happened since.

The town is essentially a busy little square where three roads meet. The fairs my uncle used to bring me to, when hundreds of farmers packed the streets and pubs, are distant history. These days you'll see the West Cork company car – a tractor – parked up among the Toyotas and VWs, while its dishevelled bachelor farmer owner buys frozen meat and tinned vegetables in the supermarket, but that's progress for you.

Like many West Cork towns, Dunmanway was developed in the seventeenth century as a plantation, or settlement, by the English; records show that, by 1700, thirty English families were living there. In recent years the town has once again been settled by the English: not the well-heeled yachties you find in nearby Kinsale, Glandore and Schull, but by alleged Crusties, hippies, druggies, pagans and New-Age travellers. In both cases, you could say an English politician was responsible for the influx: first Oliver Cromwell, and then Margaret Thatcher, whose gimlet-eyed disapproval, and riot police, caused many unconventional young Brits to take their troublesome lifestyles across the Irish Sea. This must have pleased her no end.

On an Irish talk-show recently I watched a millionaire businessman describe how he had once met Mrs T at an official reception in London. 'And where,' she'd asked him, 'are you from?'

'Cork,' he replied.

'Yuk!' exclaimed the Iron Lady, and turned on her heel.

'Never mind, old chap,' volunteered Denis, by way of consolation, 'have a G and T.'

I check into a small hotel and bar on the edge of town, variously described as 'family run', 'two star', and, more worryingly, 'Class B'. My room has a small TV, mounted on a metal bracket so far up the wall you'd have to sit on the wardrobe to watch it. Tea and coffee-making facilities, including those tiny sachets of UHT milk that have done so much to make the world a happier place, are there, as advertised. I have an unobstructed view of the roof of the disco. I wolf the complimentary custard creams, one of which is broken, and hit the street in search of Dominic.

Here's my plan. I'll wait until I see someone with dreadlocks, or any scruffy bastard with an English accent and a dog on a piece of string, and ask if he knows Dominic. I'm intrigued that of all the places they might have chosen, the new-wave émigré English have turned up here, in a backwater from my past. Walking back towards the square, I realise I'm passing Auntie Annie's house; she was my grandmother's sister. She lived here, always dressed, in my memory at least, entirely in black, in what seemed like medieval poverty: no running water, cooking range fired by turf, poor old invalid Uncle Willy under a blanket on the sofa.

We went to visit her one Sunday afternoon, straight after a massive lunch of chicken and ham and cabbage and potatoes back in Drimoleague. The moment we arrived there were bottles of stout for my dad and me, even though I was only fourteen, and hated it. There were soft drinks for my mum and sisters and little brother; then Annie served us a massive lunch, of chicken and ham and cabbage and potatoes. Pogged to the eyeballs from the lunch we'd just finished, and racked with guilt at being given enough food to keep her and Willy for a year, we forced it down with clenched fists and the backs of spoons, while Annie looked on, smiling, desperate to serve the trifle. There was just time for a quick pray, then it was back to Drimoleague, and a table groaning with cold meats and hot potatoes. Sandwiches were served at bedtime for anyone who was peckish.

After half an hour wandering round without spotting anyone remotely resembling a drug-crazed hippy, I give up, like many an intrepid explorer before me, and go to the pub. Anyone unfamiliar with south-west Ireland, and most Americans, will presume this indicates an alcohol problem; but I can't see that a pint or two during the day is a sign of moral turpitude, especially far from home. It's certainly better than going to some unique and exotic island, as so many eejits do these days, and playing golf. And instead of the depressingly corporate environment offered by pubs in the English countryside these days, where a retired estate agent or policeman presides over a muzak-polluted repro-furniture showroom in which furtive couples sit side by side eating microwaved baked potatoes, in Ireland you can still find idiosyncratic, family-owned hovels with no food, or décor, that remain temples to hospitality, conversation and drink. They'd be priceless institutions even if they only served coffee, but I can't see that catching on.

I'm the only customer, so I sit at the bar and read the paper. The landlady adopts the unusual conversational gambit for this part of the world of letting me make the first move; but I doubt she'll know Dominic. She's of an older, more God-fearing generation, and seems unlikely to be intimate with a bunch of pagan English party animals. Mind you, she is selling snuff behind the bar, 69p a box, so you never know.

It's a big day for alcohol-related stories. LONGER DAYS BRING THE PROSPECT OF LATE-NIGHT OPEN-AIR BOOZE PARTIES enthuses a front-page headline, though on closer examination it seems to be suggesting that this is a bad thing. There's also a court case that sheds interesting light on official policy to late drinking. 'A publican who allowed people to be on his premises after hours was fined £50 . . . Delaney had nine similar convictions for similar offences.' He'll be terrified about getting caught again, then.

But the landlady can't resist her natural curiosity for long. I ask for a packet of nuts and she's in like a flash, wondering if perhaps I'm on holiday. If you're the sort of person who likes to project an air of cool and remote mystery, or even if you just prefer to keep yourself to yourself, you should avoid small villages in south-west Ireland like the plague.

'I'm looking for someone I know from England. I don't suppose you'd—'

'One of the lads from Wild Mountain, is he? They're not a

bad bunch. Marvellous places they've built up there. Sure, all this nonsense about them living on the dole. Well, fair enough, some of them do, but they're getting a lot less in subsidy than the farmers, and you don't hear anyone complaining about them. And at least it's all going back into the local economy. I see it as God's way of redistributing wealth from Dublin, and anyway aren't they a lot better for the place than these rich English and Germans buying up the houses and leaving them empty fifty weeks of the year. I'd say they've got their own ways of relaxing and having fun, but haven't we all, and did you know now that they have their own cricket team? First year they entered they won the league. Look!'

I'm struggling to keep up. She takes down a framed photo from a shelf by the gin optic. There they are, eleven hairy men in white cricket flannels, smiling, enthusiastic, and, as far as you can tell, as straight as Bob Marley.

'You don't know someone called Dominic, do you?'

'Wasn't he in here last night playing with the band. Been very ill, you know, with the pneumonia, but he's looking better now. Lovely boy.'

'Could you tell me how to find him? He said it was a bit complicated.'

'Sure, it is, I suppose. But I'd say it's easy enough to find once you know where it is.'

Fair enough.

'Or I could give you his cellphone number, if you like.'

Two hours later I'm in Dominic's house, pondering the complexity of life with a mobile, but without a bathroom or toilet. The place is like a junk shop that's recently been ransacked by burglars who were interrupted before they could take anything away. Guitars, fishing rods, tools, plates, toys, hats, sticks, vegetables, an accordion, books, a bridle, some reins, a crossbow, a PA system and some animals all jostle for space among the battered pieces of furniture. There's a Belfast sink, and a cast-iron cooking range like Auntie Annie's, only older. Seven-year-old Merry runs in and out, occasionally catching me a friendly blow between the eyes with a shot from his spudgun.

'I know it looks a mess,' grins Dominic, opening two cans of Murphy's, and producing a packet of cigarette papers from underneath a cat, 'but I know where everything is.'

He's not had an easy life, and not always looked after himself, and it shows in his face, which looks older than his thirty-four years. After living as a traveller in England, he came to Ireland for a weekend festival. Twelve years, three kids, and a gypsy caravan later, he's a home-owner. And in a country that's traditionally exported its young men to work in the English building trade, he's a builder.

There's an uninterrupted view north-west to the mountains. It's six miles into town. The house and a big chunk of land cost £12,000, which wouldn't have bought a garage back in Brighton. It's a one-up one-down in need, as the estate agent would write, stifling a smirk, of some modernisation and improvement. To someone from a carefully preserved English cottage, or a freshly carpeted Irish bungalow, it might look like hippy squalor; but it could suggest something else. The intricate jumble of life's essentials, tools and fuel, children and animals, music and alcohol, crammed together under one roof with not quite enough money to go round, is like a re-creation of a rural Irish way of life that has all but disappeared.

'Have y'seen me hat?'

He takes down a thickly woven bonnet from a shelf where it's been sitting, along with a photo of his parents, some carrots, and a sword. I try it on. It's snug and warm, and feels like raw wool, possibly from some obscure Peruvian llama-goat hybrid.

'It's me dreadlocks. Wove it myself, when I had them cut off. Won a few pints off farmers in town, trying to guess what it's made of.'

He picks up the squeeze-box and starts to play and sing, head thrown back, eyes closed, rocking back and forth and roaring in a gruff, tuneful voice. His hands, scratched and ingrained with concrete and brick dust, are as battered as the keyboard of the old Italian accordion. Merry comes and sits on my lap, pulling funny faces, cheeks puffed out as if by giant gobstoppers. Then he puts his fingers into his mouth and produces the two widgets he's hacked out of the Murphy's cans. I'm impressed. I've never seen a widget before.

We've been joined during the music by two women, one Irish, one Scottish, vividly tattooed, and extravagantly pierced about the face. They're affectionate to Merry, who likes his hugs. Dub reggae is booming out of the sound system now. Dom says it's always been a party house. The couple who lived here before him were into all-night card sessions. When he first moved in, an old man used to turn up with a bottle of whiskey in the middle of the night, looking for a game of poker. He'd tap on the window, then see Dominic and remember the other people had moved. 'Ah, feckit,' he'd say. 'D'you fancy a game anyway?'

Around seven o'clock we bump-start a car that has an unusual open-plan area where the front passenger seat used to be, and I follow them to a party that's going to run until Sunday night.

It's Friday.

'The way I see it, we're repopulating a place that lost its people to famine and emigration,' says Dominic.

We're walking up a long potholed lane towards a stone ruin on a hill. I don't think the repmobile would have coped. Midges are biting, and Merry is talking to his Granddad on a toy cellphone. Music of the Afro-Celtic-Anarcho-Psychedelic persuasion is drifting towards us on a chill evening breeze, and I feel as inconspicuous as Prince Charles trying to score at the Notting Hill Carnival. I try to loosen up. After all, what's the worst that can happen? That someone will take me for some sort of narc or undercover snooper, beat me senseless, pump me full of crack, magic mushrooms and superglue, and feed me to the enormous lurcher-wolfhound thing that's just knocked me into a fuchsia bush?

Maybe it'll be worse than that. Maybe I'll be forced to join in the fire-juggling.

'Come on,' says Dominic. 'I'll introduce you to Danny.'

It's Danny's house and birthday party. He got an even better deal than Dominic – £7,000 for three acres and four stone walls, which he's spent six years restoring, in between working five-day weeks as a builder. How many English builders are there out here, anyway? And if an Irishman on an English site is a Paddy, what do they call these fellas? Nigels? Jeremies?

He's a lean man in his thirties, with close-cropped black hair, a silver earring, and black leather trousers, but I'd never criticise anyone's dress sense on their birthday. He's got a strong Norfolk accent, though he's been out here nine years. Couldn't afford to live in Norfolk, he says, because of commuters pushing prices up; couldn't contemplate a council house in town; couldn't live a travelling life because of prejudice, legislation and complaints about loud parties. But there's space here. He says the house has been habitable for six months. He's been living here with his wife and children for six years.

'But look at that, man.'

We're on a hilltop that falls away sharply into a small valley, with mountains beyond.

'When you wake in the morning, and look out there, and it's all full of mist down below you . . . we could never live like this in England.'

So does he feel part of the local community?

'The Irish community? No. They tolerate me, but I'll always be on the outside. Might be different one day for the kids. I wouldn't be here if I didn't like it, though.'

He gives me the guided tour, proud as any first-time buyer. There's no electricity, just candles and oil lamps. No mains water, so he's dug a well. The fireplace in the living-room is so enormous it's burning eight-foot logs. An eight-foot log is a tree, isn't it? There's a half-built minstrel gallery around the living-room. And a party going on.

There are maybe twenty-five or thirty adults round the place, and almost as many children. The adults, like adults at parties all round the world, are crowding into the kitchen for no apparent reason, where they are shouting, laughing, and getting intoxicated in the manner of their choice. Like a Friday night any-where, I suppose, only with more body piercing. I'm intrigued that the adults are happy to get wild in front of the kids. A lot of people would disapprove, but on the other hand the kids haven't been dumped with an unmotivated teenager who's on £3 an hour.

They also don't look like part of an alternative subculture. Not like the hippy kids who used to plague the fairs and festivals I used to perform at with Cliffhanger Theatre in the 1980s. These were wild-eyed, tie-dyed, sub-*Lord of the Flies* monsters, many of whom, I'm told, are now earning small fortunes as DJs and producers of ambient grooves for the post-E generation. Christ, they were bastards then, though, walking all over the stage, destroying performances. Then one day a psychopathic performance artist opened his show by urinating on the hippy kids. Some people say Flower Power died when Hell's Angels killed a member of the audience at Altamont in 1969, but for many of us, this was the defining moment.

But these kids aren't like that. The boys are just kick boxing, the girls polite, inquisitive, and dancing whenever the music isn't too weird. They all seem to have English accents, but when I ask them are they English or Irish, the answer's always the same.

'Irish, of course.'

An hour has gone by, and Dominic is standing and swaying, belting out obscure ballads in the middle of the kitchen. Danny opens a birthday present to reveal a lavender-coloured bra. He strips off and puts it on, to cheers, laughter, flashbulbs and tequila. A very big, very loud, very wild man passes me a bottle of clear liquid, but I pass it on when he's not looking, paranoid that it may have been spiked with something. Then I start to wonder if my paranoia means I've already been spiked. I start to feel foolish, pootling around in my hire car, with my sentimental memories, in the country where they're actually living. I'm the one who should have bought the ruin, but I'm so clueless I'd have had to hire a builder. English, probably.

I find myself in the glow of the eight-foot fire talking to Dessy, one of the handful of Irish people here. Behind us, a man with a radical hairstyle and an Essex accent is swaying, eyes shut, to an imaginary soundtrack, while his son holds his hand.

There's a cheer from the kitchen, as Danny puts the bra on again. Dessy and I are reminiscing about the Christian Brothers. He tells me about his Latin teacher, Brother Theodore.

'A tall bastard, so he was. A tall, thin, mean bastard, with a baldy head, like a lightbulb. He'd make us mark each other's work, then for every wrong mark we got, we'd get a thump. That way' – he paused – 'we were implicated in each other's pain.'

Most of us who've been through this kind of education say, 'Well, it never did me any harm.' With Dessy, I got the feeling it probably did.

'There was a feeling of abject fear in that class. Whatever happened, you'd know that twenty minutes of each lesson would be dedicated to physical violence. Then, after that, he'd lighten up. Like some dreadful tension had been released.'

We had a Latin teacher who liked to dish it out too, a lay teacher, not a brother. He'd feign a blow to your head with his right, then belt you one from the blind side with his left when you weren't braced for it. He inspired fear, but also admiration, as most of our class were hardened rugby league supporters who recognised a world-class act of brutality when they saw one.

Dessy is in his forties, with piercing green eyes, and a sense of danger about him; educated, but you get the feeling he's been damaged somewhere along the line. He takes a lemonade bottle from his jacket and offers it.

'Poteen. Best for miles around.'

This part of Cork has always been renowned for the quality of its moonshine. But how do I know I'm getting the right stuff? What if it's been adulterated with bleach, or boot polish? Or Bailey's Irish Cream?

'He's been making it fifty years. You'll not get purer. Better than commercial whiskey, that's for sure. Go on, give it a try.'

I decide to sip, but not inhale. It's smooth, and smoky, and I don't seem to be going blind.

'Fancy a chaser?'

Dessy has two pills on his hand. He pops one in his mouth, and chugs it back with some poteen. I cling to the possibility that he's a health fanatic who always takes his multivitamins in the evening.

'No thanks. I'll have to drive back soon.'

'You shouldn't go yet. This is very mellow acid. Things'll be getting a lot livelier here soon.'

Livelier. Yes indeed. The old poteen-acid combo should do the trick. It's at times like this that a lifetime's exposure to the British gutter press comes into its own. I make my excuses and leave.

Back at the Grade B there's no sign of paralysis setting in from the poteen, so I order a whiskey from the bar. It isn't a patch on its illegal cousin. I'm too late for food, so I nip out to the repmobile for the soda bread I forgot to give Dominic, and smuggle it up to my room under a jacket. If you've had the right kind of education, it's amazing how many things you can find to feel guilty about.

I watch a bit of TV while drinking the whiskey and eating the bread. There's a late-night discussion programme, in Irish, about subsidy in the arts. A trendy-looking young woman in trainers, with a ring through her eyebrow, keeps punctuating her elegant-sounding Irish with 'like' and 'y'know'. It's kind of, like, interesting? that this sorta, y'know, inarticulacy, like, transcends, languages? The weather in Irish follows, but my lids are drooping and my chin's nodding on my chest. I climb down off the wardrobe, and go to bed.

Next morning the reception desk is staffed by two pallid, grey, plump young women who've had no recent exposure to daylight or unfried food. One of them guides me to a small dining-room with a mock classical archway, but no windows. There are seven tables. Every place-setting is festooned with the boak-inducing debris of previous breakfasts – congealed bacon fat, rigid egg yolk, cold toast, curdled tea, evil Weetabix that's sucked up all the milk. This stuff should already be landfill. Only forensic examination could determine how long some of it's been here. The carpet's sticky grip hints at rare agricultural diseases.

'D'you want to find yourself a place?'

'What? Where?'

She gives a giggle.

'I've not had time to clear them all yet.'

You've not bloody cleared any of them, you lazy lump, I think, as she gets stuck into the nearest table, using an impressive forearm as bulldozer. I catch a nightmare glimpse of cold black pudding and tea dregs sluicing into a half-eaten bowl of muesli that's already begun to set, and avert my gaze. She brushes some recalcitrant crumbs to the floor with a hand on which a Band-Aid is well overdue for renewal.

'Full breakfast, is it?'

I nod, and she goes away. I can't bring myself to make a fuss after the goodwill I've had this week. Suddenly the stereo crashes on, a traditional Irish medley that includes 'Skippy the Bush Kangaroo' and 'Theme from Match of the Day'. Poteen and LSD would be less distressing. The heart-warming ping of a microwave – always a winner, wherever the restaurant – indicates reheating is now complete.

'Careful, the plate's hot,' she says, putting it down on my hand. Two rock-hard fried eggs stare up, rigid and unforgiving as tiny silicone breasts. They are turning purple from the heat of the plate, and threaten to explode at any moment. An overtly hostile sausage, and bacon raw as Parma ham, complete the spread. She plonks down a cup and saucer, and one of those stainless-steel teapots that pour tea down the side of the pot, before shooting off to the kitchen to take some more of whatever she's on.

I pick up the teapot, and pour tea into the cup, and on to the tablecloth. The tea in the cup turns a dark shade of khaki. Hang on, though. I haven't put any milk in. There must have been something milky in it already. Dear God, no. *She's given me a cup of someone else's dregs!*

Out at the reception desk I tell her friend I've decided to check out.

'Ah, ya couldn't have stayed anyway. We're fully booked. There's a wedding.'

That'll be nice for them.

Prices start at £28, which includes breakfast.

There may still be some soda bread in room 7, on top of the wardrobe.

I saw a sign for a hostel yesterday, a couple of miles out of town on the road to Dominic's, so I've reluctantly decided to give it a try. As I drive through the square, wedding guests in tail coats and wing collars stand poised on full alert, waiting for the pubs to open. One elderly man is holding a golden walking-stick.

I suppose I never really got over my first experience of a hostel. We stayed in one on that school trip to Stuttgart. We were all in a dormitory together. On the second night, I was woken from a deep sleep by Mr Chisholm, our criminally insane German teacher, who told me to stop feigning sleep and pretending it hadn't been me making the silly noises. He laid me across the top bunk and beat my pyjamaed bum with his slipper, in front of all the bigger boys. Two nights later Mengele showed up with the suppositories. Just not my week, I suppose.

Since then I've always avoided hostels, telling myself they'd either be full of buck-toothed ramblers with well-polished apples and creases in their socks, or groovy young backpackers swapping addresses, drugs and girlfriends, either of which would be far too depressing. My years as a budget traveller were spent instead on the living-room floors of unfortunate strangers whose addresses had been passed on by indiscreet drunken Australians, if you can imagine such people.

The Dunmanway hostel has only two other guests. One is a pear-shaped Englishman who looks, and I know one really shouldn't generalise about these things, like a paedophile on the run; the other is a dark-haired German cyclist with an ill-considered toothbrush moustache. I'm shown round by a charming Frenchman called Eric. I admire the magnificent view, and pick my room – a converted gypsy caravan in the grounds, for a tenner a night. I sit in the caravan for a bit, because there isn't room to do anything else in there, then set off to find Dominic.

After driving to his house and finding him not in, and trying to find Danny's house and getting lost up a mountain, I have a brainwave, and phone him on his cellphone. I've never really come to terms with the wretched things. It seems to me that life is much better if there are times in the day when no one can find you; though, of course, like most people, I've often wondered how businessmen used to cope before they were invented. How did they tell their wives they were on the train?

Anyway, Dominic turns out to be about fifty yards away, in the car park of a supermarket in Dunmanway. I've had to drive back there to find a phone, on account of not having a mobile. Though a tad hoarse, Dom is in good shape for a man who stayed up till dawn, then slept on some rubble. Merry has stayed on with the other kids at Danny's for the daytime session, so Dom and I pop in for a pint with the wedding guests by way of a loosener, then set off for Wild Mountain.

The travellers started arriving here in the eighties. At first there was an outcry, fuelled by the local press; but since then things have quietened down. As you approach the hillside, a few unusual structures, some thatched, some tarpaulined, and a couple of mobile homes, are visible. An old converted ambulance is parked off-road, looking as though it may once have been used to sell silly hats and tofu at Glastonbury. But there's no shanty-town squalor, or industrial-sized marijuana plantations guarded by junkies with machetes. If you were a vindictive small-town moralist looking for something to deplore, you'd be struggling; but then the sight of an overgrown and decaying cement farmhouse, its windows falling, or already fallen, out, would give some grounds for optimism.

We park in the lane and walk through the gap where the gate used to be, into a jungle of giant fuchsia and supernettles. No weed has been cut, no half-hearted paintbrush wielded for twenty years or more. The back of the house, facing south, is in brilliant sunshine. Two ginger cats are asleep among the cans. Sitting in the doorway on a wooden chair, staring at the floor, is a man of about fifty.

He's wearing a soiled white shirt with a blue and yellow

check, under a green cardie buttoned all the way up, under a battered sports jacket. Gumboots, worn over dark grey trousers that might have been another colour when they started out, suggest an authentic bachelor. His face is full and round, and his brown hair, though matted, is thick and luxurious, with a hairline almost down to his eyebrows, like a badly fitted wig. It can't be though, because he's too drunk to put one on.

'Peter, this is Stephen, landlord of the mountain.'

He looks up and smiles. Dominic passes him a can of strong Dutch lager from a carrier bag, and cracks one for himself. I decline, hoping not to appear antisocial, though it doesn't seem that etiquette will be a problem. Stephen's thick long hair gives him the look of an older Oscar Wilde, but with dandruff. He's fuddled but functioning, his engaging wry smile acknowledging that, despite his semi-coherence, he's fully aware of his semi-coherence.

I sit down next to the cats on the overgrown concrete path.

'Cats are looking well, Stephen,' says Dominic.

'Yerra . . . mmm . . . ngg . . . kittens . . . blerrh, just yet.'

'How many kittens?'

'Ah sure, don't know, haven't looked yet. A few, by the sound of it.'

He gestures to a cupboard door under the stairs behind him. I want to go and see what else is in there, behind the blistered wainscoting and rotten doors, or up the shattered staircase, but I fear it will be just too terrible. There's a powerful stench, as if something's died in his house, or trousers. He offers me a 'Major' brand cigarette, and smiles and says it's nice to have visitors. I'm moved by his pitiful situation. The family farm has been sacrificed to the bottle.

On the way over Dominic told me how Stephen had owned much of the mountain, and the land around it. Fifteen years ago he started renting plots to the new English arrivals; then, to raise cash, he started selling the land. And so it's gone on, hand to mouth, to pub, to mouth again, renting and selling to keep himself afloat. Suddenly Stephen starts complaining to us

that people haven't been paying their rent. Dom gently points
out that perhaps they have paid, but he hasn't remembered.

'Ah sure, I suppose that's possible.' The grin again.

He perks up for a few minutes, and becomes quite animated
while calling his solicitor a gangster and a cunt. Then he takes
me by the arm.

'I'll tell ya something now, boy. If it's true what they say
about whiskey, that it's bad for you, then I'd have been dead
years ago.'

We leave him staring out towards the ruined McCarthy castle
in the valley, the spectacular view completely obscured by six-
foot nettles.

'Come again, boys, it's nice to have company.'

Dominic puts an arm round him.

'Take care now, Stephen. And good luck.'

I suppose I was expecting some sort of commune, but what
they've built is a village: different families, and couples, and
singles, living on their own plots of land, sharing similar aspira-
tions, but living their own lives. And, like a village, everyone
knows everyone else's business.

'That's no bad thing. It's the way village life used to be, back
home, but isn't any more.'

Davie is a broad-shouldered man in his thirties, originally
from Devon. We're sitting on the grass outside his battered
mobile home. Next to it is the house he's building. Below us,
he's planted an orchard. Ponies are grazing off to our left.

'It all changed in England some time in the seventies. Everything modernised, and became homogenous. You all had to live
the same way, and local differences started to disappear. Townies
moved in, and wouldn't speak to you if you were local. It's all
burglar alarms now, and four-wheel drives to take the kids to
school. I hate the way England is now. I could never go back.'

We go inside to make tea. On the wall is a poster of an alien
smoking a spliff, captioned 'Take Me To Your Dealer'. I ask
about the gardai.

'Ah, they know what we're about. It's a small place, and news travels. Y'know, if we started a cocaine factory up here or something, that'd be different, but that's not us and they know that. We look a bit rough, and we like a party, but we have to work hard just to survive, and we love our kids. I think people round here can relate to that.'

Further up the hill is the community centre Dominic helped build. There's a stone floor they cut from the mountain and laid themselves. There's a coffee bar, and toys for the crèche, and a big Bob Marley quote on the wall: 'One world, one love, let's get together, it'll be all right'.

We pass cabins, roundhouses, a yurt-like affair, and dome. I can't help wondering about planners, and whether they're likely to move in with the bulldozers.

'I don't think anyone's going to evict us. They'd have thirty families, more than a hundred people, to rehouse, for a start.'

Laurence is a mild-mannered, dreadlocked father of five. He lives in the most spectacular house I've seen – a thatched Hansel and Gretel fantasy. Inside the huge living-room, a tree trunk, still rooted into the ground, serves as a chair among more conventional furniture. He's recently added a conservatory on the front. Again, the floors are native stone, except for just below the conservatory window, where flowers are growing through bare soil. We're high up the hill. In England, you couldn't buy this view for a million.

'Anyway, if a building's been up five years and there've been no objections, you can get retrospective planning permission.'

He works as a thatcher all round Cork. There aren't many people left who can still do it. People come and watch, he says, and want to talk about it, and about the past that's disappearing. His kids are in the village school – one of the women from the mountain is a teacher there – and this is home now, for good.

'But do you feel you belong?'

He pauses and smiles. 'Well, I've no family links so I'll always be an outsider. We're a community within a community, I suppose, but I can live with that. They're good people, the Irish.'

The kids are reading, or watching cricket on the TV. I ask their dad if he's going to Danny's party at all.

'I'm getting a bit old for that sort of thing. Think I'll stay in and watch a video tonight. Would you like more tea?'

I drop Dominic at the foot of the lane leading up to Danny's at around nine thirty, and head back to Dunmanway. I'm starving. But by the time I park in the square, it's well after ten, and my best bet might be to hit the hostel and devour whatever the paedophile and the cyclist have been naïve enough to leave in the fridge. Mind you, the Shamrock Bar, facing the square, looks inviting. I've a vague notion that I might have been in there with Uncle Jack on market days. A board in the window says, 'Lunches served, 12–2.' I'm eight hours and twenty-five minutes late.

Inside, the lights are dim and mercifully there's no TV, no juke-box, no Van Morrison or Shane McGowan or Saw Doctors, just the gentle hum of about twenty people talking to each other. As the landlord lets my pint settle, I say I realise there's probably no chance of food at this time on a Saturday night.

'I could do you soup and a sandwich, if you like.'

'That'd be great.'

'Hang on, I might do better than that.'

A quarter of an hour later he arrives at my table with a huge plate of hot chicken and ham and cabbage and potatoes. It's the Auntie Annie memorial dinner, on Saturday night, at twenty to eleven, in a pub that isn't serving food. I go back to my caravan a happy man.

The wind builds up and rattles the shutters, and the rain starts to come down, but I feel secure inside the caravan. It's a bit like going camping for the first time as a kid, and enjoying the sound of rain on canvas, knowing it can't reach you. I sit up and try to read a history of Dunmanway I've found on a shelf in the hostel, but find myself preoccupied by the present.

I'm struck by the strong sense of empowerment of the people I've met, by the control they've taken over their lives. It seems to me that if they're rebuilding ruins, and repopulating an area devastated by emigration, there's a good case for saying they should be subsidised rather than persecuted. And – if you leave Catholicism out of the equation – you can see them reverting to the values that much of Ireland has hurried to leave behind in the last thirty years. It's a basic, hands-on way of life, where crops are planted and dug, old machinery is repaired or cannibalised for parts, wells must be dug, roofs somehow kept on.

I'm sure that, for some older Irish people, this dirty-finger-nailed, electricity-free existence is an unwelcome reminder of a past they've left behind. Yet most people seem happy to accept them. No one points in the street any more. Scruffy? Noisy music? Parties? A weekend on the drink? It's not exactly unknown round here.

I find myself reading and rereading a page about Dunman-way's origins as an English plantation, and realise that, in a sense, history is repeating itself. Those immigrants were rapidly ab-sorbed. This new generation have made a life as a separate community; but gradually, through work, music, pubs and school, they are being integrated. Crucially, their children see themselves as Irish, and within a generation or two their English antecedents will have melted away. Heritage tourists will be taken up to the mountain to see the strange old houses. 'This is where English hippies used to live,' the guide will be able to say. 'It's all Irish here now.'

As I turn out my electric light, an eerie screech cuts through the night: a fox or bird, perhaps. Or one of my fellow hostellers crying out in ecstasy. I get up to fasten the lock on the caravan door, but there isn't one.

The next lunchtime I head over to Danny's place to say goodbye to Dominic. There's a campfire smouldering outside, but no one's dancing to the drum 'n' bass that's booming from a small marquee that's appeared since my last visit. A handful of people are sitting round, sipping hot drinks and looking partied out. Dessy is asleep, or dead, on a cart. But the kids seem to have as much energy as ever. A twelve-year-old is teaching a seven-year-old to fire-juggle. It seems to be going well. Neither of them is on fire yet, at any rate.

I've got to know Dominic better than I ever did in England, and I admire him for making something positive and unusual and right out of a life that at one point had seemed to be going nowhere. Over the weekend, a lot of his friends have said they envy me my family links, that my ancestors give me a real connection with this area. And maybe there's some truth in that; but I can't help feeling Dominic has made a deeper connection.

He's standing at the top of the lane as I drive off. With his weathered, lived-in face, his thick tweed jacket, rough pants, big boots and flat cap, he doesn't look like part of some English subculture any more, but like what he's become: an old-style countryman, doing his best to raise a family, make ends meet, and have a good time, on a wild patch of Irish ground.

Chapter Five

Boats and Planes

'So, Liam, what river do you think Luxor stands on?'

'Er, the Danube?'

The sun's shining and the gorse is blooming as I head back towards Cork airport. A day shy of two weeks and I finally manage to override the perpetual search mode on the repmobile radio by pressing the same button I've been frantically jabbing at for a fortnight. One day someone will reinvent twiddling a dial to find channels and be hailed as a technological genius.

The decline of the Catholic Church's influence in the last two decades has coincided with the rise of the phone-in on Irish radio, where a nation confesses its darkest heresies and most startling sexual unorthdoxies to a new priesthood of silver-tongued disc jockeys. Radio confers a cathartic anonymity, and a sense of self-justification, that can't be had from confessing the same stomach-churning filth to a steely-hearted alleged celibate in a Saturday night confessional, while your neighbours sit in rows outside, adjusting their underpants and trying to listen.

'Now, Kathleen, you're on your way to Sligo for your twenty-first. Can you tell me who wrote *The Importance of Being Earnest*?'

'Er, Ernest . . . Ernest . . . Ernest Hemingway?'

These days, you can normally rely on Irish talk radio for an engrossing catalogue of out-of-court settlements for testoster-one-crazed bishops, or guilt-ridden farmers owning up to serial gusset-twanging with semi-literate babysitters. Instead, I've got round two of the morning quiz. And the Sixteenth Rule of Travel says: *However Exotic the Country, the Local Radio Phone-in Quiz Induces in the Traveller a Sudden and Dramatic Downturn in the Will to Live.* But passing through Bandon half an hour from the airport things take a turn for the better, with news of a plan to put a great big light on the top of Croagh Patrick, Ireland's holiest mountain up there in County Mayo. The light would shine out across the world, or at any rate Mayo, as a symbol of Ireland's faith. The organisation behind this controversial plan turns out to be a bloke called Gerry, who seems to have it well thought through.

'So, Gerry, have you thought how you'll be getting the power up there?'

'Well, we've considered all the possibilities, like, but the best way will be if we dig a trench there, right up the side.'

'A trench up the side of Croagh Patrick, Gerry?'

'That's it, yeah.'

'So have you talked to the fella with the digger yet?'

'Er, well now, I've got me own digger, y'see.'

'So what'll you be putting up there on the top of the mountain then, Gerry? Will ya—'

'Just a, y'know, a great big light, like.'

'Will there not be a burger bar or some other kind of refreshment outlet?'

'Ah, sure, no, just a picnic will be nice.'

'What did St Patrick have to drink up there? Do we know that, Gerry?'

As I pull into the airport poor Gerry's taking a terrible drubbing from enraged listeners accusing him of blasphemy, congenital idiocy, and ignorance of the fact that the top of Croagh Patrick is under cloud ninety per cent of the time. Gerry's morale goes into free fall, perhaps because work on the sacrilegious trench has already begun, and he's thinking it might be quite hard now to go back and fill it in. Maybe he's already bought the electric cable.

I park the repmobile in a potholed wasteland among dozens of its clones and head for the terminal.

Apart from once absent-mindedly eating a whole packet of stale crisps in the Dar es Salaam departure lounge before looking in the bottom of the bag for crumbs and discovering it was full of live ants, I can think of few travel experiences more depressing than returning a hire car to an airport dealership. The desk will be unmanned as you approach, because the partially trained company representative has seen you coming and hidden behind the counter in the hope that you'll drop the keys in the box and go away. This way they can post you a pre-paid credit card slip, which is infinitely preferable to standing there watching your reactions as you read the bill.

After standing my ground for two or three minutes, a young man suddenly pops up from underneath the counter, feigning surprise. According to his label, his name is Ruaraigh; and he's very red. Either he's already embarrassed at the answers he's about to give me, or he's got someone down there with him.

'Ah, hiya, heh, didn't see you there just now. Looking for some fax paper. Can I help ya at all?'

Standard industry practice then prevails, as Ruaraigh denies all knowledge of my, or the repmobile's, existence, and elaborately fails to find the paperwork.

'Sorry about the delay there, Mr McCarthy.'

I've already done the mental sums on this one. Thirteen days, call it two weeks, at what was it? Twenty-two pounds ninety-five pence a day. Say £165 a week. Add on some tax, and there are always some insurance extras the bastards haven't told you about, £380, say £400 tops, which still seems a lot for cheap seats, no central locking and pariah status, but there you go, that's the world we live in.

'Here it is now, Mr McCarthy. Sorry about the hold-up, like.'

But instead of a simple invoice saying 'Car Two Weeks 400 quid' the printer is pummelling out unfeasible columns of figures on, at the last count, three sheets of corporate paper. It's taking on the look of the extras on a Keith Richards hotel bill. As the machine runs out of puff, Ruaraigh rips off the account, detaches the side perforation and glances at it, before passing it to me with a nervous grin.

'Jeezus, Mary and Joseph, that can't be right!'

The anguished howl comes from nearby, where a big woman in a state of shock, and inappropriate velour leisurewear, has just received her bill at the ironically-named Budget counter. I glance down at mine and feel physically sick.

'Six hundred and thirty-two pounds?'

'Yes, sir. Six hundred and thirty-two pounds thirty-four pence. But that's punts remember, Mr McCarthy, sir.'

Everything's turning woozy with the nausea. For a moment I can't think straight. Punts? What's he on about? Perhaps it's rhyming slang and he's talking about his bosses.

'So, if you allow for the exchange rate, sir, that's only . . .'

'Six hundred and thirty-two pounds to hire a tiny bloody embarrassment of a car for two weeks? Why the hell is car hire so expensive in this country?'

'Well, sir, it's not two weeks, it's only thirteen days.'

'That's right, so there should be at least a day to knock off then, shouldn't there? This can't be right.'

'Well, sir, no, sir, because you got the first week at the weekly rate, which was, let's see, £210 plus tax, but the second week isn't a week at all now, if you follow me, it's only six days, and at the daily rate, I'll just check on the calculator, that'll be £223.95 plus tax.'

'So, it's more for six days than a week?'

'That's right, sir, yes, because of the discount, you see, sir.'

'But can't I just pay for a week and give you a car back a day early and then everyone gains, don't they?'

'I can't do that, sir, not unless you hang on to it until tomorrow, and then it'll be cheaper all right. Would you like to do that?'

'But, bloody hell, what are all these extras anyway?'

'Well sir, there's £11 a day insurance.'

'What?'

'Ah y'see, you initialled for that, here and here. It's fully comprehensive and there's tax here and here and here.'

And on it goes. A litany of charges. Optional insurance, special insurance, roadside insurance, home contents insurance, booking fee, room service, adult video, gas bill, optional tip and two Four Seasons pizzas, all adding up to the final breathtaking total.

'But what's this here?'

'The daily rate, sir. That's the special BBC rate.'

'But I'm not working for the bloody BBC.'

'Well, the computer has you down as BBC, Mr McCarthy.'

'I'm not from the BBC. I worked for them here once a couple of years ago. That's all.'

'Well, that'll be it then. It'll be in the computer and you qualify for that rate.'

'But it's £30 a day. I booked at £22.95.'

'Well, that is the special BBC rate, sir.'

'Seven quid a day more than the standard rate?'

'Seems to be, sir, heh, heh. I'd say it's time they renegotiated that deal now. They probably haven't looked at it for a long time there.'

Suddenly a shifty youth with spots, jug ears and a company polo shirt materialises from out the back and hands a slip of paper to Ruaraigh.

'Look, what I'll do, Mr McCarthy, is I can put in a request to Head Office to bump your rate down from the BBC rate to the normal rate, like. I can't promise anything now, but maybe they'll send you through a discount on the old credit card.'

'Thanks, Ruaraigh. I appreciate that.'

'But the thing is, sir' – looking ominously at the paper Jug-ears has slipped him – 'it seems there's damage to the car, sir.'

'But there can't be. I only just bloody parked it outside.'

'I know that, sir, but our operatives have just been checking it out, sir.'

Jug-ears is out the back, staring like a vindictive gargoyle.

'And there's a cracked windscreen, sir.'

'A tiny crack, yes, the size of a match head. A pebble hit it but I've got your comprehensive insurance.'

'You still have to pay the first £75 of any claim, Mr McCarthy.'

I'm near to tears now, realising the only thing round here that's comprehensive is the way I've been stitched up.

'And the tank's not full, neither, sir. So there'll be £7.50 for petrol. You're always better off filling up before you bring it back because we have to charge top whack.'

The bloody thing hadn't been full when I drove it away. Hire cars never are. The needle drops from full to three-quarters when you've barely left the airport, because behind the phoney smiles of the front desk, in airport car parks all over the world, spaced-out jug-eared school-leavers, whose meals taste of nothing but petrol, are sucking on siphon pipes to swindle you.

'So that makes it £714.84 to be exact.'

Less non-BBC discount, of course, if it comes through. I could have bought a car for less.

The flight, on the other hand, was £21.30 one way, Cork–London, one of the new no-frills deals that makes you wonder how they can afford a pilot who's passed his test. Just before take-off, but well after take-off time, the family we've all been waiting for finally turns up. I spotted them in the bar earlier: three kids, mum and dad, and an out-on-parole brother-in-law, all in various combinations of Manchester United replica kit, except for mum, who's gone for Glasgow Celtic, though I think one of her tattoos is United.

Seats on these flights are unreserved, like being in a bus, or the casualty department of a hospital. The family, who are clearly in high spirits, having presumably given Social Services the slip earlier in the day, base themselves a few rows up to my right; the eldest boy though, a nine-year-old sociopath, is banished down the aisle to sit next to me. When he complains, then shrieks, his uncle – carry-on beer in hand ready for take-off – comes down and threatens him, then gives him a can of Coke and a family-size bag of what smell like prawn cocktail and Russian cigarette-flavour cheesy corn snacks. The kid chugs the Coke and guzzles the technicolour chemicals in the few minutes we're sitting on the tarmac, then as we begin to taxi, he starts wailing, 'Ma, Ma, Ma' in a monotone crescendo that goes unnoticed by the increasingly lively, and indeed arm-wrestling, family group up front. He blurts out the words, 'Ma, I'm gonna do a sick,' just a split second before blurting out the Coke and cheesy snacks from, I can't help noticing at such close range, nose and gob simultaneously. Fortunately a woman across the aisle is quick to react with a no-frills sick bag, and I get away with minor traces of splashback.

As we gain altitude and my pebble-dashed chinos begin to crisp up nicely, I consider the reasons for this hiatus in my journey. I'm planning to spend a lot more time travelling round the west of Ireland, but not in a hire car; and I can't make the Loch Derg pilgrimage before they open for business in June. And anyway work calls.

Well, not work exactly, but one of the management-imposed charades that plague many industries these days, and television more than most. Every few months the senior executives at BBC and Channel 4 and ITV leave to take up similar jobs at a rival channel, where they immediately sack the existing staff and bring in their mates from their last job. They then cancel programmes, and commission focus groups of unemployable daytime TV-watchers with personality disorders to try and find out what viewers want.

Meanwhile, writers are summoned from all over the country to dream up ideas for vibrant, new, original programmes, which are then ditched in favour of the braindead pet, cookery, gardening and home improvement shows that have come to dominate the British airwaves. This time I'm considering pitching an idea about two sick dogs who swap homes. While they're away they get looked after by sexy vets, and their gardens and kennels have makeovers. Then they die and get barbecued by Ainsley Harriott. I'll need about a month in England for meetings with various chancers, charlatans and posh boys calling themselves producers, then I can go back to Ireland for as long as I like.

As we come in to land at Stansted there is a vicious fracas

involving the three-year-old in the middle of the row in front of me, who has spent the entire flight standing on her seat slam-dancing and head-butting the shoulder of the woman in the window seat. The child's mother, sitting in front of Sick Boy – now working his way through his second Snickers Bar with 7-Up chasers – is an odd one, and no error.

Thirty-something, white and Irish, she's dressed in a full-length embroidered biblical gown with striped pyjamas showing underneath, desert sandals, and a blue nativity-play headdress. The whole ensemble is nicely complemented by two-inch-thick orange foundation – like one of those scary women at a department store cosmetics counter – pouting pink lip gloss, and Dusty Springfield mascara, which appears to have been applied with a table tennis bat.

In England, we're used to being able to place people socially at a glance and it's frustrating when, as with this woman, the totality of the image simply does not compute. The best I can come up with for now is that she's from one of those obscure fundamentalist Christian sects who don't believe in books or paracetamol. The poor woman has probably endured baptism by immersion, possibly in red-hot coals, and has been forced to practise serial polygamy with thin blokes with white beards and crocheted hats in poorly heated outbuildings in places like Sligo and Suffolk.

This lifestyle has clearly had its effect on the child, who is disturbed, and enjoying every minute of it. For the duration of the flight, her mother has half-heartedly attempted to control her by repeating the mantra, 'Do you want a smack?' fifty or sixty times. Or perhaps it was 'some smack'. It's hard to be sure. In any case, mum was the one who got the smacks: first, when the child carefully considered the hard-edged plastic toy she'd been given to placate her, then launched it at her mother's face from a distance of two feet; and a second time, when, without warning, she landed a sickening right cross to her jaw. You got the feeling that once she got her on her own back at the ashram, she'd really lay into her.

'So what was that on the plane about a smack?'

'Nothing, dear.'

'Come here a minute would you, mother?'

As the wheels come down and we're preparing to land, mum, the woman by the window, and two hosties are still trying to force the kid to sit and fasten her seatbelt, while she emits a stomach-churning keen. At any rate, it's stomach-churning for Sick Boy. This time he dispenses with the formality of a warning. He simply honks once, like a poorly goose, then chunders with tremendous violence. Foaming Snickers fragments hit the back of the nativity headdress like a flock of starlings. Then the kid's mother runs down the aisle and belts him.

The glamour of airline travel is beginning to wear off. Next time I'll recapture the serene atmosphere of my childhood.

I'll go back to Ireland on the ferry.

A little more than six weeks later and I'm in a pub in Wales waiting for the night ferry to Cork. It's more than two decades since I last arrived in Cork by boat, and I have a strong sense of what I can only describe as nostalgic anticipation. For reasons I cannot fathom, the telly in the corner above the bar was showing Jimi Hendrix in black and white when I came in. He was playing 'Purple Haze' then. He's doing 'Hey Joe' now. Look – there's Noel Redding standing next to him. The half-dozen men in the pub are watching as if they're a new act. Perhaps driving to the ferry has somehow taken me through a time warp to the 1960s. This bar contains no indication that the last thirty years have happened. The most modern things in it are Formica and pork rinds. I've never understood the appeal of a snack that has hair growing out of it.

Hope the car's safe outside. It's a big tank of a Volvo saloon, nearly twenty years old, chunky, blue, deeply unfashionable, and it only cost £290. How do you like that then, Ruaraigh? Less than a week's hire price. I found it in Brighton in a little back-street garage up from the station. I test-drove it, knocked him down from £400, did the deal and drove off. Six hundred yards away the clutch failed, the gears wouldn't change, and it broke down in the middle of the Old Shoreham Road. I had to call the AA – the Automobile Association, not Alcoholics Anonymous. As I hadn't yet worked out how to open the hood, it was quite embarrassing. The AA man didn't disguise the fact that he thought I was a twat. Yet, when I was a kid, they used to salute you if you were a member. What went wrong there then?

Still, it's a bargain, I keep telling myself, especially if you don't count the £720 I've spent so far on repairs. Plus tax, road test fees, punitive insurance, add Ruaraigh's bill – and the non-BBC discount never materialised, by the way – and I'm almost two grand down already. And I'm not even in Ireland. As I've said, I'm in bloody Wales.

When I came in I had to ask three times for a pint before the barmaid understood me. They've never liked me, the Welsh. I went to a Wales–England rugby game at Cardiff Arms Park once, too crowded to move, and at half-time the people on the tier above us pissed on us for being English. I tried to explain I was a fellow Celt, but had to settle for turning my collar up.

Oh Christ, Hendrix has finished now and Marmalade are on, singing 'Ob-La-Di, Ob-La-Da'. This can't be what all the telly's like down here, can it? Mind you, these blokes don't seem to notice. They're up playing darts now, four of them, big buggers, with enormous beer bellies poking through skin-tight leisure tops. That one there, you can see the shape of his navel through it, and Christ, can they swear. These people swear more than the Irish. The only words I can hear as they're throwing the arrows are swear words. The barmaid's swearing now too. They probably think I'm some terrible ponce, sitting here with an English accent and writing things down. Hope they don't come over.

'Hey, what are you writing, butt? Give us a look, will you?'

'Oh, it's nothing. Just some stuff about what fat bastards you are. Hey, come on, lads, only joking . . .'

Nah, smashing people the Welsh. St Patrick came from here, didn't he? There you are then. Nancy Sinatra's on now; this is all getting a bit weird. Better not have any more to drink till I'm on the boat. Walk to the door. Whatever you do, don't look back. They might take it as a sign of weakness.

8.20 p.m.

I'm sitting in the queue to get on the ferry between a Saab turbo and a Land-Rover Discovery, listening to the top news story of the hour.

Thirteen members of the Ivory Coast youth rugby team have defected, or at any rate run off, during a tournament in Cardiff. One went after the match, six during dinner and another six during a shopping expedition the next day. They've no money, no English and only the clothes they were standing up in: bright turquoise tracksuits. So police are looking for thirteen enormous black youths in dayglo suits who don't speak the language and have no money.

'They seem to have disappeared without trace,' says a senior Welsh cop 'So far we have no leads. We are taking this very serious.'

I've just had the third degree from a policeman or customs officer or some such. He was Welsh too. They've always had it in for me. I was in a pub in Merthyr Tydfil once, years ago, with my friend Rod, and people in the public bar heard a rumour there was an Englishman in the lounge. They came through and formed a little queue to make fun of me. Mind you, I did stink of urine at the time, having been at the Cardiff Arms Park that afternoon.

The bloke just now was asking all kinds of questions about the purpose of my visit. Naturally I wasn't going to tell him I planned to wander around for an unspecified length of time going into every pub I saw called McCarthy's and undertaking a sadomasochistic pilgrimage, while trying to work out whether I was on some metaphysical level Irish, due to the collective genetic memory of my ancestors living on in the innermost reaches of my soul. So, I just said, 'Holiday', and he thought, sad lonely English bastard, then started asking questions about the blue Tank. How long had I had it? Made a note of its registration. Clearly thought I was exporting it illegally, which I may well be, but I'm not about to give him the satisfaction of telling him that.

9.20 p.m.

Happy Shillelagh Theme Bar on boat. We've just left port.

Thirteen tall black blokes in bright blue tracksuits are standing at the bar trying to get served. Nah, just joking. It's actually weirder than that. The place is like a Hogarth engraving. It's as if hundreds of alcoholics who've been drinking all day have been given massive injections of adrenaline and amphetamine and herded into an enclosed space with cattle prods. The din is deafening, the energy level terrifying, but Guinness is only £1.75 a pint, so, as it takes so long to get served, I've just got two. I'll need a few more to have any hope of catching up with everyone else. If this lot get seasick it'll be a catastrophe. On balance, I'd settle for the vomiting cattle.

It's a ten-hour voyage and I haven't got a cabin. Neither, it seems, have hundreds of other people. On the way up from the car deck, every acre of available floor space, and this is a big boat, is covered with sleeping bags, pillows, duvets and air-beds. Airbeds? Don't people know how to rough it any more? They've got foot pumps some of them, the mollycoddled bastards, and I saw one lump of a lad with pyjamas on. All I've got is one of those hopeless little velvet aeroplane pillows, and I've left that in the Tank. Too late now. The plan was to find a nice comfy sofa or luxuriously upholstered banquette to sleep on, but there'd be more chance of that in a refugee camp. Cholera might be an option though. I was swept along in a tide of thirst-crazed bug-eyed humanity to the bar where I now find myself. The barmaid here didn't understand me the first two times either. Bloody Welsh, I suppose, though I have to say she sounded more – what's the word – Russian?

The tables are all packed with great circles of career drinkers, laughing and shouting and generally behaving as if they're celebrating early release from a secure mental institution. There are hordes of marauding children, all acting as if they're drunk too. Some of them have crept up on a laughably optimistic woman who has lain down on an air-bed in a corner, and are trying to make the sound of an air-bed deflating. When she doesn't react, they jab it with a fork. Several dozen tellys seem to be on, all showing different football matches and pop videos simultaneously. There's clearly nowhere to sit, let alone lie; but then, against the odds, I spy a five-foot length of cushioned bench seat free, slightly removed from the vortex of the mêlée. I decide to stake my claim and, despite the pints I'm carrying, I narrowly beat two crack addicts in an exciting foot race. Pausing only to buy a *Big Issue* from a passing busker and his dog, I get stuck into the Guinness. So this will be my bedroom tonight. Ideal.

9.50 p.m.
I now realise why this seat was the only one free on the entire boat. Sitting, standing, and dancing on tables immediately behind me are thirty men in matching green polo shirts who I now know to be Yokel Rugby Football Club from Nether Sheepshagger in Mummerset. They're going on an end-of-season tour to Ireland, and seem quite excited at the prospect. I have chosen the worst seat in the whole of the Irish Sea. Some of them have just taken umbrage at my writing things down in a book, a process which, in their village, is probably associated with witchcraft, and are shouting things at me and clearly contemplating reprisals. I decide to drink up and go for a wander round the boat.

As I leave, a shrieking gang of eleven- and twelve-year-olds turns up. They are black and white, boys and girls, one on crutches, one wearing some sort of leg iron or calliper – an Equal Opportunities gang. For some reason they're all dressed in Tam o' Shanters and ginger wigs. Not an hour out of port, and the voyage is already taking on an unpleasant hallucinatory quality. Is this what the prospect of arriving in Ireland does to people? God knows what it must be like in August at the height of the tourist season. They must need water cannon, or issue the bar staff with Mace.

10.20 p.m.
Out in the main thoroughfare two nuns are saying the rosary outside the disabled toilet. The booze supermarket is as packed

as Safeway on the Friday night before Christmas. Four fifteen-year-old girls in stilettos, with pierced navels and goose-pimpled cleavage, are sharing a joke, and a bottle of Bailey's, with two guys who look like South American death-squad hit-men.

I seek refuge in a tiny bar near disco hell and order a drink. Sitting on a stool in the middle of the room is a man who looks like a parody Irishman from a Hollywood movie: red face, battered trilby, threadbare tweed jacket, clumpy boots, wooden stick. It's unclear whether he's a passenger, or some manner of traditional ornament or themed decoration laid on by the tourist board.

As I take my seat, the Tam o' Shanter gang march past the doorway, clapping and chanting like goblin football hooligans looking for a ruck. Look at us all, English, Irish, Scottish, Welsh – raucous, wild-eyed, up for it, bouncing off each other like actors in a surreal pageant of the history of our islands. What would Italian, or Cantonese, ferry passengers make of these appalling visions?

There are two crew members over there, eating ice-cream and drinking vodka. Perhaps they're Russian too.

10.40 p.m.
I take a short stroll outside, past the lifeboats. There don't seem to be many. Hope I don't have to fight all the other mad bastards on the boat to get in one.

10.50 p.m.
Last orders in a restaurant on B deck. I've ordered two starters, on account of wanting to kill some time, but not being hungry. There are two restaurants to choose from, one Irish, one Greek, both serving exactly the same menu. I'm having garlic mushrooms and Caesar salad, neither of which is Greek, or Irish. Together with the French house red, they are vibrating alarmingly from the motion of the boat, which creates the interesting effect of making you feel sick as food goes down, rather than up.

On being asked which part of Greece he is from, my waiter tells me he is Polish. There are many Polish on this boat, he says, also Latvian and Russian, confirming my suspicions. At the moment, my waiter and two of his colleagues are standing in a line, backs to the wall, staring intimidatingly at me in an eerily accurate reconstruction of restaurant service in the old Soviet Union. To be fully authentic, there'd have been a fourth member of the team, to stop me getting into the restaurant in the first place.

A curious trade-off is taking place here. In the late eighties and early nineties the Irish got a foothold in Russia, running pubs and hard-currency supermarkets in Moscow and other major cities. Duty free and airport catering were all run by the Irish. So you could eat Irish stew and drink Guinness at Moscow airport, while waiting a couple of days for your internal flight to find fuel, or a sober crew. Nowadays, all the amiable Irish barmen who used to staff boats like this are on their way to their first million in Warsaw, St Petersburg and Budapest, leaving the displaced persons of the Soviet catering empire to recreate an authentic cold-war dining experience in the middle of the Irish Sea.

Midnight

Back in the bar, the rugby club have joined forces with the ginger-wigged midgets and are teaching them the obscene version of 'Allouette'. Many of the rugby players have the strange walk of gym fanatics – no neck, shoulders hunched, arms curved out from the body like cowboys poised for the draw – an absurd self-conscious affectation exacerbated by too many steroid milkshakes.

On a plush banquette not ten feet from the caterwauling rugger buggers a young couple are making elaborate preparations for sleep. He's your standard grey-faced, brutal-haircutted contemporary youth in a torn Blur T-shirt. She is slender, brunette, dark bob, angelic smile, twenty years old, the most beautiful woman on the boat. While she coyly takes out a hairband, he removes his trainers and sniffs them. Next off are his pale-blue towelling socks, so moulded to his feet you can hear the skin peel off with them. These he doesn't so much sniff, as ingest. Bafflingly, she then kisses him firmly on the lips and they lie down in a face-to-face embrace, the socks three inches from their heads. I lie down on the carpet underneath a table and ponder the arbitrary cruelty of life.

6 a.m.
What's left of the air is filled with the horrible sounds of people with chest infections regaining consciousness.

When you wake up hungover, or on the floor of a bar, or both, it's important to remember that this is the worst you're going to feel all day. Nothing will top the moment you press down on the carpet with one palm in an attempt to sit up, and stale beer oozes up between your fingers as if from a giant sponge.

All around me on the floor are people who weren't there when I went to sleep – except for the woman behind me, whom I remember lying down with her son in one hand and a cigarette in the other. She's lighting up again now, while the lad sleeps soundly on the scorched carpet. Across the room are several rugby players, in comas, on window ledges. Of the ginger midgets, there is no sign.

It has been, by the most optimistic definition, a fitful night's sleep. Though I barely stirred when the drugged-up public schoolboy spilled the ashtray on me, I was jerked bolt upright by the sound of the fire extinguishers going off, and the screams that accompanied them. I looked up to see several rugby players standing on seats in clouds of dense white smoke, lit from behind and shrieking with laughter, like demon kings in some kitsch opera. Suddenly through the smoke a vision appeared in peaked cap, gold epaulettes and braided uniform, gesticulating and shouting in an East European accent, distracted from his purpose only briefly by the sight of a naked yokel carrying an ornamental potted palm. Showing immense courage in the face of overwhelming odds, the former Warsaw Pact officer threw down the gauntlet to the unacceptable face of rural English team sports, and confiscated their bottle of

Jameson's. An 'ooh' of foreboding echoed round the bar. But Mummerset's finest decided to leave it there and backed down, mumbling curses. From across the bar came a flurry of sneering abuse from the twelve-year-old Tam o' Shantered underclass. 'Chuck 'em off, chuck 'em off, chuck 'em off,' they chanted, their faces contorted by hate and E numbers. Maybe I'm mistaken, but two of them appeared to be waving crutches in the air.

God help us all when they start drinking.

Now though, through those windows that aren't obscured by the reclining bulk of liver-damaged rugby players, I can see the day's first light. I pick my way unsteadily across the room through the human flotsam that litters the hideously stained carpet. Half-finished pints afloat with fags and partially digested food clutter the sticky tables. The TVs are showing the shopping channel, motorcycle scrambling and a Daniel O'Donnell video. A bewildered multiply-pierced youth, hair matted like a sheep's arse, peers out anxiously from his skidmarked, joint-singed sleeping bag. He seems genuinely baffled by the ragbag assortment of truck drivers, labourers, students, tinkers, businessmen, schoolgirls, nuclear families and second-row forwards scattered on the floor around him, looking and smelling like victims of a late-night poison gas attack. It's possible he has no recollection of how he got here.

I go to the toilet to make a token stab at freshening up but recoil in horror, driven out by the throat-tearing retching sounds of a six-foot-five man wearing a T-shirt that says 'Irish Pub Berlin'. I head for the nearest coffee bar, where I join a queue so morose it brings to mind a meal scene from *One Day in the Life of Ivan Denisovich*. Spotting an espresso machine, I ask for an espresso.

'No! Espresso! Feeltah coffee!' barks the former KGB agent behind the counter. He is partnered by a brown-haired woman of such severity that I am powerless to resist when, against my will, she dumps a croissant-shaped object, that I now know not to have been a croissant, on to a paper plate, where it lands with the appetising thud of a cheap Polish brick. It's accompanied by a heavily perspiring pat of foil-wrapped butter bearing the incomplete legend 'Best Before', and I'm sure it was.

Up on deck, we're gliding along the river estuary past the same fields I saw as a child; but television and condoms have arrived in Ireland since then, so today there's no one out there waving. Cobh Cathedral dominates the hillside in front of us, surrounded by brightly painted houses.

'Fucking hell. Last time I was here they were all grey,' says the man next to me, a priest in his mid-fifties.

Down on the car deck, all the other vehicles seem to be occupied by sober, well-rested, mentally stable people who must have been airlifted aboard in the last half-hour, because there was certainly no sign of them last night. I'm starting to wonder if I didn't dream the entire freak show when, lying in a patch of oil by the rear wheels of a Dutch lorry, I spy a soiled ginger wig in a tartan hat. Of its tiny psychotic owner, though, there is no sign. The bow doors open, we rev our engines, and traffic pours from the bowels of the enormous ship, campers, minibuses, caravans, trailers, several coaches and dozens of private cars, many of them with the D nationality sticker that indicates 'GERMANS IN RELENTLESS PURSUIT OF RELAXED CELTIC FUN'. We're all funnelled into one tiny road that leads away from the port like a single-lane M25.

Unfortunately, the radio is still tuned to the BBC, which sounds all wrong in Ireland. The writer Lord Bragg is trailing his programme later that morning, in which he will argue that the latest developments in science and theology show that he is very clever indeed. I retune frantically, hoping to get an update on the Croagh Patrick trench. But instead, it's a tragic news story about a ninety-year-old lady being mugged on her way to early morning mass. The thieves got away with her prayer book and rosary beads. Sounds like Christian Brothers, if you ask me.

Suddenly, I look up, which I try and do as often as possible when driving, and realise that the lorries and camper vans that moments ago had packed the road ahead have miraculously disappeared. A glance in the rear-view mirror reveals an empty lane winding away down a hill. I appear to have Cork completely to myself. Hundreds of drunks, a lesser number of clean-cut families, a rugby team and some Germans have disappeared into the countryside without trace.

Ireland's ability to absorb incomers should never be underestimated.

Chapter Six

All-night Hooley in MacCarthy's Bar

The Convent sits on a hillside on the edge of the village, looking down on a ruined abbey and a spectacular tidal inlet of the Atlantic Ocean. It has twelve acres of grounds, a walled nineteenth-century vegetable garden, and a restaurant with stained-glass windows – once the nuns' chapel – where the cooking is the equal of any in the country. You can stay there for less than the cost of a dodgy B&B in Lowestoft; but it isn't actually called the Convent, and I'm not going to tell you where it is.

I withhold this information, not out of malice, but enlightened self-interest. The Third Rule of Travel says: *Never Bang on About How Wonderful Some Unspoiled Place is, Because Next Time You Go There, You Won't be Able to Get In.* When you're travelling, it helps to know a place where you can recover from the last place, and I've known about the Convent for a few years. Fortunately, it's less than an hour's drive from the Cork ferry, so I'm there in time for breakfast. Dizzy with sleep deprivation, stinking of ashtrays and other people's feet, I take my seat next to the only other guests, an American couple in their fifties. They smile politely, and recoil.

I'm tempted to ask them why so many of their fellow

countrymen continue to mispronounce *Monty Pie-thonn*, when we don't have a problem with *Cheers*, but realize this would be unnecessarily confrontational; so instead I set about a life-affirming spread of free-range eggs, home-baked soda bread, sausages from the Convent pigs, and kippers cured by the woman up the road. Service is refreshingly un-Soviet. After flirting briefly with a walk down to the abbey, I decide to do what you're allowed to do with a clear conscience in Ireland, Spain and other countries not founded on the Protestant work ethic, and go to bed for the day.

Unfortunately, though, as I'm half-English by birth, and wholly so by environment, it's impossible to sleep. Mind you, the electric saw in the room below doesn't help, shrieking and grinding away in what later turns out to have been an ecologically disastrous and ultimately doomed attempt to create a cold-storage room by sawing a fridge in half. One of the seductive things about West Cork is that stuff is done in an altogether less by-the-book way than it is in, say, Oxford; as I'm sure Jeremy Irons – whose castle near Baltimore has been undergoing renovation for several years now by all manner of odd people you bump into in bars and, well, bars mostly – has realised.

Con and Karen, one Irish, one English, have been at the Convent since the late seventies, when they bowled up from Antwerp with a multinational crew of maverick chefs, psyche-delically-enhanced waiters, and their lovers, and set up a com-mune. I bet that pleased the parish priest. The building and grounds, once the home of the Sisters of Mercy – the nuns, not the prostitutes in the Leonard Cohen song – were bought at a knock-down price from a disillusioned Californian mind-control cult who just couldn't seem to control minds out here the way they did back home. Over the years commune evolved into backpacker hostel, into B&B, into guest-house with great restaurant. TVs, trouser presses and mini-bars haven't arrived yet, but if you're the kind of person who enjoys gourmet cuisine in a deconsecrated chapel, while a fridge is sawn up in the room next door, then you'll struggle to find better at the price.

Downstairs in the chapel I have a coffee, and eavesdrop on the mid-morning debate about what should be on tonight's non-laminated menu. Fishermen are phoned to check what they caught last night; ducks are ordered from some dishevelled duck bloke up a back lane somewhere; and the garden is checked for leaves that look ready for plucking. I don't think you make much money with this sort of carry-on, but it appears to be very good for the soul.

'Organic Dan's on the phone.'

'Great fella, Organic Dan,' enthuses Con, while Karen orders the mushrooms. 'Blew in from Germany about ten years ago. Couldn't leave, of course, so started up in the organic vegetable business. Completely assimilated now. More Irish than the Irish. Supplied vegetables to us the whole of last year and forgot to send a bill. Marvellous. Wouldn't last a week in Munich now.'

It seems Ireland has always had the ability to render incomers harmless by making them Irish. When the English, or Normans as they were at the time, first invaded in 1171, they were clean-shaven and close-cropped, as they liked to fight, and didn't want nasty tweaks from hair getting caught in chain mail and helmets. But within a couple of generations those Normans left behind to be in charge had adopted the long hair and wild beards of the native Irish. It wasn't long before they were speaking the language, singing the songs, and presumably showing a reckless disregard for the licensing laws. If there'd been fridges, they'd have been as keen as the next fella to saw them in two. Anyway, by Edward III's time the situation had got so out of hand that the English introduced the Statutes of Kilkenny, observing that 'many English of the land of Ireland forsaking the English language, fashion, mode of riding, laws and usages, live and govern themselves according to the manners, fashion and language of the Irish enemies.'

So this new law forbade the English from marrying the Irish or listening to their storytellers and musicians who, long before James Joyce or the Chieftains, already had quite a reputation. They weren't allowed to sell horses to them, or ride bareback like the locals, or speak Irish; and they were told to get a bloody good haircut and generally smarten their ideas up. These statutes remained law for 200 years, and had no effect whatsoever. 'They were in essence an admission of the failure of the English conquest of Ireland and an acknowledgement of the Irish conquest of the English by absorption,' as Leonard Patrick O'Connor Wibberley has written.

I know he has, because by lunchtime I'm sitting in a pub in the village, just down the road from the Convent, reading his excellent and amusing history, rather wonderfully titled *The Trouble with the Irish (or the English Depending on Your Point of View)*. I reckon if I can't spend the day sleeping, the next best thing is to spend it reading and drinking. I found the fading green hardback in a second-hand shop in a fishing port in Nova Scotia last year. I know nothing about Leonard Patrick O'Connor Wibberley except that he also wrote *The Mouse that Roared*, which went on to become an Ealing film classic; and I only know he wrote that because it says so in the front of *The Trouble with the Irish*.

It was published in 1956, and for all I know I've got the only copy still in existence. Because of its age it seemed an appropriate choice to accompany me on this journey; it delivers a history of the country that ends at exactly the time my boyhood visits began, which has a pleasing symmetry. It also carries a distinct flavour of the fifties, that long-lost era before Guinness was chilled, when cows were milked by hand, when a priest could still fumble beneath an altar boy's cassock without fear of being pictured in the local paper getting out of a meat wagon with a blanket over his head.

And he was no mug, old Wibberley. This is the final paragraph of his book, written, remember, in 1955: 'So it would seem that North and South will finally be united. But the Irish must surely have learned that union brought about at the point of a gun is not union but suppression and thus any attempts of the IRA to force the North to unite with the South will but stiffen resistance and prolong the eight-hundred-year-old problem, now approaching solution, of the trouble with the Irish.'

But it's his theme of absorption of the outsider due to what he calls 'that particular property of Ireland, that intangible but forcible magic of the land' that intrigues me. What if all the family time I've spent here over the years means that I'm partially absorbed, and the country is calling out to me to complete the process? This seems more credible than genetic memory, and less shallow than my having simply fallen for Ireland's well-marketed image of the Celt and the craic; or at least it does after three pints of stout. But if Ireland absorbs everyone – or at least everyone who's open to it – then does that mean that ancestry doesn't matter? Is there no difference between me and, say, a German tourist on a cycling holiday with a Corrs album playing on his Walkman? This is an ugly possibility that's difficult to contemplate, so I decide to order some food instead.

I cast an eye on the blackboard. Salad of marinated feta cheese with roasted red peppers. Stuffed chicken fillet with tomato tequila sauce. Hake with chicory and orange in filo parcels with prawn sauce. If any absorption is going on on the food front, it seems to be in the other direction. I decide to go as native as the menu allows, and order a plate of smoked wild salmon from the wonderful smokehouse up the road whose name I can't tell you, but the old boy who owned it dropped dead last year at the primary school Christmas play, and his son runs it now.

The village is tiny, so there are just the six pubs. I've picked the one best suited to Wibberley's theory of absorption. There's a French landlady and a Belgian barmaid, both with spectacularly confused accents. A young builder with a scar on his face is sitting at the bar eating a very rare steak with garlic butter. As I make my order he deftly initiates a conversation, and in less than a minute has confided that, although he's never actually worked on Jeremy Irons's castle, he once sold him some timbers, over the odds like, in the boatyard at Baltimore.

A lull in the conversation means that it's my turn now. Unfortunately, a lifetime spent in England has rubbed off on me, and I can't think of anything to talk about except the weather.

'See it's started raining again.'

'You know what, best feckin' thing about this country, the rain, you know why? Cause if the sun was always feckin' shiny every bastard would be coming here. That beautiful waterfront over there at Glandore – d'you know that? Well, feckin' high rises all up the feckin' hillside, that's what it'd be like there now if the weather was like Greece. And then the place would really be shagged now, wouldn't it? This way, it keeps most of them away except for the ones who really want to come, like, and anyway I think it's more interesting, isn't it, when every day isn't the feckin' same?'

'The weather is God's way of keeping Ireland Irish,' chips in the French woman.

'What's that you're reading over there anyway, stuck away in the corner like you don't want anyone talking to you?' says the builder.

So we discuss Wibberley, and genetic memory, which he reckons is a sound enough idea.

'So what are you doing here anyway? On holiday are ya? Or are you looking for a nice cheap old house to buy? Because if that's yer game you should have been here ten years ago. Them days are gone now.'

I say I'm visiting my family and travelling around.

'What? Looking for ya roots are ya? Like all them poor feckin' Yanks in Killarney? Jeezus Christ, the trousers on some of them fellas.'

I'm cringing to be categorised in this way. I've got nothing in common with American heritage tourists, but for the moment I can't think why; so I decide to stand there, saying nothing and chewing salmon, until someone else says something, which obviously won't be long.

'Where are you heading next then?'

'West, I think, then north.'

'Have ya ever been out to the Beara Peninsula?'

I never have; a piece of news which is greeted by sighs of pity and incredulity all round. I've heard about it all right, a wild strip of land poking out into the Atlantic at the western fringe of Cork. An Australian alcoholic I know once tried to spend the winter there, but his foot went septic and he had to go back to Darwin. These things happen.

'It's a beautiful place. You'll find plenty of McCarthys out that way to make you feel at home.'

It's a nice idea, but I've already decided to leave Cork tomorrow. There just isn't time to go to Beara.

'And there's a McCarthy's pub out there, real old style, never been changed.'

'I really couldn't change my plans now.'

'Why the feck not?'

I'm just going to ask him whether he's always said feck or was it invented by the guys who wrote the *Father Ted* TV shows, when the Belgian woman suddenly joins in.

'I reckon there's only two kinds of people, the Irish and the wannabe Irish.'

Clearly she's now one of the former; but what if I'm one of the others?

'Sure, we had some Germans in the other day, didn't we, Yvette, and weren't they desperate to be Irish? Couldn't get enough of the place.'

'Why do you think that is then?'

'Well, I asked them that, and they said it's because the Irish know how to have fun.'

'That's it? Fun?'

'Yeah.'

'No sort of mystical union with the land, Celtic twilight of our ancestors kind of thing?'

'No, just fun. So I says, so you like fun, but do you know how to have fun? And this woman stares at me, all serious like and says, "Off course not. Ve are German." '

Huge peals of laughter all round. In its way, this is quite a telling symbol of the new united Europe: an Englishman, an Irishman, a French woman and a Belgian, all sitting round having a good laugh about the Germans.

I leave the pub and go for a moist walk past the post office, the butcher's, and the other five pubs, down to the abbey at the water's edge. You can still see the side door where lepers had to stand, and a well that's supposed to cure warts. Because of the huge numbers of wine casks that were found there it's believed by some historians to have functioned as both a haven of monastic contemplation, and a massive illegal off-licence. It was burned, along with the whole village, by the English army in 1642. Irish children were considered fair targets, on the grounds that one day they would grow into Irish adults. Some soldiers testified to having stripped Irish corpses and found pointed tails on their backs, proving they were devils.

Soft drizzle, a few pints and a good old wallow in the injustices of history is a powerful combination, as the Irish know better than most. As I head back up the hill to the Convent, my English half and my Irish half are distinctly ill at ease with each other. I have to give them a good talking to, and tell them there's no point living in the past, but I'm not sure they're convinced.

After a light supper of langoustines with whiskey mayonnaise, chervil and carrot soup, well-hung fillet of rare local beef marinated in Thai spices, and rhubarb crème brûlée, all washed down with a galumphing chocolatey Aussie red, I sleep the luxuriantly deep, guilt-free sleep that comes only to those who've had too much to eat and drink, and just don't care.

I wake with sun streaming through the curtains, and realise almost immediately that it must be morning. I pull the curtains back and see that the tide is in, twinkling brilliantly. The landscape looks luminous, and a glorious day is beckoning; so I go back to bed for an hour, then get up again.

Out on the landing, at the top of a grand staircase with a huge Gothic ecclesiastical window, are the American couple who almost gagged when I arrived for breakfast yesterday.

'We've been up for hours,' says their body language. 'We've already had a healthy breakfast of wholemeal toast and 'erb tea. We've explored the grounds and we're dressed up like this because now we're going on a massive walk that will help turn us into better people. You look like shit, by the way.'

Then they actually say, 'Beautiful day.'

'Sure is.'

They go on down while I go back into my room because I've

forgotten my map. I also grab my copy of the tourist board's indispensable *Guide to 100 Best B&Bs Run by Mad Nosey Religious Fanatics*. Downstairs, the front door opens, and the Americans blow back in, pursued by the climate.

'Problem?'

'Yeah, gotta change. It's started to rain. Now I remember why we usually go to Hawaii.'

Yes indeed.

Over breakfast, I hatch a plan. I will definitely leave Cork today. I've no idea why. The still dominant, but increasingly rattled, English half of me just needs a plan, and this is it.

As I ease the blue Tank round the turning circle and head down the drive, I look back at the Convent in the rear-view mirror. I'm abandoning this house, this view and the best cooks in the country to take my chances once again among the Mrs Goggins of this world. With luck I'll be somewhere up the Kerry coast by nightfall.

Eight miles on there's a fork in the road. Right for Killarney, Kerry and the north; left for Bantry Bay and the Beara Peninsula.

I turn left. No point in being too rigidly Anglo-Saxon about these things.

The rain has cleared and it's a bright blustery day. The gorse is still in bloom, and occasionally there's a burst of its distinctive coconutty-vanilla aroma. The road west goes through Skibbereen again. On the western edge of town it runs alongside a river for a little way. A bank of black clouds, backlit by sunlight, has given the choppy water an unearthly charcoal and silver sheen; the wind compounds the surreal effect by making the river appear to flow backwards. I pull over to the side of the road and get out to admire the view.

Immediately across the road is a ruined abbey and cemetery. As I haven't visited one since late yesterday afternoon, I decide to take a look. On the whole, it's fair to say that, if you're travelling round the west of Ireland, an interest in ruined abbeys, however slight, will stand you in better stead than a passion for rollerblading, say, or a penchant for showbiz gossip.

The sign says that this is Abbeystrowny – the monastery of the stream – a Cistercian community ruined since the thirteenth century. The graves are more recent. Flanked on three sides by the churchyard is a plot of lush, neatly mown grass, about fifty yards by twenty-five, its surface gently undulating like the windblown waves on the river over the road. Some sort of garden of remembrance, perhaps?

There's a white painted wrought-iron monument, all ornate flowers and petals, incorporating a harp and a Celtic cross. It was erected in 1887 to the memory of the victims of the famine. A plaque says, 'Made by Eugene McCarthy, blacksmith, of Ilen Street, Skibbereen.' The significance of the patch of thick grassed lawn begins to dawn on me. It's a famine pit – an unmarked grave of victims of the potato famine. I find an inscription on stones nearby.

TO THE NAMELESS DEAD WHO LIE HERE AND IN WAYSIDE GRAVES

Nerve and muscle and heart and brain,
Lost to Ireland, lost in vain,
Pause and you can almost hear
The sounds echo down the ages,
The creak of the burial cart.
Here in humiliation and sorrow,
Not unmixed with indignation
One is driven to exclaim
Oh God, that bread should be so dear
And human flesh so cheap.

There isn't a soul to be seen; no cars passing. The black clouds pass from the face of the sun, and a granite boulder sprouting a huge gorse bush on a hill looking down on the churchyard is suddenly illuminated. The rock, and probably the bush as well, have been watching this spot since long before these terrible things happened. I look down at the patch of grass beneath my feet. The undulations in the ground suddenly look like long human shapes, as if the ground is too full, and they're rising to the surface. How many must be buried here? Dozens; hundreds maybe. The famine was never mentioned when I was a kid. I think older generations were still in some way ashamed back then. 'Humiliation' – that was the word on the stone. The inscription continues: 'Ireland's worst single disaster 1845 to 1850. One million dead. One million emigrated. Skibbereen, epicentre of this horror, suffered more than most. Here in the famine burial pits, were placed the coffinless remains of nine thousand victims . . .'

Nine thousand.

I cross the road back to the car in subdued mood and take a look in Wibberley. According to him, parliament in London voted £100,000 to famine relief, in the same year it gave £200,000 to the beautification of Battersea Park. 'Anyone who knows Battersea Park,' he observes, 'will quickly admit that such a sum was totally inadequate for the purpose.'

Cheered by the bleak humour of my guide, I leave Skibbereen behind and drive west towards Beara.

Glengarriff sits on Bantry Bay on the armpit of the Beara Peninsula. Sheltered on three sides from the winds by lofty wooded hills, it's reputed to have the best climate in Ireland, and both the mainland and the islands offshore in Bantry Bay luxuriate in rich subtropical vegetation. When Thackeray first came to Ireland and visited the town in 1842 he wrote of 'the astonishing beauty of the country', even though it was pissing down and they'd lost his luggage. 'What sends picturesque tourists to the Rhine and Saxon Switzerland?' he wondered. Sweet white wine, over-hyped sausages and an obsession with cleanliness, William Makepeace, that's what.

I stop to buy a bar of chocolate at a shop that appears to be open, but whose door is locked. It's opened begrudgingly, then locked again behind me to deter other customers, by a hatchet-faced lady who glares at me while I select the best Kit Kat in the shop. In a corner a couple of intimidated Americans lurk in the shadows, examining tea towels covered in pictures of leprechauns, or possibly the shopkeeper's relatives.

Glengarriff is a busy tourist town, with menus in Dutch, and woolly sweaters and ornamental shillelaghs on permanent offer at knock-down prices. As I drive through, a small huddle of men with assorted nautical headwear and cigarettes on the go lurk near one of the boating concessions, touting for business from a family of recently arrived smart-but-casual Continental income opportunities pushing a polka-dot pram. The town has a sense of heightened Irishness that gives it an air of unreality, but there's no denying it's in a gorgeous spot.

Turn left at Glengarriff and you enter Beara. 'Within five miles there is a country of the magnificence of which no pen can give an idea,' wrote Thackeray, who clearly couldn't be bothered trying to describe it, as he was behind schedule on a *Vanity Fair* script for the BBC at the time. Suddenly the lush rolling farmland of West Cork and the verdant Celtic jungle of Glengarriff are just memories, and you're in an altogether wilder place.

The road west has the massive expanse of Bantry Bay to the left, and stark mountains of biblical ruggedness on the right. Sheep are attached to unlikely precipices as if by Velcro. Radiant shafts of sunlight pierce the dark bruise of cloud cover and hit the water with a metallic flash, as if to prove there is a Creator, and his taste is for random and terrifying beauty. By heading for Beara instead of following my intended route I suppose I'm hoping to leave the world of plans and arrangements behind, lay claim to my share of Ireland's spontaneous and disorganised ebullience, and see if I really fit in. I'll simply turn up at McCarthy's Bar, and see what happens. If nothing does, I can go away again.

Entering Castletownbere I notice that the Tank has developed a niggling exhaust rattle. I consider pulling in at O'Sullivan's garage, but the new-found spirit of the journey persuades me to ignore it until it gets really bad, then tie it up with a bit of old washing-line I'll find in a ditch somewhere. O'Sullivan's garage is just along from O'Sullivan's estate agent, next door to McCarthy's solicitors on the one side, and MacCarthy's – with an 'a' like my grandfather – Bar and Grocery on the other.

Deferring the first pint of the day to enhance its flavour, I park on the waterfront and go for a stroll through town.

Castletownbere – or Castletownberehaven to give its full name – is a proper working fishing port. Thirty or forty small boats moored on the waterfront just yards from the main street are swarming with fishermen doing things I don't understand with cables and hawsers. A lad in a woolly hat with a mad gleam in his eye is moving crates of monkfish with a forklift, tearing around the quayside with all the caution of Keith Moon driving a Rolls-Royce towards a swimming pool.

Blowing in the breeze along the water's edge is an exotic-looking row of what visitors believe to be date palms, thriving in the Gulf Stream, but which are in fact cunning impostors imported from New Zealand. Framed by the stark mountain-sides behind, the houses and shops leap out in vivid shades of yellow, blue and dayglo. O'Donoghue's Bar is two shades of purple. The bank is green and pink. 'Jack Patrick's Restaurant and Butcher' proclaims a sign. 'In memory of the men of the Berehaven battalion who fought for the Irish Republic' says the large grey Celtic cross in the market square opposite Mac-Carthy's. A fresh tricolour wreath of lilies lies next to it on the pavement.

There's a B&B sign on a big old house so on impulse – I'm getting the hang of this – I go and knock on the door. After the sort of pause that usually suggests someone inside is destroying evidence, the door is opened by a bespectacled, guilty-looking man who hasn't recently showered. He squints malevolently round the door and says, 'Yes?' meaning, 'I don't want you to stay here.'

'Do you have a room for the night?'

He peers out over my shoulder to the street. 'On your own are you?'

'I am.'

'I only have a double.'

'That's okay. I'll pay the double rate.'

He shakes his head. 'No.'

'Why not?'

'I don't usually do that.'

He goes to shut the door, to stop me seeing whatever is hanging from a meat hook or decomposing in the acid bath behind him; but suddenly we're interrupted by two returning guests, a good-looking, fresh-faced couple in their twenties – Dutch cyclists, I'd say at a guess – who go in past him, smiling. As the door slowly closes, my last glimpse is of him watching them go up the stairs, with the brooding gaze of a serial killer of Dutch cyclists.

Half an hour later I'm unpacking in a hygienic bungalow on the edge of town. As I close the gilt-embossed door of the white melamine wardrobe and sit down on the polyester and fibreglass duvet cover, I can gaze out through the double-glazed UPVC windows at the untamed mountainside beyond. Smack in front of it a technicolour plastic leprechaun stands by a tiny Renaissance-style fountain on a crazy-paved patio. The casual brush of bare foot against the maroon, yellow, black, green and orange swirls of the brushed nylon shagpile generates a bracing burst of static, and sparks leap from my forehead.

I am not the first to observe that the landscape of rural Ireland has been badly defaced these last thirty years by the slapdash construction of suburban housing in places where there are no suburbs. On mountainsides, cliff tops and riversides, by secluded loughs, ancient bogs and neolithic monuments, the Invasion of the Killer Bungalows has swept all before it. Strict planning regulations are now rumoured to be in force, but the faux-Spanish haciendas, neo-Kelloggs dream homes, and mini-Southforks are already here. At times it can seem that the booming Celtic Tiger economy must be driven entirely by the manufacture of net curtains and plastic Doric columns.

But before sneering at Irish bad taste, smug outsiders who live in twee English villages, like me, should bear in mind that the bungalow blight is simply the logical outcome of Ireland's history of poverty; a poverty for which English landlords living across the sea in their carefully preserved villages must shoulder their fair share of the blame. Ireland simply does not possess the picturesque old housing stock that's to be found in England and France, because for many centuries, and until very recently, this was a desperately poor country. Those houses were never built. The census of 1842, for example, records that eighty-four per cent of the population of the Beara Peninsula at that time were living in one-room mud huts. Visitors like Thackeray, though used to the deprivation of Victorian London, were staggered by the poverty and squalor they witnessed.

The self-confident synthetic consumerism of the new houses is a response to this history of deprivation. 'Look,' the bungalows are saying, 'we're not peasants any more. We buy things now, rather than digging them up. We've been sitting on bare wooden benches for centuries, but we've got Dralon sofas now, just like you.' So people whose parents made do with bare concrete floors are now mad for fitted carpets, preferably in epilepsy-inducing designs. Grandchildren of turf cutters who never saw an indoor toilet can't wait to install turf-effect gas fires and en-suite avocado bidets. Often you'll see an inappropriate-looking new house built right next to the ruin it's replaced. 'We were that,' it's saying, 'but now we're this.' It's a very Irish paradox that modern houses and bungalows can speak so eloquently of the nation's past.

When I arrived here Mrs O'Sullivan greeted me in textbook style.

'Where are ye from? Are ye working or on holiday? Are ye married? Do ye have children? Why aren't they with ye? What work is it ye do, clearing off and leaving them behind? Will ye be wanting mass times? Half eight all right for breakfast?'

Then she let me in.

She showed me round, making sure to point out the carefully concealed switch and red light without which, bitter experience has taught me, showers in B & Bs just get colder and colder, even with the dial all the way up to red. Then she, her husband and two kids set off in a people carrier with a fish symbol on the back for half six mass, Saturday night mass now fulfilling the once inflexible Sunday obligation.

'Crazy, really, isn't it?' said Mrs O'Sullivan. 'But I suppose it's good for the supermarkets and golf clubs. Sure, I expect soon we'll be able to go to Sunday mass Monday to Friday as well. Will you be late?'

'I shouldn't think so, no.'

After all, I don't know a soul. I'm taking Wibberley out in my pocket for company.

'I'll make some sandwiches, so. They'll be there whenever you come in.'

On the wall in the hallway, where the previous generation would have venerated the Pope and JFK, is a photo of Manchester United, who seem to be more popular in County Cork than they are in Manchester. Pausing for a moment by the front door to admire the traditional Celtic craftsmanship on the glow-in-the-dark Virgin Mary holy water font with integral night light and thermometer, I step outside into dazzling sunshine and heavy drizzle, and set out to walk to MacCarthy's.

On the main street, lots of swarthy, tough-looking men, heavily stubbled and tattooed, and that's just their heads, are prowling round in groups. As I'm wondering what gay package tourists from Brighton and San Francisco are doing in Castletownbere, I notice they're speaking Spanish and Portuguese, and are probably fishermen ashore for the night. Round here, they've been arguing about monkfish quotas with the Spanish for at least 500 years.

Outside the church half a dozen shifty-looking men are lurking by the porch, observing their obligation to attend mass, but without actually entering the building and being spotted by the priest. Two of them are smoking, cigarettes clutched between thumb and first finger, lit end in palm, in the tough-guy style favoured by mean hombres, and boys behind bike sheds, the world over. Hunched and restless, their furtive, well-practised body language doesn't say 'Church' so much as 'Unemployment Office' or 'Magistrate's Court'. Ireland may be becoming a more secular society, but some deeply ingrained vestige of belief has convinced these guys they're more likely to avoid eternal damnation if they spend an hour every Saturday night having a few smokes outside the church before going out for a skinful. It's a complex business, modern theology.

The Second Rule of Travel in Ireland says: *The More Bright Primary Colours and Ancient Celtic Symbols Outside the Pub, the More Phoney the Interior.* Reassuringly, the sign outside Mac-Carthy's is plain white lettering on black. I wasn't expecting the 'a' before the 'cC' but detail isn't going to hold me back now. In any case, the ornate period tiling on the floor as you go in proclaims 'McCarthy's' which creates a comforting air of confusion, and gives you something to talk about. Even at seven o'clock in the evening, damp, friendless and without a plan, I can sense that this place might be a contender in the Best Pub in the World competition I have been privately conducting since 1975. For the Ovalau Club in Levuka, Fiji, the pressure is suddenly on.

MacCarthy's is an effortless compromise. The front half is a grocer's shop with seats for drinkers; the back half, a bar with groceries. On the right as you enter is a tiny snug, once a matchmaker's booth where big-handed farmers arranged marriages between cousins who hadn't met. Aluminium kettles and saucepans hang from the ceiling, not for show, but for sale. Drinkers sit under shelves of long-life orange juice and sliced bread. There is a fridge full of dairy products. The well-stocked shelves behind the bar display eggs, tinned peaches and peas, Paxo stuffing, custard creams, baking powder, bananas, Uncle Ben's rice, nutmeg, onions, olive oil, spaghetti, Brillo pads and soap: good news for hungry drinkers who need a wash.

The dense, luxuriantly-sculpted pint of stout is five minutes in the pouring, the precise amount of time needed to confess your entire life history to the skilled Irish bar person.

I feel rather pathetic telling the woman serving me that I've come in because my name is McCarthy. Presumably I'm not the first lonely heritage-obsessed saddo to turn up from overseas claiming to be part of the diaspora and hoping to be made a fuss of. But I'm made as welcome as any local, and no traveller can ask for more. In fact, unlike the locals, I'm not allowed to pay for my drink. She introduces herself. It's her pub. I blurt out something embarrassing about perhaps being cousins, like I'm some dewy-eyed policeman from Boston who's never set foot in Ireland before.

'Actually, it's my birthday today and there's a bit of a party later. Maybe you'd like to come?'

Trust me on this one. If you ever manage to turn up, by chance, in a strange town where there's a pub with your name on it, on the night of the landlady's birthday, and she invites you to the party, then this is God's way of telling you to forget about going back to the B&B for sandwiches and an early night.

It must have been around four in the morning that I spilled the whiskey on the social worker. Earlier on things had been more sedate. For a while, at least.

I was introduced to neighbours and friends, a sister, and an eighty-two-year-old mother, who'd flown over from England for the birthday, but was planning to move back permanently, she told me, while buying me a pint to follow the one on the house, and the one the social worker, or was it the sister, had bought. Then someone turned up and said she'd just seen a woman put up her umbrella outside the church and a bread knife had fallen out.

I stood up about then and cracked my head on a shelf of sugar bags and jam, but by then someone had arrived with the menus and they were all ordering starters for the birthday dinner. So I said goodbye as they got up to leave and, 'What are you talking about?' said someone, and 'Has he not ordered?' asked another. So I ordered the garlic mussels and the sole and next thing I know we're all outside and walking down the street carrying our drinks to the sister's restaurant, where they sit me down at a specially laid table. I'd gatecrashed the private family party.

'Ah no, this is just the meal, the party won't be till later.'

I was handed a glass of white to go with my pint, its creamy head now mottled with rainspots. Someone else passed a glass of red. Suddenly I realised I was the only male on a table of high-spirited females, assorted ages forty-something to eighty-two. One of them raised a glass.

'Well, Peter, blessed art thou amongst women,' which really is an excellent joke if you know your Hail Mary.

I recall very fine ratatouille, potatoes *and* chips, so you didn't have to make that difficult choice in advance, more wine, and seventy-two flash photos, unless they were only twenty-four-shot films, in which case there were just the forty-eight.

My credit card caused some hilarity, on account of there being no bill. Walking down the street some time after eleven, all the pub doors were shut and curtains drawn. True, the tremendous hubbub coming from behind the curtains suggested there might be the odd straggler still trapped inside, but of course they'd only be observing the statutory drinking-up time, licensing laws in the west of Ireland being painstakingly observed, as anyone will tell you. We went past MacCarthy's, continued along the street, then through the door of a house, where we proceeded in a northerly direction along a darkened passageway, before emerging behind the bar of the most crowded pub I have ever been in in my life. Young women, gnarled old men, lads with Vinny Jones haircuts, animated old ladies, extended families were all yabbering and laughing and generally observing the statutory drinking-up time with impressive commitment.

Moving in any direction clearly wasn't an option and the pub, as I've said, was shut. Unsure what to do, I instinctively ordered a round of drinks. You never know, perhaps there was an official extension, passed by the local courts for the benefit of the group of people singing 'Happy Birthday' to a glamorous, sporadically conscious young woman in the corner. Well, clearly my luck was in. An extra hour's legal drinking must have been granted, because my round duly appeared.

'That'll be £18.47.'

This was the first money I'd been allowed to spend all night. I handed over a twenty, happy to be paying my way at last.

'Ah wait, you're with the MacCarthys. Sure, put that away, these'll be on the house.'

We extricated ourselves from the crush just before midnight, when the legally extended closing time would certainly be enforced and everyone sent home, whether they liked it or not. Somehow you could feel it in the air.

Back at MacCarthy's, however, no such restrictions applied, because this was a private party. I was in the dream Irish pub of the popular romantic imagination – dimly lit, past midnight, shelves piled with obscure groceries, a buzz of conversation and whoosh of energy coming off the crowd. On a bench by the wall two musicians were playing 'Happy Birthday' to announce the arrival of a giant strawberry gateau. For a moment I had a vision of Michael Flatley bursting from it in a shamrock posing pouch, his taut nipples glistening with baby oil.

But fortunately, this wasn't a road we had to go down, and it was just cut into slices. The musicians played a raucous set of songs that nebulous half-Irish like me recognise, but can't name. The guitarist's massive voice cut effortlessly through the noise of the crowd and the bearded mandolin player, eyes closed in passionate supplication as he hit the high notes, was the very essence of the traditional Irish musician.

Turned out he was German. He just bowled up here five years ago wearing a sarong, and never left. The audience clearly didn't resent his playing their music; if anything, I'd say they took the imitation as flattery.

I found myself envying this outsider who's now an insider in a place where I desperately want to belong myself, despite the outrageous hours they keep. I was jolted out of my introspection by a seventy-two-year-old woman who stood on a chair and sang 'The Fields of Athenry'. She was a bit wobbly on her pins, on account of having suffered a stroke the previous week, but it went down well anyway. Everyone followed with songs of their own, except me, because we just don't carry on like that in England; and this, more than anything else, made me feel like an impostor.

But then singing turned to dancing and I no longer felt English, just awkward, as I was swept up in a distant relative of the waltz. By now, there were just a dozen of us, the hardcore survivors of the seething mob who'd been here four hours ago. Christ, was that really the time? As I swivelled my wrist to look at my watch I tipped the glass of Jameson's I was holding over the social worker, but of course it wasn't a problem, it was only whiskey, she said, and didn't I look at home here? And would I ever think of coming to live here, because it's clear that I belong? I hadn't even told her what was going through my head or the reasons for my trip.

As Stroke Lady was loaded into a taxi of which she would have no recollection next day, but that's the medication for you, I noticed the birds were singing, and decided to try and fit in a short nap before breakfast. Saying goodbye to my new-found family and friends, I realised with a shock that I now knew more about some of them than about people at home I'd known for twenty years. As I can't now remember what these things were, I can't say whether or not this was a profound and truthful insight, or just gibberish.

I walked back along the high street, past pubs that were either long closed, or full of people who'd calmed down quite a lot since last night. It was half past five as I walked up the gravel drive to the front door of the B&B. After several frustrating minutes trying to open it with my bedroom key, I tried the front door one instead. As I lurched inside, Mrs O'Sullivan appeared, just in time to see me pause to admire the luminous Virgin again, and knock it off the wall. Politely declining the six rounds of ham sandwiches on the tray she was holding, I edged gingerly along the hallway to the wrong bedroom door, and opened it.

If it weren't for the fact that the pubs had been closed for six and a half hours, she'd probably have thought I was drunk.

Chapter Seven

The Children of Lir

I wake the next morning around eleven. Two Italian motor-cyclists in blue and yellow suits are staring at me, and grinning.

I've woken once already when, two and three-quarter hours after she'd offered me the plate of sandwiches, Mrs O'Sullivan knocked on my door and announced it was breakfast time. To my distress, the fry-up featured puddings, both black and white, and an unforgivable kidney. I palmed the offending items into a napkin, and slipped the obscene bundle into my trouser pocket for disposal later. Out in the polished parquet hallway, Mr O'Sullivan was bolting the Blessed Virgin back on the wall with a Black and Decker, while his son played Robopriest on the computer. I paid Mrs O'Sullivan and thanked her.

'Ah,' she said, 'you're looking grand, considering. Isn't it true that Mrs Thatcher only used to sleep three hours a night when she was in charge of you?'

Perhaps so. If she went round all day feeling like this, it would explain an awful lot.

I went outside into a biblical deluge with no plan beyond having a big snooze in the car. Negotiating the steep driveway in the Tank was like white-water rafting, only without a big Kiwi to rely on if the going got tough. Making sure not to knock the eagles off the gateposts and really spoil Mr O'Sullivan's day, I turned right down the lane, with the tide. My eyes felt as if I'd slept with someone else's contact lenses in. Perhaps I had. I gave them a good rub and crouched forward over the steering wheel like Mr Magoo.

The road ahead was all but invisible in the apocalyptic gloom, and the exhaust rattle had upgraded itself overnight to a bassy blowy sound not unlike a tuba. All things considered, it would be a good idea to stop soon. Suddenly a dog ran out of a driveway and started to run along beside the car, snapping and yelping at the wheels.

I waited until the barking had stopped, indicating either that I had outrun the high-spirited little dog, or squashed the bastard, and pulled into the gateway of a mist-shrouded field. I remembered the heated seat, an impressive feature in a £290 car; so I turned it on, closed my eyes and was asleep in seconds, only quicker.

I think the bikers have come to view a stone circle in the field and found me parked in their way. I don't know how long they've been knocking on the windscreen; long enough to find it amusing, at any rate. There's a considerable amount of drool on my chin, but they look sensational. Doesn't it make you sick, how Italians always look so good? In Verona, I've seen pensioners wearing Gucci shades and canary-yellow mohair suits. Where I live they have on-the-spot fines for that sort of carry-on.

There's nothing like a couple of Italians staring at you to make you feel ashamed to be part of a nation that thinks polyester is a good fabric. They wait patiently for me to reverse out of the steaming quagmire.

'Iz no problem,' says the guy, who looks like a particularly handsome Serie A footballer, while his presumably cello-playing supermodel novelist girlfriend hugs his arm. The sun's out now, and I fancy a look at the stone circle myself, which is now clearly visible in the field, but I can't bear the thought of them seeing that I'm wearing brown shoes with black trousers; so I drive off back towards town, exhaust trumpeting stylishly. There's an enormous single standing stone about fourteen feet high in the garden of a bungalow. These things must be ten a penny round here, I think, swerving to avoid an object in the road, which may or may not have been a dead dog.

There are no Singapore noodles in the Beara Peninsula; however, they do a decent bit of cod in the Old Bakery Café, which is where I find out about the Buddhists. Half an hour later, I'm looking down from my window on the cliff edge, past the fluttering prayer flags, on to one of the most spectacular stretches of coastline I've ever seen. Five craggy headlands stand in a line between me and Castletownbere. Blue sky is followed by yellow mist, then by an enormous broad rainbow, as the weather goes into convulsions on hitting land for the first time since leaving America.

A Buddhist retreat centre seems like a good antidote to the excesses of last night. It's unlikely I'll attain Nirvana, but there's a fighting chance it might keep me out of the pub. When I arrived I was welcomed by a mild-mannered, smiley man with a faraway look in his eye, as though he were watching a particularly pleasing spider on the wall behind my head. He explained that the people in the centre itself were on year-long silent retreat, but there was a hostel, an old converted farmhouse that was open to anyone.

I was early enough to claim the only private room, for twelve quid a night. It's finished in polished wood, like a chalet, with a hand-made double bed and wardrobe. There's a book in my pocket called *A Doctor's War* by Aidan MacCarthy. I have hazy recollections of someone passing it across the bar to me last night at the author's daughter's birthday party. I lie on the bed while the weather runs amok outside, and finish it by dusk. It's a jaw-dropping account of life as an RAF doctor during the Second World War. He survived Dunkirk, capture by the Japanese in the Pacific, and being held prisoner in Nagasaki the day the atom bomb dropped, before cruising home in triumph aboard the *Queen Mary*, only to find his brother, a parish priest in London, had been killed in the last bombing raid of the war.

The book throws intriguing new light on life in the prison camps of the Pacific: 'The Japanese and Korean guards had no scruples about masturbating in public, either solo or in dual operation. This form of sexual relief did not necessarily mean they were homosexual.'

You'd have your suspicions, though, wouldn't you? I've decided to pay a lot more attention to the background action next time *Bridge on the River Kwai* is on the TV.

Around seven, I go downstairs to make an austere sandwich from some depressing ingredients I've picked up in town. A scary-looking man, gaunt but muscular, with a close-cropped scalp covered in tattoos, is sitting on the sofa reading.

'Hello,' I chirp breezily, thinking a bit of chat might help obliterate the haunting image of oriental prison guards tugging in tandem. He just stares at me, then turns back to his book.

At the kitchen end of the communal room two couples are serving dinner – two Spanish lads in their early twenties, and their Spanish and French girlfriends. Spotting my melancholy pot of hummus and half a cellophane-wrapped cucumber, they invite me to dine with them. Just like that. Haven't even heard me speak. Then they top this by giving me the last of the bottle of red wine they're sharing. It's a simple, delicious meal of linguine with a fresh tomato sauce, and green salad dressed with olive oil. To follow, the French woman produces about a third of a Camembert, enough for a few slivers each. It's sensational.

'Did you buy this here or in France?'

'Oh, in France.'

I try to explain my theory that the French and Italians keep all the good food for themselves, and send us all the substandard crap, only with the same labels on. I'm not sure they understand, but they've been delightful company.

And then it strikes me that they must be sleeping in the dormitories, which are single sex. Young love deserves better than that. The least I can do after their generosity is offer them my room, so they can cuddle each other while the storm rages outside. I could take one of the beds in the dorm with Tattooed Scary Man.

'Goodnight,' I say, and shoot off up to my room before

anyone else has the same idea. I mean, it wasn't as if they'd laid on a pudding or anything. Pudding might just have swung it.

Next morning they're down at breakfast before me. Tattooed Scary Man is outside on the clifftop lawn, stripped to the waist, doing vigorous early morning trained killer exercises. As far as I can tell from a quick headcount, he hasn't taken anyone out during the hours of darkness. It's around eight thirty. A card on the notice-board says there's a meditation class at nine fifteen each morning in the Shrine Room, open to anyone. A young Australian guy I said hello to yesterday afternoon is sweeping the kitchen floor, so I ask if the meditation would be suitable for novices. He tries to conceal his contempt, but fails.

'I guess. However – inexperienced – you might be.'

Right.

'Are you here to study, then?'

He stops brushing and gives a big sigh. 'Study isn't the right word.'

Oops. Sorry.

'I'm here to do more practice.'

He resumes broom duties. Clearly I'm a right nuisance, so I decide to bombard him with small talk.

'What part of Australia are you from, then?'

'Melbourne.' Sweep sweep, sweep sweep.

'Really? Melbourne's one of my favourite cities.'

He looks at me like I'm sick in the head. I give up and go for a shower.

There are two shower rooms next to each other on the ground floor, both empty. I go into one, and walk around barefoot for a bit in pools of other people's second-hand water, before realising I haven't brought a towel. So what's the etiquette? Do they provide them? At twelve quid a night I shouldn't think so. And I'm not about to go and ask my Aussie mate and look like a complete loser. There are two towels hanging by the sink. Are they communal or privately owned? By Scary Man, perhaps? In any case, they're moist and warm, ideal for cultivating rare fungus and malignant bacteria; one of them also features an impressive collection of small dark curly hairs. In the airing cupboard I find a crisp piece of cloth that had been a towel in a former life, but has since graduated to plumbing maintenance. I dry myself on my T-shirt, put it on a radiator to dry, and head off to meditation.

Aussie has got there before me. He's framed in one of the floor-to-ceiling windows that look out on the Atlantic. There's an elaborate and colourful altar in one corner; a raised dais with some kind of lavishly upholstered throne; and assorted embroidered prayer cushions and moulded plastic chairs. The floor and walls are varnished wood.

'Is there anything I need to know?'

This really makes his day.

'You could take . . . a mat, I guess, or maybe a . . . plastic chair . . . would be better for you. It just depends oh . . . whether . . .'

He just tails off and stops talking in mid-sentence, like he can't be bothered dealing with me because I'm not sufficiently spiritual; or maybe that's paranoid and says more about me than him. I'd say, though, that a bit more contact with the Irish, and a bit less contemplation of his inner self, would give him better value for his Qantas round-the-world Apex supersaver. Mind you, he probably knows I think that, which is why he despised me in the first place.

The class is taken by a German woman of about thirty. There are just the three of us. She gives little readings from *The Tibetan Book of Living and Dying*, and, for my benefit, explains it's better to keep eyes open as I look ahead. Apparently I shouldn't be trying to think of anything, but I shouldn't be trying to think of nothing either. Every few minutes she tings some finger-cymbals for us to take a little break, then tings them again for us to continue. It feels good. In my peripheral vision I get glimpses of a fishing boat bobbing below on turquoise sunlit water. There are three ponies grazing on scrub on the precipitous hillside. Mizen Head looms across the water. I feel myself slipping off into a place of deep spiritual calm, which is disturbed at regular intervals by worries about my exhaust.

When we finish after forty-five minutes, Aussie blanks me and leaves. I head out for the Tank.

Either a bird has flown up my exhaust, or someone's put one there; there's no other explanation.

I've pulled in at a scenic-view lay-by halfway along the road back to Castletownbere. The tuba-like tones of the exhaust seem deeper and louder. If I'm the young Australian Buddhist, then the exhaust is me: it's getting on my nerves. I've never understood how cars work, beyond a long-standing conviction that petrol is crucial; so when it comes to identifying faults and fixing them, I haven't got a clue. However, I do realise that it's important for a man to be able to display the body language of the DIY mechanic if he is to command the respect of his peers, and avoid being mocked, or set upon with baseball bats; so I'm quite capable of giving a tyre a sharp tap with the toe-end of my boot, or saying, 'Lift up the bonnet,' and shaking my head pessimistically. Masculine protocol now requires that, without having the faintest idea what I'm looking for, I must lie on the ground and look under the car.

Imagine my surprise, then, when I'm able to diagnose the fault immediately. The end section of exhaust pipe, though shiny and uncorroded, has sheared, or been sheared, off; protruding from the rectangular box to which the pipe had been attached is a swathe of thick black feathers. There's a dead bird stuck up my exhaust.

I give the feathers a tentative tug, like a Korean prison guard who's new to the job. I'm afraid that the rotting carrion, decomposing in the poisonous fumes, will come away in my hand; but it won't budge. The feathers are stiff and matted, and make my hand filthy. I seem to be holding the wing of some sort of blackbird or rook, whose large body must be wedged inside the exhaust box, the wrong side of a one-and-a-half-inch hole. How on earth am I going to get it out? And how the hell did it get in there in the first place?

As the Tank thunders down the hillside to Castletownbere, I consider the options. Either the bird just took a wrong turning and flew up the exhaust with tremendous force; or someone put it there. But who? The Italian bikers? Perhaps that's why they were laughing when I woke. But why would they do that? Revenge for British taste in soft furnishings, perhaps; or punishment for putting tinned pineapple and chicken tikka on pizzas? Possible, but it doesn't seem likely. I suppose Mr O'Sullivan could have done it for inflicting structural damage on the Virgin at half five in the morning. Or maybe I'd been targeted by some trainee youth wing of the IRA who'd seen the British registration plates on the car and, unaware of my Irish ancestry, had lashed out at British imperialism by, I dunno, sticking a dead bird up it.

This paranoid nonsense is all going through my head as I reach town. There are two garages by the main square. I park by the nearest and go in. Suddenly I realise who's done it. Tattooed Scary Man! He's obviously using the hostel as some kind of hiding place while he conducts a guerrilla campaign against society. He started by staring me out and refusing to speak. Now he's ramming dead wildlife up my pipework.

'Can I help you?'

A big red-faced man in his forties, wearing oily navy-blue overalls, is facing me. He's got an assistant half his age, with a squint.

'What? Oh, I've got a Volvo outside . . .'

There's no easy way to say this.

'What's the problem?'

'It's . . . there's ehm . . . there's a dead bird up the exhaust.'

The assistant snorts so hard that a bubble of snot appears from his nostril and bursts on his lip. He wipes it with a freckly forearm. His boss tries to glare at him but only manages a smile.

'Here, give us the keys, I'll take a look at it for you. Come back in half an hour?'

The local school has just broken for lunch and the street is full of teenagers eating chips and chocolate, in some cases simultaneously. Clusters of lads are making a big production out of having a furtive smoke. They're lurking outside phone boxes and by the public toilets on the waterfront, cigarettes in hand, rehearsing for the day when it'll be their turn to slouch outside the church porch ingesting nicotine during mass.

I nip into a mini-mart to buy a paper. There's a flier in the window advertising a raffle. 'First Prize – Pilgrimage to Lourdes. Second Prize – Bottle of Brandy.' I head for MacCarthy's, order a half, and hide in the snug with my paper. I'm immediately spotted by Mrs MacCarthy Senior, who does what any self-respecting Irish woman of her generation would do, and makes me four rounds of ham and cheese sandwiches. Auntie Annie would have made eight, just to be on the safe side.

When I leave, the kids are on their way back to school, and the blue sky has turned overcast with an ominous build-up of dark cloud out to sea. With any luck they'll have it out by now. Will they have had to take the exhaust off, or do they perhaps have some kind of special tongs or forceps to poke up the pipe and pull birds out, bit by bit if necessary? It could get quite messy. There's a lot more to being a mechanic than I imagined.

The kid with the squint is sitting on an oil drum eating a doughnut, while his boss works on a Peugeot. He shouts across to him. I don't quite catch it, but I think he says, 'Michael, Bird Man's here to see you.'

'Ah, hello, sir, she's all ready for you; not a lot I could do, I'm afraid.'

'So, the bird's still up there?'

'Well, ya see, it wasn't a bird. Come on and I'll show you.'

'But it had feathers.'

Squint Boy goes into a major coughing fit at this. We walk to the car, which is parked outside near the art deco petrol pumps. Michael peers knowingly underneath and I copy him, doing my best to exude an air of mechanical knowledge.

'See that?'

He's yanking hard on the blackbird wing, which appears to be unravelling. As he pulls, several feet of the black feathery stuff come out in a long sooty string.

'It's just the lining like, from inside the exhaust. Sound insulation, I suppose. You'll need a new rear section but I don't carry them here. Ah, you'll be fine, no problem driving, just a bit noisy.'

I smile and nod in a final attempt to preserve my dignity.

'What do I owe you?'

'Ah, there's no charge. Just keep an eye on it, but I'd say you'd be fine.'

I decide to get in the car quick before a crowd gathers.

'And watch out for them low-flying herons. They'd be a divil to shift. Good luck now.'

He bangs twice with the palm of his hand on the side of the car, and I phutt off. So that's why Volvo spares are so expensive. They're hand lined with blackbird feathers by skilled Swedish craftsmen. That'll be why they always start on frosty mornings.

Driving out of town past the semi-derelict Silver Dollar Bar – closed for years by the looks of it, but still with a yellowing poster of an International Cabaret Star and Recording Artiste in the window – I realise that embarrassment hasn't been a great price to pay. I know garages where they'd have scraped a dead bird off the road, produced it as evidence, and charged me £167.50 plus tax. I drive for another five minutes, then turn left off the road at the sign saying Dunboy Castle.

The crenellated gatehouse is impressive, if a little dishevelled; nature is threatening to take over. There's no one about. A notice, handwritten in felt-tip on a scrap of card, suggests admission charges. There's an open box to drop coins in, if you want to. I pay up and drive into the grounds, where I find two castles for the price of one.

Puxley's Castle is a nineteenth-century Romanesque mansion, all Gothic arched windows and marble-clad pillars. It was built by the Puxley family, who made their millions in copper mining, or at least in owning the mines in which other people went mining. Their colourful family history, with little altered except the names, is told in Daphne du Maurier's novel *Hungry Hill*. From the front of the castle there's a glorious view across a tidal channel to the real Hungry Hill, which looms high behind Castletownbere.

Inside, chunks of stone and marble litter the ground. The

roof's gone. Shrubs and wild flowers are growing in impossibly high places. Some rooms are thick with hoof prints and cowpats. It was burned and gutted by the IRA during the Civil War in 1921.

A few hundred yards away, facing Bere Island across the channel into Castletownbere harbour, is Dunboy Castle, the rugged stone ruin of a thirteenth century fortress. After the English hammered the combined Irish and Spanish forces at the Battle of Kinsale in 1602, this was the next target. The entire garrison of 143 men was slaughtered, including – and some people are still a bit miffed about this, even 400 years later – the priest who walked out carrying the white flag. There are plaques to him in Irish and in English. I sit on the mossy remains of a wall that was destroyed while Shakespeare was writing *Hamlet,* and contemplate this landscape that for centuries was the stronghold of the O'Sullivans. Before them the ruling clan here had been McCarthys.

Suddenly I know there's something I must do. I stand up slowly and deliberately, and walk to the water's edge. Across to my right is the last lighthouse before America.

I know our memories serve us poorly sometimes – but how could I have forgotten this? I reach into my pocket, pull out a greasy and unpleasant bundle and throw yesterday's black pudding and sausage into the sea.

Even before I get to Windy Point, it's easy to see how it got its name. Heading west from Castletownbere towards the end of the peninsula, the gusts threaten to pull the Tank across the road into the path of an oncoming sheep. At one point the road ahead is blocked by a car and a post office van that have stopped alongside each other. As I approach, a hand appears through the window of the post van and passes a clutch of letters to the car driver. It's like a carefully composed moment from a sentimental film about the quirks of living on the Celtic fringe. Perhaps there's been a general alert that there's a tourist in the area, so they rushed out and laid on this little cameo when they saw me coming.

'Look out for a blue Volvo with a bird up its arse.'

It's a spectacular coastline where rugged mountains give way to small fields that are farmed to the cliff's edge. There's been no indiscriminate house-building. Every couple of minutes you pass some ancient monument, a standing stone or ring fort or mass rock, just lying there, as if these relics of the past have been randomly scattered across the landscape by some ancient giant. In such a place, where thousands of years of human continuity is laid out, random and unadorned, in an unchanging landscape, I'm sure it's only natural to feel a strong sense of belonging, whether your name is McCarthy, or Mitsubishi.

You know you've reached Windy Point, and the end of the line, when you see a sign saying: 'Moscow 3,310 kilometres'. If this is a joke, it's impressively deadpan for a venue with such a small audience. But having said this is the end of the line, it isn't; or not quite. Two hundred yards offshore sits Dursey Island, the furthest you can get from Dublin and still be in Ireland. The size of the population varies, from seven to fifteen, depending on who you ask. The only way on and off is by cable car, which is swaying precariously 100 feet above the treacherous waters of the Dursey Sound.

I park next to the only other vehicle, a Volkswagen with a yellow crook lock on the steering wheel, presumably to protect it from any joy-riding fishermen or shepherds who might be hiding in caves nearby, waiting to pounce. The cable car looks like it's seen better days, though you'd be hard pressed to put a date on them. The Perspex window in the sliding door is broken, and the metal floor seems to be held in place by what can only be described as a stick. There's clear fresh air between it and the wall.

'It's licensed for six adults,' says Paddy, the operator, as he takes my fare. 'Or one cow. Mind, we did have fifteen sheep in it once.'

The gap between the floor and the rest of the cable car is clearly a sensible precaution, given the likelihood of terrified cattle looking down on the churning depths and crapping themselves. 'Ah no, it doesn't bother the animals at all. Before this was built cows had to swim across, with the farmers in a boat alongside.'

It sounds unlikely, but he's telling the truth. There are photos to prove it. Paddy and his wife own a B&B overlooking the water a couple of hundred yards away. He says that there are queues for the cable car in the summertime, but residents and livestock always take precedence over tourists and go to the front of the line. 'The Germans don't seem to mind, but the Brits get a bit pissed off.'

I'm the only passenger, which is a relief. You wouldn't want to be cooped up in a space like this with a nervous sheep or incontinent heifer. The seats are plain benches, rather than upholstered plush, which must make them easier to hose down. To reassure any traveller who has suddenly become aware of his mortality, prayers about death have been pinned to the wall. A bottle of clear liquid, possibly holy water, maybe poteen, is laid on for emergencies. As we rattle off, I look down on the rocks at the water's edge below me, and see the previous cable, fraying and rusting where it fell.

We make a smooth landing on Dursey, but the weather is closing in. Two cars are parked, or abandoned, close to the cable car. It's fair to say that their bodywork is in need of some attention; so is the gaffa tape that's holding them together. In the rear window of one of them is a sticker saying 'Looney Car Sales'. Cars on outlying Irish islands are driven till they disintegrate, before being abandoned in bogs and ditches, where they'll be discovered one day by a future civilisation and venerated as relics of an ancient and mysterious culture.

Dursey is about four miles long by a mile wide, and I'd had a notion to do a circular walk, with no clear aim in mind. Maybe I could count the people. But there's no pub or shop, and I haven't thought to bring any provisions, so as the first drops of rain begin to fall a long hike isn't looking like a great way to spend the day. The rugged hillsides provide grazing for sheep, but no shelter.

I plod on for ten minutes trying to enjoy a view which is disappearing before my eyes. Down the slope to my left, close to the water's edge, is a ruined church and graveyard, so I head towards it out of force of habit, and cower in the lee of a wall. My supposed all-weather hat, purchased in Babbitt's General Store at the Grand Canyon, is hopelessly out of its depth this far from Arizona and behaves like a blocked gutter, pouring cascades of water down the neck of my coat. I like a walk on a wild hillside, but I'm not a fanatic; I don't own a plastic pouch to hang round my neck with a map in. I don't feel guilty about heading back to the cable car.

There's no system I can see for summoning it from the other side, so I'll just have to wait. The doorway of a maintenance shed offers protection from the worst of the weather, and having a different place to cower from the rain adds variety. As the mainland recedes into the gloom, I try and remind myself that if it weren't for the weather, it'd be all feckin' high rises over there. I find an old mint in my pocket, carefully peel off the fluff and oose, and suck it slowly for lunch.

Luckily, I've trained myself over the years never to go any-where without something to read, just in case someone turns up late, the meeting ends early, or I'm inadvertently imprisoned for thirty-five years and put into solitary confinement. I'm actually quite worried about those people you see on long train journeys with nothing to read, just staring blankly into the middle distance. What the hell is going on in their heads, then? Perhaps they've got excellent memories, and they're just remembering a particularly good book they once read, which saves them having to carry one round. Because there's a danger in carrying a book round: you might leave it somewhere before you've finished it. I once left my copy of *Get Shorty* in the back of a drunken farmer's Jeep in Costa Rica when I was only two-thirds of the way through, and it completely ruined the trip. The rainforest is a much duller place without Elmore Leonard. And I've lost *Angela's Ashes* twice. Does that poor kid ever grow up? Do they persuade his dad to go into rehab?

Tucked in my inside pocket is a history of the island I picked up in town. There's no better time to read about a place than when you're marooned there in a monsoon. After waiting till

I've finished my mint, so as not to use up two pleasures at the same time, I immerse myself in the book.

I soon discover that 'the island is often the first landfall for birds accidentally flying from America'; and that in the ninth century, when the Vikings were constantly ransacking the Cork coast, Dursey was used as a staging post for kidnapped villagers who were then sold into slavery in Scandinavia or Spain. And in 1602, after the Battle of Kinsale and the storming of Dunboy Castle, terrible things happened here.

It seems that the British troops advancing from Dunboy found that many villagers from the mainland had taken refuge on Dursey, in hope of escaping the invading army. It was not to be. The book quotes from a contemporary account by Philip O'Sullivan:

> they shot down, hacked with swords, or ran through with spears, the now disarmed garrison and others, old men, women and children, whom they had driven into one heap. Some rammed their swords up to the hilt through the babe and mother who was carrying it on her breast, others paraded before their comrades little children, writhing and convulsed on their spears, and finally binding all the survivors, they threw them into the sea over jagged and sharp rocks, showering on them shots and stones. In this way perished about three hundred . . .

I'm standing next to the cliff from which they were thrown. This cheers me up no end.

The explicit dramatic reconstruction of the massacre playing inside my head is suddenly interrupted by the rattle of the cable car. Paddy has obviously decided that a death by exposure would be bad for business and has come to my rescue. The car clatters ashore, and two tall blond men in pastel Gore-Tex waterproofs clamber out. I decide not to mention the cruel things the Vikings did around here provided they say nothing about the British army. I try some satire instead.

'Nice day for it.'

'Yes. Iz very good. Some rain but . . .' He shrugs and smiles while deftly sealing a dozen flaps with Velcro.

'Where are you from?'

'We are coming from Brussels. Yesterday we are hearing that a very rare bird is landing here. So we make phone call, find it is true, and now . . .'

To emphasise his sanity, his mate joins in.

'Now, we make long walk. See if we can find him. Haf a nice day.'

And off they go, striding purposefully into the deluge. Quite frankly, this kind of behaviour alarms me.

Back on the mainland I get straight into the car, steam up the windscreen, and drive back towards the hostel. When I reach the turning I carry straight on and drive to MacCarthy's where, during the next few hours, at least three people I've never met before will make jokes about the bird up my exhaust.

A fuggy bar in a fishing port is a great place to spend a rainy afternoon. It's some time after dark when I realise I've drunk enough to ward off the pneumonia and would be better off in bed. Driving's out of the question, so I go to the pay phone in the hall and call a taxi. Is there, I wonder, any chance of a cab in the next half-hour or so?

'I will be outside in three minutes. You will be outside? Three minutes?'

For West Cork, this seems an unusually urgent approach to time; still, I drink up, say my goodbyes and sure enough there he is, outside in a minibus, three minutes on the dot. The rain has eased off into a dewy, garden-sprinkler kind of affair. As we head up the main street, a parked car full of kids pulls out suddenly and almost clips our wing mirror.

'That was close,' I say.

'No,' says the driver.

'What?'

'No. I am not Klaus.'

'What?'

'You say I was Klaus. I am not Klaus. My name is Hans.'

'So you are Hans?'

'Yes. I am Hans, not Klaus.'

'Where are you from, Hans?' As if I don't know by now.

'I am from Germany. Twenty years my wife and I are coming here. Two years ago we make opportunity to buy this business. So here we are.'

I'd sing him 'Please Be Nice to the Germans' but I can't remember the words. Clearly, this part of Ireland holds genuine attractions for German people; but unlike me, still just flirting with this sense of belonging, Hans has actually done something about it and moved here. Perhaps he deserves it more than I do. I ask him what he likes so much about Ireland. He thinks for a long time, then speaks slowly and deliberately.

'The people. I loff their carefree imperfection.'

I pay the fare and ask for a receipt, a life-long instinct among the self-employed. He produces a receipt book with Receipt Book printed on the front and carefully writes one out, noting date, time, pick-up point and destination; then whips out an ink pad and rubber stamp from the glove compartment, validates the receipt, and hands it to me. Not much sign that the old carefree imperfection is catching, then.

He drives off to collect his next fare, who is expecting him in eighteen minutes and thirty-two seconds precisely. By then I'll be fast asleep, but that's the Great Outdoors for you. There's nothing quite like a short walk in the rain, followed by four or five hours in the pub, to make you appreciate your bed.

Next morning I have to move out of the hostel because the room's booked. I pay my £24 to a young French woman, then take a walk along the cliffs. There's been a transformation in the weather: the sky is blue, the water calm and aquamarine, the sun warm on my face. I chat for a while with a nice man from Norwich who's behind the counter in the Buddhist paraphernalia shop. He says they've got a couple of cottages to rent, with the same spectacular view. I may come back and rent one.

But not until I've seen a photo in the paper confirming that Tattooed Scary Man has been arrested and charged.

The story of the children of Lir is one of the most celebrated of Irish legends. Lir, a king of an ancient Irish race called the Tuatha de Danaan, had four children: a daughter, Fionnuala, and three sons, Aodh, Fiacra and Conn. When their mother died Lir married again, but his new wife was jealous of the love the father had for his children. Enlisting the help of a druid, she turned them into swans, condemning them to spend 300 years on the cold water of Lake Darvra in Westmeath, 300 years on the Sea of Moyle between Ireland and Scotland, and a final 300 years on the Atlantic off the west coast of Ireland. At the end of this time the spell was broken by the tolling of a church bell, St Patrick and Christianity having arrived in Ireland during the 900-year interim. Transformed back into very old human beings indeed, they died close to the spot where they came ashore.

I knew the story already, but it wasn't until yesterday evening in MacCarthy's that I realised that the place where they came ashore and died is reputed to be at the village of Allihies, a twelve-mile drive from Castletownbere on the northern side of the peninsula. It's just eight or nine miles if you walk across the mountains.

Con, the man who'd told me the story, had arranged to meet me down in town. He turns up with a reassuring little backpack of water, chocolate and apples, and his trousers tucked into his socks, like a serious hiker. I feel in safe hands. When we got chatting in MacCarthy's it only took a few minutes to establish an unexpected connection. As a young man in the sixties he'd been a teacher in Drimoleague, where he'd lodged with a close friend of my mother's. We used to visit there all the time. When I was a small boy, I'd almost certainly met him.

We spend the day walking a section of the Beara Way, a route that runs 100 miles around the peninsula. Away from the road, you're travelling through history. We begin in the ruins of a Bronze Age settlement, where the shapes of houses are clearly visible in the boggy land; then go down to the stone circle where the Italians found me sleeping. There are thirteen stones.

'Always an odd number, we don't know why.'

And so it goes on. Famine houses abandoned in the 1840s; then a ring fort sitting in a field of sheep with wooden pallets leaning against it. We pass through an old-style farmyard, turkeys and chickens running free, yard and stone outbuildings so comprehensively covered in manure it looks as though they've been sprayed with the stuff. And then there's a steep climb, and Castletownbere is twinkling far below us in the afternoon sun, like a Mediterranean resort. Just a day later, and Dursey would have passed for Crete.

We've risen a long way very quickly, and suddenly, without warning, we're on top of the world, looking down into a huge natural amphitheatre enclosed by mountains on three sides and the Atlantic on the fourth. Across to our right, snaking up the foot of a hillside, is a row of garishly painted houses, all bright reds, blues, greens and pinks. Behind and above the village on the gaunt grey mountainside stand several stone towers, like ancient temples: the copper mines of Allihies.

They've mined copper on these mountainsides since the Bronze Age. The mines have been closed since the late nineteenth century, but at one time this was the richest copper-producing area in Europe. Between the barren rock, tiny overgrown fields are still visible, where they tried to grow potatoes to feed the 6,000 people who once lived here. There are fewer than 600 in the area today.

We drop down into Allihies and stop for a pint at O'Neills. O'Neill himself isn't in, but out campaigning for the Euro elections. I've seen his face on the telegraph poles. We sit outside on a south-facing bench in the evening sun. Below us is a beautiful beach, formed not from sand, but from the residue of the copper grindings from the Allihies mines. In the playground across the road, children are swearing loudly. It's quite idyllic.

'Will I show you where the children of Lir are buried?'

We walk another five or ten minutes round some confusing lanes, then stop by the roadside.

'Now look at the road there. Perfectly straight, isn't it? But follow the fence along the side and you'll see it curves in, then back out for no reason. When the men were putting up that fence years ago they wouldn't touch that spot. That's where the children of Lir are buried.'

We cross the road, two grown men in search of hard physical evidence that four children had been turned into swans for 900 years.

'I haven't been here for twenty years or more. Not since my children were small. See. There.'

He's pointing at a large round white stone on the grass by the roadside. A tarnished Irish penny and a small dead flower are lying on it.

'That's the biggest of them. That marks Fionnuala's grave. But I'm sure there used to be three others.'

There's no sign of them. It's just an overgrown patch of coarse, tufty grass, but I feel compelled to look. Dropping to my knees, I start tearing at the grass with my fingers, looking for the shape of a stone. Nothing. I tear off more layers of grass and earth then, suddenly, a gleaming white stone the size of a bowling ball is looking up at me. I pull at the grass again, more carefully now, and fold it back to reveal the other two. 'There now,' says Con triumphantly.

I feel the hairs on my neck rise. I look around. Nothing. No one. No sign. No plaque. No little grotto selling books and souvenirs. The grass and soil have been undisturbed, I'd say, for a decade or more.

I get down on my knees and replace the earth and grass as carefully as I can. We tamp it down with our feet, leaving no sign that we've been there. Walking back into town we come to a T-junction. From our right, a ten-year-old girl rides past on a horse, bareback, eating a packet of crisps. A fork-lift truck comes swerving down the hill from the opposite direction. It's being steered by a two-year-old boy sitting on his father's lap. Real life is taking on a vivid, mythic quality.

Con's wife has driven over from Castletownbere to take him back, but I'm not inclined to leave. After a drink and some home-made seafood chowder, I get a room in a B&B along the street and sit up in bed for a while reading. A double-page spread in the local rag catches my eye. ADVERTISING FEATURE says the headline, a form of words usually seen above a flattering review of a restaurant that's been written by its owner. It's a piece about a new hotel development. My heart sinks.

'The Beara Peninsula has been famed for its wild beauty for many long years and although its enormous potential for tourist development' – Aagh! – '*tourist development* has yet to be fully realised, the Hideously Inappropriate Brand New Wilderness Hotel will go a long way to helping that situation.'

I'd stay away if I were you. Don't go. There's no tourism infrastructure, you see. Nothing to do. It rains all the time. You can't get Singapore noodles, even with money to burn. And there's a Tattooed Scary Man on the loose. All in all, you'd have a terrible time. I'd go somewhere else if I were you.

I'm told Killarney's very nice.

Chapter Eight

Dead Kid's Room

Singapore Prison is close to the international airport, and they're both called Changi. I once visited the memorial to the allied prisoners of the Second World War just outside the jail. It was a humid, sweltering day, when the slightest movement left you drenched in perspiration and reflecting how it must have been to be a prisoner of war here. It's still rumoured to be a cramped and oppressive place, airless and moist, where strangers fester side by side in the half-light amid the stench of overripe human flesh.

Just like the hostel in Killarney, then.

It's hot in the street, but even hotter in the dorms. On either side of the upstairs corridor, doors open on to tiny rooms containing three or four sets of bunks. In one of them, two Australian prisoners – sorry, travellers – lie smoking, while trying to outdo each other with tales of beaches in Indonesia. One of them is also boasting of having got lucky last night with a local girl, but his friend doesn't believe him, and neither do I. There's barely room to pick your way to the door through the rancid T-shirts and socks that appear to have been fired like shrapnel in all directions by exploding backpacks. The room is imbued with that deep, bass-note stench of male feet that, once absorbed, can never be exorcised. The French girl on reception says that for twelve quid I can have the bottom bunk in the corner, but, quite honestly, I'd rather pay to get shingles. The fake eighteenth-century country house hotel across the road doesn't stink, but it does charge £135 a night for a single room. Maybe coming to Killarney was a mistake. I blame Thackeray.

The drive from Allihies via Kenmare and the Connor Pass took a couple of hours. Before leaving, I had a morning walk round the copper mines on the mountainside above Allihies. It was clear and bright, and suddenly warm, as if there might be a chance of Ireland having a summer this year. Out to sea, the Skellig Rocks were clearly visible for the first time since I'd arrived. On one of them, Skellig Michael, are the ruins of a ninth-century monastery. Centuries ago, people would gather on the cliff top on Dursey or at Allihies, kneel and face the Skelligs at mass time and pray along with a service they couldn't see or hear.

I headed east along the northern side of the peninsula towards Kenmare and Killarney. The views looking north across the Kenmare Estuary to the mountains of the Ring of Kerry are sensational, especially when an absence of weather means you can actually see them. I stopped at one point to climb the hillside and take it all in, and to pull another couple of yards of sooty feathers out of the exhaust. Lying in the road, near where I'd parked, was a large dead animal – possibly a badger – that had been skinned. It was a gruesome sight. I looked around for a culprit, but there was nothing except a large horned sheep, also in the middle of the road, watching me. Sheep don't skin badgers, do they? It's not mentioned in the *I Spy* book.

I drove on, stopping a couple of times to go ferreting up mountainsides looking for mass rocks and standing stones. I know this passion for old stones is beginning to seem like an obsession, but when there are no sushi restaurants or art-house cinemas to hang out in, you have to make your own fun. At one point I followed a waterfall up the hillside through ferns and thick woods. At the top, I stopped to gaze out over the mountains, lakes and islands of Kerry, but found myself instead gazing in wonder at the beautiful emerald moss that covered the rocks at my feet. Wow, I thought. At home I go mental trying to get rid of the moss in the garden, but here I realise how beautiful it is. It was a moment of great realisation. I realised the solitude and the natural beauty were turning me soft in the head. It was time to go somewhere with lots of people and buildings, so I could get back in touch with my uncaring, cynical side. I needed quality time in a major tourist trap. I went back to the Tank and hit the road for Killarney.

It was gorgeous moss though.

'A hideous row of houses informed us that we were at Killarney,' observed Thackeray, and you know what? He wasn't wrong. 'Killarney – Looking Good', says the sign, but, whichever direction you approach from – and I tried several, in a vain attempt to escape the gridlock – you are greeted by rows and rows of B&Bs. Many are suburban semis and terraces, small family homes that, Tardis-like, have miraculously created the space to accommodate big-boned American families reared on hormone-enriched all-you-can-eat buffets. Others are grander, executive-style homes that look like they were assembled last week from a doll's house kit. All are festooned with signs proclaiming their attractions. 'All Rooms En-Suite! TV! Car Space! Tea And Coffee Making Facilities!' they shout. But why stop there? People shouldn't sell themselves short. Tourism's a cut-throat business. You need to get all your selling points up there on the board. 'Sheets On All Beds!'. 'Legs To Keep Bed Off Floor!' 'Drawer To Put Underpants In!' 'Walls!'

It was a shock to the system after Beara, but it was also the reason I was here. After wandering in glorious, deserted land-scapes, and being treated as long-lost family in fantasy small-town pubs, a dose of mainstream tourism would be good for the soul. If anything could expose my feelings of belonging as phoney sentimentality, Killarney might do the trick. A few days hanging out with wannabe Irish from all corners of the civilised world, and Australia, might put things in perspective, and make me deny my heritage. 'What, me, mate? No, I'm English, can't stand the place. I just sell 'em the plastic windows.'

I am also here because of Thackeray, whose *Irish Sketchbook* I've been reading ever since Beara. It's always a good idea to travel with an unfashionable and preferably out-of-date guide-book, otherwise you end up like all those poor sods you see reading the *Lonely Planet Guide* in real, authentic places that are reassuringly full of other people just like them.

Thackeray came here to go stag hunting, but didn't get a glimpse of one. All he saw all day were four dogs and a German. Even then, in 1842, Killarney was a major tourist trap, with prices to match.

> The town of Killarney was in a violent state of excitement . . . and attracted a vast crowd from all parts of the king-dom. All the inns were full, and lodgings cost 5 shillings a day, nay, more in some places; for, though my landlady, Mrs MacGillicuddy, charges but that sum, a leisurely old gentleman whom I never saw in my life before, made my acquaintance by stopping me in the street yesterday and said he paid a pound a day for his two bedrooms.

It's quite likely that this sort of thing still goes on; that wild-eyed visitors lurch up to complete strangers in the centre of town, grab them by the sleeve, and say, 'Look, you don't know me, and I'm sorry to bother you, but I'm going to go mad if I don't tell someone! Look at this receipt! Look how much I'm paying for a single room. Unbelievable, isn't it?'

Leaving the hostel, I see a hotel on New Street has a sign advertising, 'Special B & B Rates', but the young English woman at the reception desk actually laughs when I ask for a single room. 'I've only got rooms with three beds in, so I'd have to charge you the same as for three people. It'd be ridiculously expensive.' I ask if that's what they mean by special rates.

'It's just a revenue thing. We're very greedy in the hotel industry in Ireland.' She even repeats it for me when I ask her, so that I can write it down. They should put it on their headed notepaper.

Outside the big hotels, pony and trap drivers with the faces of medieval assassins are touting for business among gaggles of befuddled recent arrivals who are wandering around in a collective trance, like Stepford Tourists. 'Will the horse expect extra oats?' enquires an admirably self-aware American, who, at a guess, has won a trip to Europe as first prize in the Fattest Arse in the Midwest competition. Perched on top of the cart in baseball cap, stripy stretch fabric polo shirt and vast architect-designed shorts, he looks like Tweedledum. It takes two of the assassins to hoist his wife up there to join him, like Tweedledee in drag. The horse craps ostentatiously in derision, and off they trundle, to provide a bit of comic relief for the people stuck in the traffic jams.

The shops are impressively well stocked with leprechaun ashtrays and shamrock rosary beads, and there's an Italian restaurant where you can get a steak and still have change from twenty quid. Vegetables are extra. By seven o'clock, when I'm still tramping round looking for somewhere to stay, the streets are packed with people of all nationalities. As well as the hordes of Americans, I hear Spanish, Portuguese, Russian, Italian, Welsh, Scandinavian, French, Ulster and Dutch, but no Germans, because they're all in Cork driving taxis and singing folk songs. A ripple effect passes along the street, as groups of people pause to look at the menu in the window of the Italian restaurant, then recoil in horror as they realise they could send a taxi to Cork city for a Singapore noodles carry-out and still save money.

I'm beginning to realise that the parts of the country I've been in so far have been deserted because every bugger's here. Suddenly the gridlocked traffic is overtaken by Tweedledum and Tweedledee, careering along in their souped-up tumbril as the assassin cracks his whip. To show they've been assimilated into Celtic society, they're both now draped in tartan picnic rugs. He's smoking a large cigar, while she's opted for a packet of fudge as big as Dobbin's nosebag, to tide her over till dinner in half an hour's time. Irish hotels catering for Americans are aware of the need to serve American-sized portions, so she'll soon be tucking into a whole spit-roast pig, followed by a main course, all washed down with pints of Diet Coke to stop her from getting fat.

As the Tweedles pass from my field of vision, a handwritten

'Vacancies' sign is revealed on the frosted-glass front door of a small and unsympathetically modernised terraced house. The auburn-haired teenage girl who answers the door smirks when I ask if they've got a single room, as if there's a private joke I'm not in on. 'You'll have to ask me mother.' Mum duly appears in the narrow hallway and corners me by the foot of the stairs.

'There's only my son's room. He's away for a couple of days in, er . . . in Dublin, and everything else is full.' She leads me up the steep, vividly carpeted stairs and across the landing to a magnolia-painted plywood door which is splintered, as if it's been hit with a blunt instrument. We look at each other. She shrugs.

'I'm afraid the door's broken.'

Inside, there's a magnolia-painted plywood wardrobe, a narrow divan with no headboard, a tiny pink washbasin, and nothing else. Spots of glue pepper the walls like acne. The posters, sneakers, socks, tissues and pizza that are the very fabric of a teenage boy's life have presumably been bound and gagged and forced, still struggling, into a cupboard under the stairs where they will remain until he gets back. Either that, or the family have topped him, destroyed all his stuff, broken the door getting him out, and dumped his body in one of the famous lakes. After all, Mum didn't seem too sure about the Dublin alibi, and the girl did have a weird smirk.

'So, how much for the room?'

She hesitates, then plucks a figure from the air at random. 'Twenty pounds?'

'That'll be fine.'

She punches the air in triumph, does a back flip and slides across the room on her knees; at least, in her imagination. At any rate, she's clearly delighted. So it's true what they say about the English: they'll stay anywhere and not complain.

'Well, you'll be the first, you know, since we, er . . .'

Our eyes meet across the deserted room. 'Since your son went to Dublin?'

'That's right. Dublin. Now, what time would you like breakfast?'

★   ★   ★

142

By the time I hit the street it's almost nine and lots of places will stop serving food soon. I had a quick shower before coming out. I'm sharing the family's bathroom, for which they apologised profusely, though I'm quite happy. There's hair in the plughole, family-sized shampoo hanging from a rickety shower over a dark-brown bathtub, and the wiring on the shaving socket is held together with Band-Aid. I'm not complaining. It's all refreshingly non-corporate. I'm a great believer in putting your cash directly into the local economy rather than giving it to the International Global Chain of Hotel Evil. My hosts could use the money, and they're homely, natural and unselfconscious, whether they've murdered the boy or not.

Town is buzzing and seems to be getting fuller and fuller the later it gets. I enjoy a splendid dinner of freshly-caught, local, organic, free-range toasted cheese and ham special, and a bowl of chips, on the window ledge of a friendly pub with a mostly local clientèle. As I'm about to leave, the crowded room is suddenly filled to bursting point as the Tweedles come in with great commotion, accompanied by an even heavier couple. The four of them appear to have dressed for a cocktail party hosted by Zsa Zsa Gabor on a yacht in Acapulco, but if the locals have noticed, they don't bat an eyelid. I suppose they must have seen everything by now.

'So how are you enjoying your holiday?' asks the barman, as he pours whiskey for the men, and something green for their partners.

'Oh, it's just gorgeous,' says Tweedledee.

'Yeah, terrific,' agrees Tweedledum. 'So old-fashioned.'

'And so unspoiled,' says Dee. 'Say, do you have a rest room?'

'Upstairs.'

'Guess I'll wait then,' says Dee. 'We don't do stairs.'

'So, where are you folks from?' asks the barman.

'Oh, we live in Chicago,' says Dum, 'but my father was Irish.'

There's a general murmur of approval and I feel ashamed. This man I've been mocking as a stereotype of mindless tourism turns out to be as authentically Irish as I am. I feel like apologising, though we've never even met.

'Sure, that's great,' says the barman. 'So where exactly was your daddy from?'

'He was from Texas.'

Outside, the streets are really heaving and I've half a mind to go back to Dead Kid's Room for an early night. However, I realised many years ago that, home or abroad, whether I go out or stay in, I'm temperamentally incapable of going to bed before the local closing time, for fear that someone out there is having fun, and I might miss it. So I prowl the streets in search of good things to say about Killarney, and realise that, if you took all the visitors away, you'd be left with a beautiful and virtually intact eighteenth and nineteenth-century country town, unvandalised by planners and developers.

I walk past a big, white, posh hotel called the Killarney Bay. In an attempt to present itself as authentically Oirish, its bar, which looks out on to the street, has been christened 'Scruffies'. Through half-open picture windows I can see elegantly dressed young people, with lifestyles and unnecessarily expensive wrist-watches, nibbling olives and sipping wine and designer lager. A couple of bouncers with brutal haircuts and black bomber jackets stand in the doorway, presumably to stop anyone scruffy getting into Scruffies.

Round the corner, in the front bar of the Killarney Grand, a saintly-looking young woman and a rather debauched-looking young man are playing fiddle and guitar. Immediately in front of them, several rows of French, Italian and Scandinavian tourists sit and stare in reverential silence. One of them is taping the session. Behind them stand the English, Americans and Australians, listening all right, but also occasionally chat-ting, much to the annoyance of a sour-faced, curly-haired Viking in cycling shorts, who keeps shushing Nordically. Further back still, stretching the full length of the enormous and luxuriously refitted bar, stand the young professional Irish, chattering like speed freaks and ignoring the music completely, as they discuss work and house prices while trying to get off with each other.

Sitting on her own in a corner at the music end of the room is a wild, red-faced woman in her fifties who'd never get into Scruffies in a coat like that. She's drinking pints of Pils lager, and giggling and chatting to herself in an amiable enough way. In between songs, she launches into a traditional ditty of her own, originally recorded by Dean Martin. The fiddle player smiles as she retunes her violin, but the intrusion is too much for Viking-on-a-Bike, who hasn't travelled to the mystical Celtic heartlands to hear 'Li'l Ole Wine Drinker Me.'

'Ssh!' he hisses, bringing half a century of Scandinavian social engineering to bear on the situation.

'Ah, feck off, ya silly tourist cunt,' comes the laconic reply. The musicians crack up.

I fall into conversation with a thirtyish couple, perfectly turned out in the Barbour 'n' Brogue style favoured by rich young Italians. They come from Venice. 'It must be nice to get away from all the tourists,' I joke.

'But I think there are also very many tourists here,' says the woman, impassively.

To loosen things up, I offer to buy them a drink, and find myself in the unprecedented situation of ordering two glasses of mineral water in an Irish pub at half past ten at night. My new friends watch with fascination as I take a gulp from my pint. I feel like an exhibit. This must be what it's like to eat sausage and chips in a bus shelter while Princess Anne watches and takes notes.

'In Venezie, there is nothing like this' – she gestures gracefully with one hand, taking care not to spill the precious water – 'where many people meet to, how you say, get drahnk?'

I tell her I like Venice very much, and, for some reason, she tells me that her mother, who is a countess, has Alzheimer's, and that she is caring for her. As my first joke has gone down badly, I decide against the Alzheimer's gag, even though it's a cracker. Her husband, who's a journalist, speaks five languages, the flash bastard, but seems happy just to observe us talking. I become paranoid that he's weighing me up so he can write a vicious caricature after I'm gone. I'll probably play a key role in his article about xenophobic, monolinguistic, heavily perspiring Englishmen boozing their philistine way round the cultural hot spots of Europe. Just as I'm thinking it's unethical for people to write about you if they don't tell you that's what they're up to, she asks me what I'm doing in Ireland; so I tell her I'm a physics teacher on holiday.

'So, why are you travelling alone?'

I'd have thought that was fairly obvious. I mean, how many friends do physics teachers have, apart from the reps who sell them the lab equipment? But solo travel is a deeply puzzling concept for Italians. In many years of travelling I've never met any Italians away from home on their own. Indeed, the Twenty-sixth Rule states that *Any Italian Travelling Abroad Will be Accompanied by an Even More Glamorous Person of the Opposite Sex.* When two couples are travelling together, at least three of them will be wearing sunglasses on top of their heads.

I tell her I'm on my own because my wife has left me.

'But why did your wife go away?'

'Because I am a physics teacher.'

She's uneasy now, not certain whether I'm joking or not. I decide to make amends by telling her something true. I confess I'm fascinated by the worldwide boom in all things Irish, and I'm wondering whether it's possible to belong in a place where you weren't born and didn't grow up. Perhaps she can shed some light on my dilemma?

'Oh, I think this is true, yes, many Italians are now coming to Ireland. We feel very close.'

'What, because you're both Catholic countries?'

'No, no, eez more than that. I think in both countries we have – how you say – healthy disrespect? for authority? This makes me belong.'

Oh God, no. She's misunderstood me. I meant can *I* belong, not her. People can be so self-centred, can't they?

'And also here in Ireland they value? Yes, value, the important things in life – children and grandparents. The very young and the very old. This too is much like Italy.'

But not much like England. Mind you, the bloody Romans never even came to Ireland. Much too scary for them. She takes a careful sip from her mineral water and looks out across the sea of alcohol.

'So yes, I think I can belong here.'

'Oh, right, no, what I was thinking, and I don't know what you think about it, but an outside opinion might help' – she's starting to look a bit baffled – 'but is it possible for me with, you know, Irish ancestors, that I can belong here? Or am I just a sort of romantic fool?'

She pauses to think, then gives me a big, friendly smile. 'Why, yes.'

Phew.

'Yes, fool, I think. You are English, yes? So you are always wanting to fight with Irish, to beat them.'

Hey, come on love, you can't pin that one on me. My granddad threw stones at the Black and Tans.

'You cannot belong, you and the Irish, you are like Jock.'

Like Jock? What the hell's she on about now? She turns to her husband for reassurance that she's using the right expression. He smiles and raises a supportive eyebrow.

'Yes, the English and the Irish, like Jock, and cheese.'

Lying on Dead Kid's Divan, I lick my wounds. I've been laughed out of town by an Italian aristo who thinks she's got more claim on the place than I have. This seems to be Ireland's power. After about ten minutes, everyone feels like they belong here, so there's nothing special about me. Diaspora: it's a romantic word, but perhaps to be truly part of it your ancestors had to walk to Appalachia or the Yukon, or get deported to New South Wales. Perhaps having a mum who came over to be a nurse during the Second World War just doesn't count: not enough romance, not sufficient active and deliberate oppression on behalf of the English, to make the story sad enough.

It can be a bloody gloomy business you know, travelling on your own.

Before I left the bar, Gianni and Hortense gave me a business card embossed with full-colour coat of arms and two e-mail addresses. I gave them half a beer mat with a phone number in felt-tip. You never know, one day they may need to call ABC Taxis in Brighton.

Lying on the bed, I decide to use their card as a bookmark, and turn to Chapter Eleven of Thackeray: 'Killarney, Stag Hunting On The Lake'. But I'm asleep within minutes. Half an hour later I'm woken up by my own snoring, which really is about as sad as it gets. I clean my teeth and undress, which people in books hardly ever do, and get into bed. It's not long enough. My feet are sticking over the end. Before I go to sleep I get up and check the walls for bloodstains.

There aren't any.

Poison, maybe?

'Yeah, yesterday was a pretty good day; we did the, er, Ring of Kerry?'

The guy at the next, indeed only other, breakfast table is a skinny, baldy, fifty-five-year-old New Yorker with two twenty-something daughters, or incredible sexual magnetism. He's talking in the fastest-spreading dialect in the English-speaking world – Californian/Australian Universal Interrogative.

'Today I guess we'll do the, er, Gap of Dunloe?'

The daughters or lovers are in agreement.

'For sure.'

'Sounds cool.'

I have come up with a plan of my own.

I will go outside, wander about aimlessly, and see what happens.

It's ten a.m., and people are struggling along the streets with their luggage, desperate to leave before the next lot arrive. The town resounds to the thwack of daintily-wrapped soap and miniature shampoo being bunged on to freshly-swabbed sinks. Outside the big hotels, the medieval assassins are shouting and touting among the traffic, while their ponies fantasise about life in a field. Inside the biggest hotel, in a £350-a-night suite, Hortense is eating *pain au chocolat* in a complimentary towelling bathrobe while Gianni taps away at his laptop and chuckles. By now, Tweedledum and Tweedledee, still on target for twelve countries in ten days, will be somewhere on the Grand Canal, in a gondola that's rapidly shipping water.

It's a warm, sunny day, with high fluffy clouds, and the light plays dramatically across the mountains that ring the town. Apart from some new shopfronts, and replacement windows, and new hotels, and the traffic, it's probably much as it was when Thackeray was here. But surely there couldn't have been this many visitors? Even the people without luggage don't seem to live here. They're all looking up at buildings, or rifling through guidebooks, or pausing tentatively on street corners, behaviour which in more ruthless countries would be taken to mean, 'I'm not from here, so please rob me.' And once somewhere has more tourists than local people, more knick-knack shops than newsagents or groceries, then equilibrium has been destroyed, the game is up, and the balance has irrevocably shifted in favour of revenue, occupancy and the forces of darkness. Real life may continue, but to the visitor it's all but invisible.

I walk along the main street, past a franchise for the surreally named fast food chain, Abrakebabra, and stop for a coffee in a meat and two veg café. Someone's left a newspaper behind on the next table, and I find myself powerless to resist the pull of the headline.

PRIEST SUES CORPORATION OVER KNEE: 'A priest who sued Cork Corporation for compensation because a fall in the street made it hard for him to kneel and genuflect, settled out of court yesterday.'

It sounds dodgy to me. I mean, the wear and tear on your average priest's knees must be tremendous. They're bound to be the first bits to go. If you bear that in mind, then there must be a fair chance the crafty old bugger took a dive hoping to get a big payday in court. Surprisingly, however, Cork Corporation's barrister ignored this sure-fire line of argument and adopted a different and ultimately flawed strategy.

'Defence complained that many members of the clergy continued with hip replacements, knee replacements and even the loss of a limb.'

Top work, MacRumpole. 'If it please Your Honour, I refer the court to the previous case of Father O'Malley, who, Your Honour will recall, had both legs flattened like Sta-Prest slacks, after falling under a corporation steam roller. These days he says mass on a converted skateboard pulled along on a rope by two nuns, but he's never asked for a penny from the corporation, so I don't see why this whingeing eejit should get anything either.'

The paper says that the priest's thinking of taking a holiday now he's got his money from the council. As I sit reading about him, he may already be in Mykonos, having his nipples pierced.

Flicking through the paper, I'm astonished at the number of references to, or articles about, British media figures, like David Beckham, Posh Spice and the cast of *Coronation Street*. Perhaps most tellingly of all, there are references to 'Prime Minister Tony Blair', and 'the House of Commons'; the prefix 'British' is not employed. An article also points out that twenty-one per cent of the Irish population now read the *News of the World*. Irish circulation of the *Sun* is also up twenty-three per cent in two years; and if you watch TV in pubs, hotels and guest-houses, you'll quickly be aware how many people are ignoring local coverage in favour of British news, sports and soap operas on satellite. Ireland may be a self-confident, independent and booming country, but the accessibility and influence of British media and culture has never been greater. People should watch out. We've been in this game a long time. We don't always need to send in the Paras.

Happily, there's no cricket on the sports pages, but one headline does catch my eye. KILLARNEY RACES, it says. FIRST RACE TWO THIRTY. Suddenly, I have a plan. I pay my bill, then find a deli, where I make my contribution to Ireland's £10 billion budget surplus by investing in half a cooked chicken and a quarter of a bottle of champagne. All I need now is a ruined abbey.

I head for the Tank, which has been sitting unmolested on double yellow lines for the last day and a half. Out of force of habit I kneel down, like a priest with top-notch knees, and extrude a particularly mucky fistful of feathers. What are you meant to do with this stuff? I can't just dump it in the gutter. It might give off fumes that will inhibit the growth of local children. Or maybe it's carcinogenic. Perhaps I should pop it in a Jiffy bag and send it to Greenpeace. I get in the car and pull out into the path of a pony-and-trap-load of Koreans, who are shooting the shit out of everything that moves with four camcorders at once, and head south into the National Park.

On race day Thackeray visited Muckross, a few miles south of town, so I reckon I may as well do the same. When he was there the English landowner, Mr Herbert, was building 'a fine house in the Elizabethan style from which you command the most wonderful rich views of the lake'. Today, the house is a major tourist attraction, drawing large crowds and performing the useful social function of preventing Killarney itself from exploding through sheer volume of people. As I arrive, a very tall woman in pink, and a very short bloke in a cabaret costume, are having their wedding photographs taken. Standing on the steps of the house, surrounded by friends, family and a couple of ill-considered bridesmaids, they are being heckled by the official photographer, a Dublin wideboy somebody must have picked out of the *Yellow Pages* with a hatpin. Dressed in a blue Max Miller suit with a vivid green check, early Pink Floyd tie with matching pocket hankie, and two-tone Doc Martens, he is marshalling his subjects with a non-stop stream of good-natured banter.

'Jesus Christ, will you move in at the edges? Can you get hold of that bloody kid? Could you not smile? It's meant to be the happiest feckin' day of yer lives. Where's that bloody priest gone now? Ah, hello, Father, just get on the end of the line there, would you?'

It costs to go in the house, so I don't, but you can wander in the grounds for free, so I do. Thackeray loved the place, his only regrets being that, like me, he had no one to enjoy it with, and, unlike me, he hadn't brought lunch.

Depend on it, for show places and the due enjoyment of scenery, that distance of cold chickens and champagne is the most pleasing perspective one could have. I would have sacrificed a mountain or two for the above . . .

So in homage to Thackeray, I sit myself down on a mossy bank under a tree with a spectacular view of the lake, and get out the cold chicken and rapidly warming champagne. It's beautiful, expansive, landscaped parkland, with an outrageously picturesque lake as its centrepiece, and it does nothing for me. The heart isn't pumping, the hairs aren't rising, and the tears aren't going to well up without at least half a bottle of supermarket gin. Somehow the view feels all wrong: Anglo order imposed on Irish chaos. One of the distinctive qualities of the English landscape is that over the centuries virtually every acre has been designed. The hand of man is everywhere, and you either like that or you don't. But here, in the elemental west of Ireland, a manicured and cultivated oil painting is the last thing I want to be walking around in. I finish most of the chicken, and all the champagne, but I'd have been happier with an apple and a bottle of water on an old rock up a wild mountainside. A couple walk past arm in arm, but break off when his cellphone rings. I get up and head back to the car park.

Going through the woods along the side of the lake, I stop and chat with a large, tweedy Austrian lady who is carrying a walking-stick and a bag into which she is putting litter. I ask her how long she's worked at the house. She says she's on her holidays. International Litter Vigilante, it says on her passport.

The wedding party have moved on, to be replaced by a milling throng of Americans who can't find their tour bus, and so are panicking in case they die. On a wall nearby, a dozen or so Irish building workers are eating packed lunches and enjoying the show. It could have been much the same when Thackeray was here. The house was still under construction, so there must have been plenty of grimy labourers stripped to the waist like these lads and having a good old laugh at the antics of the Victorian tourists, naïvely taking holiday pictures with their easels and paint-brushes.

A little way back up the road to Killarney I stop at Muckross Abbey, because Thackeray gave it such a good review.

The prettiest little bijou of a ruined abbey ever seen – a little chapel with a little chancel, a little cloister, a little dormitory [he's coming across as a little camp, don't you think?] and in the midst of the cloister a wonderful huge yew tree which darkens the whole place.

I walk a few hundred yards from the car park up a tarmacked track. Ponies and traps driven by men deemed too sinister-looking to operate on the streets of Killarney, and God knows that's saying something, are on hand for the hard of walking. Massive rooks are dining on an abundance of horse shit.

The fifteenth-century abbey is still there, just as he described it, except that . . . at first I'm not sure. The yew tree's there, sure enough, a few hundred years old now; it's just that . . . there's no roof or anything, and it's clearly a ruin, so why does it look so . . . new? I love my ruined abbeys and bits of old stone, several times a day if possible. I love their mosses, their patina, their lichen and sense of timeless decay, but these rocks look as pristine as the stone-built B&Bs on the edge of town. It's like those old banks and insurance offices and municipal buildings that have been cleaned up in Glasgow and Manchester and Leeds.

They haven't, have they?

Yes, they have. A charming young man conducting a visitor survey from a nearby shed confirms it. 'There's a restoration programme going on. It's just been sandblasted.'

Sandblasted? I can see that, for an urban building covered in Victorian soot, sandblasting can take things back to how they used to be. But for a rugged walled church by a lake in County Kerry, that's suffered from nothing but fresh air and Cromwell's soldiers for 500 years, it's an act of vandalism. Victorian soot had a limited sphere of influence. It never made it this far.

As I drive back towards town and the first race of the day, the radio phone-ins are in full swing. A woman calls in on her cellphone.

'So where is it you're calling from Marie?'

'I'm in the car, on me way to Pamplona.'

'Pamplona? In Spain? So, how's it going?'

'A bit hot, like. But it's going great. The kids have been strapped in the back since a week last Tuesday. Me husband has to get out every hundred miles or so and turn 'em so they don't get bed sores.'

'Good for him. So will he be running with the bulls when you get there?'

'He will indeed, yeah, God bless him, we'll all be watching and praying for him. He'll be running with them first thing tomorrow. Mind you, I haven't told him that yet.'

Thackeray reckoned that Killarney racetrack 'is really one of the most beautiful spots that ever was seen, the lake and mountains lying along two sides of it and of course visible from all'. It's the same today. The only suggestion that there's a town nearby is a church steeple rising behind the trees. It's turned into a warm, sunny day with occasional showers, or a showery, overcast day with occasional sunshine, depending on your point of view. The runners for the first race, the two thirty, are already coming out on to the track as I go through the turnstile behind an elderly lady in a big hat and trouser suit, who asks the guy taking the money, 'Will I do? Do you think I have a chance?' She's either looking for a man, or running in the three thirty.

At the end of an astonishingly long line of bookies is a chap called McCarthy. I go straight over and put £5 at five to one on a horse whose name closely resembles a TV executive I'd like to see run two and a half miles jumping fences while a fierce little Irish bloke whipped him. My horse leads for the whole of the first circuit, then appears to be pulled backwards on invisible wires, and comes in last with something to spare. I resolve to spend the rest of the afternoon ignoring the races and watching the people, as Thackeray seems to have done.

> The sight of so much happy laziness did one good to look
> on nor did the honest fellows seem to weary of this
> amusement. Hours passed on . . . but the finest peasantry
> in Europe never budged from their posts and continued
> to indulge in talk, indolence and conversation.

He was also lucky enough to witness a fight; though to the modern reader it sounds like something that might go on in Madam Sin's Dungeon of Pain just off the Tottenham Court Road. 'The great flagellator rode up to the groom, lifted him gracefully off his horse into the air, and on to the ground, and when there administered to him a severe and merited fustigation.'

Things have calmed down a bit since then; although between the first and second races I spot a priest in a dog-collar and flat tweed cap putting on a bet; a transvestite falling off her four-inch lilac stilettos; a jazz band playing the theme from the *Benny Hill Show*; a woman in an Armani suit eating two scoops of mashed potato and a fried egg with a plastic fork off a paper plate; and a stall selling off-the-peg prescription reading glasses for a fiver a time. The crowd is split fifty-fifty between local families and couples out for a jolly, and the serious racing fraternity. I don't see any Americans, but there's a sprinkling of young foreign-language students with those logo-covered backpacks they never take off. There's also a handful of 'posh English wankers' as a barman describes a group of champagne-guzzling punters who, I have to say, look like posh English wankers to me.

Underneath the stand, clusters of compulsive gamblers are watching TVs showing live horse-racing from England, live greyhound-racing from Scotland, and live darts from the hill tribes of northern Laos. But more vivid than the punters, and more numerous, are the real stars of the show, the bookies. With these guys around, thoroughbred Arab stallions are mere background action. Two long lines of over-the-top and frankly terrifying characters face each other along the home straight like infantry before a battle, right down to the way they scrutinise each other through field glasses.

No two are alike. Their faces have been cast with all the precision, variety and attention to detail of minor characters in an early Martin Scorsese movie. There's a French accountant, immaculate in black designer suit and open-fronted £500 raincoat; a gangster, or jazz singer, in a chalk-stripe Bugsy Malone suit and black Van Morrison trilby; a Bob Hoskins thug in T-shirt and Rolex; there are straw hats, titfers, flat caps, binoculars. 'Sterling bets paid in sterling, boys, taking bets now on Leicester and Doncaster!' There's one like a headmaster, one like a bent bank manager, and even one who looks like a bookie. This is a police line-up costumed by Shirley Russell and Vivienne Westwood. They're making strange gestures, talking into lapel mikes, and gazing through binoculars, while behind them Steerpikeish youths and no-nonsense slabs of uncompromising womanhood scribble in mysterious ledgers. As I don't know anything about betting, I haven't a clue what's going on; but that doesn't really matter. I once saw an avant-garde Polish production of an obscure essay by Goethe, and that made for compulsive viewing too.

'As for the races themselves,' said Thackeray, 'I won't pretend to say that they were better or worse than other such amusements,' and I couldn't say fairer than that. Just before the last race I drift off back to town in the warm drizzle, wishing I dared be a betting man, and thinking what a good word fustigation is.

I read my book and have a couple of pints in a cramped, dark, sawdust-strewn bar that I suspect used to be a spacious, bright, carpeted bar until the heritage refurbishers got hold of it. By the time I've treated myself to another handsome supper of toasted special and chips, and spent a little while looking up the symptoms of scurvy, it's past ten, so I start to drift back in the general direction of Dead Kid's. The rain's cleared, it's a warm evening and there's still light in the sky. I turn a corner to be confronted by the most annoying street performer on the planet: that bloke who paints his face gold, stands dead still, and then moves his head to stare at you when you walk past. I suppose it's all very well in a soft venue like Killarney, but he'd be well advised not to try it in Newcastle at half past ten on a Saturday night.

There's loud music coming from a pub next to the hotel where the English receptionist slandered the Irish hotel industry. Inside, it's mayhem. An enormous room is packed with people who lost all inhibition around the time my horse was running in the two thirty. To my left, they're four deep at the bar and

gripped with the terror that they may not get served. To my
right, an electric band is belting out Celt rock at high volume.
Last night's pecking order is reversed. The tourists, grinning and
keeping time with their heads like nodding dogs, are at the back,
where there's less chance of getting splashed or trampled. At the
front Killarney's teenies and early twenties are going mental,
pogo-ing in scrum formation and bouncing off each other and
the walls like human pinballs. Perhaps it's the last day of exams;
or maybe it's just Thursday. Right next to me a downy lad of
about sixteen and a blonde girl he's just met start snogging
carnivorously. His two mates stand eighteen inches away staring,
grinning and nodding to each other as if to say, 'Jeez, will you
look at that?' Then suddenly, they're all at it, chewing, tongue-
ing and groping in a last-gasp hormonal surge. Coincidentally,
I've just been reading what Thackeray had to say about snogging, on Race Day, in Killarney.

> And here, lest the fair public may have a bad opinion of
> the personage who talks of kissing with such awful levity,
> let it be said there are no more innocent girls in the world
> than the Irish girls. One has but to walk through an
> English and Irish town and see how much superior is the
> morality of the latter. That great terror striker, the
> confessional, is before the Irish girl, and sooner or later
> her sins must be told there.

Mind you, that was before pierced tongues, alcopops, and the
ex-Bishop of Galway's kid.

Suddenly there's an eerie moment of stillness, as if the room is
gathering its collective breath, and then the band launch into a
blistering up-tempo version of the National Anthem. All around
me people are dancing, bouncing, embracing, singing, shouting,
kissing and falling down – to the *National Anthem*. As a symbol of
a nation who know how to have a good time, it would take
some beating. Closing time in the British Legion was never like
this.

★ ★ ★

The door of the B&B is just closing as I approach, so I open it again. There's a startled Irish couple in the hall, who mumble a flustered 'hello' as they feign interest in a leaflet about something called the Kerry Experience. They don't fool me though. It's obvious they are clandestine snoggers who have panicked at the sound of the door opening, in case it's the landlady returning home. Like everyone who has stayed in an Irish B&B, they know full well that displays of lustful abandon are just not on, especially right underneath a technicolour crucifixion. All those holy pictures are on the walls for a purpose. These places are family homes, where you may sleep, and eat large quantities of pork products for breakfast, but the fun ends there. It doesn't matter whether you're here to celebrate your silver wedding, or you've just met in the pub that evening: same rules apply. Just pack it in, will you, and go and get some sleep.

On the upstairs landing, I pause outside my room. There's a strange smell of burning that wasn't there before. Immediately I sense something is wrong. It could be the intuition that only comes with years of experience, or it might be the fact that my big blue suitcase is out here in the corridor. What the hell is going on?

I look at my door to check the room number. There isn't one. So it's definitely the right room then. Look, there's the big split in the plywood where they damaged the door getting the body out.

Suddenly, I have an image of Andy Sipowicz on *NYPD Blue* breaking down a tenement door with his shoulder; once he's in he starts shooting the crack dealers as they climb out of the window onto the fire escape. Perhaps I should try a less confrontational approach. I take a tentative hold of the door knob and give it a half-hearted limp-wristed twist. The door opens gently and I flick on the light, a bare ceiling bulb, slightly off centre. The room's full of smoke and someone's in my bed.

Dead Kid?

Only thing is, he isn't dead.

He's sitting up with the duvet around him, smoking something.

'Oh, hiya. Sorry about the bed. Didn't you see the note?'

'Note? What note?'

'Me ma said she'd write you a note and put it on the door. Did she not write you a note? Thing is I came home, like, but she has another room for you so that's all right. It's en-suite 'n' all, that's if you don't mind. Or I can go along there so.'

'No, no, it's all right, I'll go. Which room number is it?'

'It doesn't have a number. None of the rooms have numbers. It's the front room. We just call it, you know, the front room. Bang the door shut then, will ya, I don't want Ma to smell.'

He takes a long drag. From the street, there's the sound of drunken teenagers hitting fresh air.

'Did she tell ya I was in Dublin?'

'Yes, she said you were away. Sorry to . . .'

'Hey, no problem. You're the one who's paying. Feckin' bed isn't long enough though, is it? Did yer feet stick out the bottom? How much did she charge you?'

Dead Kid is eighteen or nineteen, lean and tough-looking, with short dark hair and an earring. He says he works at one of the big hotels and has a girlfriend there, a French girl whom he stays with a lot of the time. His ma doesn't mind; it's just that she doesn't want anyone else to know.

'So if anyone asks, she says I'm gone to Dublin.'

It'd be hard not to like him. After all, there's no reason for him to tell me any of this stuff, so in return I tell him I'm on my way to a pilgrimage in Donegal. He stubs out the roach.

'What, Lough Derg do you mean? My grandmother used to do it every year. Sort of a holiday, only with bruises. You must be mental. Pass the papers, will you?'

As he rolls another, he tells me about working at the hotel. The Germans are the bossiest, he says, and the least friendly, but the Americans are the funniest. What about the English? I wonder.

'Too mean to pay the prices. Can't say I blame 'em.'

He tells me about the busload of Americans they had in a while ago.

' 'Twas one of those thirteen countries in ten days kind of a deal. They arrive late at night and next morning before breakfast this big lady comes to the front desk and asks do we have a map of Wales? So we look, but I know we haven't, so the girl on reception says to her, "No, I'm sorry, we just have the maps of Ireland." And the woman says to her, "Ah, don't worry, honey, I don't think we're going there this time."

He leans forward, proffering the Killarney Carrot.

'So do you want to light this, or shall I?'

Chapter Nine

Blaming the Dolphin

'Hello there, Donal, thanks for phoning in, and how are you today?'

'Well, I'm on dialysis, so not too good really.'

'Oh. Right. Well, I'm sorry to hear that Donal. What was it you were wanting to talk about anyway?'

'Calor Gas.'

'Of course you were.'

The radio's turned up loud as I sit in the traffic trying to get out of the centre of Killarney. It's a slow business. If aliens landed, you'd be hard pressed to explain to them the difference between Killarney traffic, and parking. You're dealing in very fine nuances here. I suppose that traffic implies, at least on some subliminal level, the intention of moving. But on mornings like this it's a purely academic distinction; because, whether you're sitting in it or not, the car's going nowhere.

The pony and traps are out in force this morning too. So the non-journey through town provides plenty of opportunity to stare at a stationary horse's arse, which isn't something you can do when you're whizzing through the countryside at fifty miles an hour. The cars gridlocked closest to me all seem to be brand new – no one seems keen to be seen driving an old banger in Ireland any more, except me and a few old farmers on outlying islands – and their state-of-the-art stereos are all booming out bass-heavy dance music, and adverts for tiling centres that are also happy to handle all your grouting needs. The blue Tank's own-brand Volvo radio, however, isn't keen on music. It only does phone-ins.

'So, what you're saying, Donal, is that you can't lift the gas cylinders because of the dialysis.'

'That's right. And my brother now, he used to lift them for me, but he can't any more because of the triple by-pass, d'ye see?'

'I do see, Donal. Course I do.'

The presenter's doing his best to sound concerned, but clearly this isn't what he went into showbiz for. His polished mid-Atlantic brogue can't conceal the fact that he'd like Donal's cottage to collapse on him, his phone, and his kidney machine. He obviously hasn't considered the possibility that Donal may not exist.

Someone told me a while back that a lot of the crankier-sounding phone-ins, and the most deranged letters received by producers of TV and radio programmes, come from students on media studies courses, who are encouraged by their feckless, embittered, promiscuous, drunken tutors to see how programme-makers react under extreme provocation. So it could be that Donal isn't on dialysis in a turf-fired hovel in Monaghan, as he claims, but on vodka and Nightnurse in a centrally heated flat in Dublin, killing time until *Countdown* comes on.

So I just sit patiently in the traffic and listen. There's just time to shave, grow more stubble and shave again, when suddenly we're moving and I'm out of the town centre and on to a ring road full of petrol stations, B & Bs and recently erected Ikea flat-pack hotels. As I'm turning off a roundabout on to the Tralee road, I spot a hitch-hiker who is giving a demonstration of how not to hitch-hike. Is he standing up, smiling, with his thumb out? No. He is sitting, slumped forward, with a sign round his neck, like a police mugshot of someone called 'Galway'. He's nodding his head as he listens to a Walkman, and he has a scarier beard than Gerry Adams. Because it takes so long to type books out and sew all the pages inside the cover, you are reading this quite a while after I left Killarney; but, believe me, if you go there tomorrow, he will still be by the roundabout.

Halfway to Tralee, I stop to buy a small bottle of still mineral water. It's fresh Irish spring water, just like the water we used to get from my uncle's well when I was a kid, except that it works out at £2.40 a litre now. Mind you, you couldn't read a list of ingredients on the side of the bottle in those days, so that's value for money. Looking back, it's hard to imagine how we coped before we could read the contents of a bottle of water. Calcium, magnesium, potassium, nitrate and fluorides, but not a trace of fat. That's one of the best things about water, I reckon. No fat. I drink deep, and drive on.

Tralee has depressing outskirts, but a delightful town centre. While Ireland's new prosperity has brought new building and transformed the look of the countryside, lots of small country towns have remained unchanged apart from a lick of paint and the odd rogue plastic window. You can see why they didn't use Tralee as the location for *Bladerunner*. It's a town from a children's story book, free of glass and steel modernising, and bearing no resemblance to the increasingly homogenous British high street with its depressingly familiar procession of brand names. A place like Tralee puts you in touch with a remembered but recently disappeared past, and makes you realise how long it is since you walked through a British town and thought, 'Oh good. There's a branch of the Gap.'

There are a couple of traditional-looking but un-ponced-up hotels with Georgian doors and sash windows. I go into one and find a homely restaurant, where local shoppers and business people are nattering vigorously over the comfort-food set lunch. I order from the schoolgirl waitress, then take out a set of brochures and information sheets about the Lough Derg pilgrimage.

From midnight, prior to arrival at Lough Derg, the pilgrim observes A COMPLETE FAST FROM ALL FOOD

AND DRINK [their emphasis], plain water excepted, and prescribed medication. The fast continues for three full days . . .

I actually have butterflies in my stomach reading this stuff. As I'm starting to question the wisdom of making this journey north, I'm distracted by the conversation at the next table, where two big, rugged men in suits – rough diamonds who look like they've made a few bob – are beginning to reap the benefits of the couple of drinks they had before lunch.

'Hey, did ya hear about the Corkman who went on *Mastermind*?'

His friend is shaking his head, and already laughing at the central conceit. Kerrymen like them have always made jokes about Corkmen, and vice versa; the rest of Ireland makes jokes about Cork and Kerry; and the English make jokes about the whole of Ireland, in the belief that there's nothing funny about Surrey.

'So Pat goes on *Mastermind*. He goes and sits in the chair in the spotlight, like, and they announce his special subject: "Ireland, the Easter Rising and the War of Independence, 1916 to 1921."

' "Start the clock," says yer man. "First question, name one of the leaders of the Easter Rising of 1916."

' "Pass."

' "Name the IRA leader who led the fight against the British before agreeing to partition."

' "Pass."

' "Name the first president of the Irish Free State."

' "Pass."

'And a voice shouts out from the audience, "Good man, Pat. Tell the bastards fuck all." '

There are places in the world where it's dangerous to react to other people's conversation, but I'm sure Tralee isn't one of them. They're laughing out loud, and so am I. The joke-teller catches my eye, gives a big grin, and says, 'How are ya?' and I find I'm congratulating myself on my choice of lunch venue. Once you've been around a bit, I reckon, you get an eye for these things. After all, the locals eat here. It'll be simple ingredients, simply cooked. Add on the top-notch humour, and this is shaping up to be the perfect lunch.

And then it arrives.

Cremated lamb, gravy with skin, thrice-microwaved carrots, two ice-cream scoops of mashed potato riddled with hard bits, all singed crisp for ten minutes under one of those incendiary lamps, then served on a plate the temperature of molten copper.

I try my best to eat it, honest I do. I think of how hungry I'll be at Lough Derg. I imagine I'm in prison. I slice off a forkful of gravy and pretend it's squid, but it's too rubbery to be realistic. So I'm on the horns of a painful dilemma here, the eternal and exquisite agony of the Englishman abroad, or at home for that matter: to complain, or not to complain? Of course, we're known for not complaining, because we're embarrassed by it. But if I do complain and send it back – as clearly I should, because eating it isn't an option – they'll think, Ah, supercilious English bastard, it's good enough for everybody else, but not for him. But if I don't, then the waitress will go back in the kitchen and they'll all go, 'Did ya give the English guy the joke meal? And did he eat it? Christ almighty!'

So perhaps this is where my Irish side can come into play. I won't be sneery, or snotty; and I won't be hypocritically silent either. I'll just smile like an old pal, and make a pleasant social encounter of it. I'll say, 'Hey I'm not being awkward but . . .'

'Is everything all right, sir?'

'Mm? What?'

She's appeared from nowhere.

'Is your meal all right, sir?'

We're both looking at it. As it's set, it's started to bulk up alarmingly, and has taken on the texture of one of those elephant-dung sculptures that get shortlisted for the Turner Prize. But somehow, I can't do the English thing, and I can't do the Irish thing. I can't complain, I can't not complain. I can't turn it into an amusing social encounter, and I sure as shit can't eat it. So I pretend my mouth is full, nod slowly, and give a wincing half-smile, as if I've been kicked in the testicles and I'm trying to pretend it doesn't hurt. This does the trick. She moves on to the Kerrymen, and serves each of them an enormous tureen of unidentified solids obscured by custard.

I wait till she's gone back into the kitchen, then leave the price of the meal, plus a tip, on the table next to the untouched food and dash for the door. When you're a student you run out without paying; but when you're a grown-up you pay, then run out without eating. It's one of the perks of being emotionally immature.

Out in the street, my instinct is to hide, in case someone runs out after me and tries to give me back my money, or my meal. There's a tourist board sign pointing up the street to the Kerry Experience, the thing the clandestine snoggers were pretending to read about last night. So I decide to go there, even though I don't know what it is.

It turns out to be an award-winning museum and Visitor Attraction, with a modern computerised box-office and ticketing operation. This gets up my nose for a start, as I still cling to the naïve and discredited Marxist dogma that museums should be free. Two French students, barely visible beneath backpacks the size of American fridges, are negotiating a discount as I shell out the full whack, but I try not to let it bother me.

'And may we leave our luggages 'ere?'

'I'm sorry. We have no room.'

I follow them as they lurch precariously up the stairs, aware that at any moment they might topple over on to their backs and die like sheep before the emergency services can get to them. Why do people carry these vast objects around on their backs? In my experience, most backpackers you see round the world are only interested in beach parties, nightclubs, and pizza, and have no intention of climbing a mountain or hiking a hill in their lives, unless they have to go up one to score some Es, and even then they probably get a cab. The pack is only used for carrying dirty washing around the world; so why don't they throw some of it away and get a nice little holdall instead?

The Experience affects me as these things usually do. I find myself wishing that instead of being in an audio-visual display about Kerry, or an interactive recreation of life in Kerry, I was outside, in Kerry. Mind you, there's a family from Dublin who are good value. At various points in the exhibition, life-sized figures are arranged in tableaux to illustrate life in ancient Ireland: lighting a fire, making Celtic jewellery, hunting, serving after hours, and so on. But instead of reading the information boards, the Dubliners are climbing into each display – three boys, a girl, and Ma and Pa – and taking flash photos of themselves gurning, shrieking and flashing V-signs among their Celtic ancestors. As I leave, I see one of the French backpackers wedged in a narrow gap between the Dark Ages and the arrival of Christianity.

At the end of a corridor lined with impressive photographs of ruined castles and stone monuments is a big-boned youth in a white shirt and black trousers. There's no one else around. He gives me a big smile.

'Do ya want the ride?'

It's hard to know really, isn't it? Do you, or don't you? What is 'the ride' anyway? In contemporary low-life Irish fiction it usually refers to sexual activity devoid of tenderness and long-term commitment, doesn't it? So what's this kid's game?

'This way.'

He leads me through a doorway. As I don't know what to expect, anything would be a surprise, but I have to say I hadn't anticipated little fairground carts on tracks. He sits me in one, presses a button, and off I glide into a reconstruction of medieval Tralee before it burned down in 1691. A tape plays, on which birds sing, sheep baa, and people greet you in Irish as you cruise past the market, the shops and the inn. '*Sláinte*' shouts a man. Or was it 'Wanker!'? It's hard to tell with all the birds and sheep.

Ahead of me on the track I see three empty carts moving along; behind me, two more. I'm the only person in here. I have no kids with me, no foreign students to supervise, no minibus load from an old people's home to care for. I am in here, on my own, on a sunny day, at full price, because I have chosen to be. I am indeed the saddest of the sad, and if I hadn't realised already,

I'd have seen it on Big Lad's face as he stops my little ghost train car and lets me out.

Feckin' tragic, he's thinking. That's worse than going on the dodgem cars on yer own.

I need a Kerry experience.

Back at the Tank, I look at the map. The latest version of my plan is to follow the road north, via Limerick, Galway and Sligo, to Donegal. Limerick isn't far, a couple of hours at most. I could stay there tonight, or even go further. But this page of the map stops at Limerick. I look down the side of the page to see which number to turn to next and something catches my eye.

The Dingle Peninsula.

I want to be going north and east, and Dingle is south and west. Whichever way you look at it, that's the wrong way; and the more diversions I make, the longer it will be before I get to the barefoot fasting and inflicting of holy bruises.

A couple of hours later I'm in Dingle town looking for somewhere to stay.

Dingle's Irish name is An Daingean, meaning the fortress, which it was long before the Anglo-Normans arrived here. I read on a leaflet that, 'It is often called the most westerly town in Europe,' which suggests there may be some dispute, though I can't spot any other likely contenders for the honour. There's just a handful of tiny villages, the Blasket Islands and then America.

Leaving Tralee this afternoon, I headed west along the peninsula, with the Slieve Mish Mountains to my left, and Tralee Bay to my right, which gradually gave way to the less sheltered waters of the full-tilt Atlantic. After half an hour or so I was driving parallel to an apparently endless stretch of sand. Waves a mile or more wide were rolling in, ten deep, white-topped, on to the vast sandy shallows. I followed a sign down a dirt track to Gowlane Strand. I like that word, Strand.

The trek ended at some sand dunes, fenced off from the adjacent field with old barbed-wire. There was just one other car there. A family with Belfast accents were sitting around it having a picnic. Beyond them, I had the entire beach to myself. The sense of space was astonishing – sand stretching away for more miles than I could tell, fields behind, dotted with farmhouses, then mountains beyond. The sky was blue, the sun hot on my skin, the clouds high and fluffy and impossibly photogenic. I do believe I ran and shouted and jumped for joy. But if you go there tomorrow, expecting it to be as I've described, it will be lashing it down, and the wind will hurt your face. If it's a predictable climate you're after, try the Sahara.

Back at the car, the Belfast family were playing volleyball, parents *v* kids, using the barbed-wire fence as a net. This probably had some symbolic significance, but I couldn't work out what it was.

Half a mile along the road I stopped to pick up three young women who were hitch-hiking. There was a flurry of American accents as they tried to pile their bags on to the back seat.

'Hang on,' I said. 'Let's put those packs in the trunk,' because 'trunk' is the American word for boot, and I wanted to demonstrate my relaxed familiarity with their country. Two of them got in the back, one in the front, and we set off.

'So what part of the States are you from?' I asked urbanely.

'Er, I'm not American, I was just having a bit of a laugh,' said the woman in the front. 'I'm from Tralee.'

'And I'm from Galway,' came a voice from the back, 'but we were pretending to be American all day just for the crack. She's really American though.'

The real American, who could also do a very convincing Irish accent, in case they needed variety in their hoaxes, was travelling round Europe. So far, she'd been to Paris, the Loire, the Côte d'Azur, Germany, Austria, Switzerland, Italy including Venice and Florence, Prague, Normandy, Brittany, the Camargue and then my pen ran out. She'd met the other two in Tibet last year and now they were showing her Ireland, or at any rate Dingle. So what sort of people have the time to travel round Tibet, and are crazy enough to go around their own country pretending to be American just for the fun of it?

'We're teachers. Sad, isn't it?'

Not as sad as going round the Kerry Experience on your own.

We headed south over the Connor Pass, the highest road in the country. At the summit we got out to admire the astonishing view north across the loughs to Mount Brandon. On an outcrop of rock, a gentle-eyed, bearded man was playing the harp, an act of truly selfless beauty, I thought, until I saw the CDs, tapes and Celtic jewellery his girlfriend was selling. He'd left the T-shirts and the satin tour bomber jackets in the car until there was a bigger crowd.

From the top of the pass, the descent to Dingle is sudden and direct, as if you're landing a light aircraft rather than a heavy and increasingly rattly car. I dropped them in a field at the water's edge, near the Norman tower, where they planned to camp for free. Jen, the American woman, thanked me, and said she never usually hitched, it was just this once, because she was with the others, and they said Ireland's safe and it would be okay. But she clearly felt very guilty, and didn't want anyone she knew to find out about it – especially her mother, retired schoolteacher Mrs Hilary Iverson, of Lake Side Drive, Madison, Wisconsin.

Twenty years ago it used to be a problem getting a room for two in Ireland. Stern-eyed ladies would give you the once-over. Immorality was suspected; and, if you claimed to be married, where were the children then? Sorry, no sinners. Today, though, as I'd already discovered in Killarney, it's finding a single room that can be a problem. That revenue thing, I suppose. After half a dozen refusals, I was resigning myself to finding nowhere in town, and being exiled to some bungalow in the middle of nowhere with carpets on the walls, when I spotted some slightly out-of-focus photographs by the front door of an old terraced house. They showed rooms that weren't big, stylish, or comfortable, just 1950s functional, bordering on the austere.

Five minutes later, I'm taking the key from my landlord, a nervy little baldy guy in his forties; single, I think; gay, perhaps, with wire-rimmed glasses that make him look a bit like De Valera. His house is plain and unshowy and I like it a lot. It reminds me of staying with relatives when I was a kid. There's also a pay phone in the hall that has no receiver, just bare protruding wires. He should use all this as a selling point and put a sign outside like the ones in Killarney. 'No Rooms En-suite. No TV. No Radio. No Hairdryer. No Phone. No Tea and Coffee Making Facilities. No Frilly Duvets. Just Sheets and a blanket. A Touch of De Valera's Ireland in the Heart of the Celtic Tiger.'

Up the street there's a restaurant with an illuminated sign proclaiming 'Celtic Food'. I wander up and go in. I'm intrigued at the prospect of authentic recipes, resurrected from the twilight of our Celtic past. A waitress brings me a menu. There's liver pâté and toast, garlic mushrooms, pasta of the day, fish and chips, mozzarella sticks, and cottage pie. Interesting. Perhaps these dishes once had some ritual or ceremonial significance that's been lost with the passage of time. We know the Celtic tribes originally came from central Europe. I suppose it's possible they brought cottage pie with them. Those lines drawn in the mashed potato with a fork could be based on a pre-Christian pagan design.

As I cross Main Street after my mystical meal, there's an old fella sitting on a window ledge near the post office. He tips his cap to me and enquires, 'How are ya?' then begins to sing. A shiver goes down my spine. The song is 'The Old Rustic Bridge by the Mill'. It was my grandfather's favourite song. I remember him singing it on the farm in Drimoleague. I learned to play it on the piano when I was eight. My teacher was called Sister Theresa. She used to follow the notes on the sheet music with a bent knitting needle.

So that I can listen to him sing, I stop and feign interest in a shop window display that consists entirely of tweed caps. It's an eerie moment. Either this is one of those meaningless coincidences in which we invest meaning because it makes the world seem a more ordered, yet at the same time more mysterious, place; or he's the reincarnation of my grandfather. Come to think of it, the old boy does look familiar. I take a good look at him, and suddenly I realise who he is.

When I first came to Dingle in the 1970s, its recent, and indeed only, claim to international fame was that the movie *Ryan's Daughter* had been shot a few miles out of town, at the tip of the peninsula, near the village of Dunquin. The stars of the film, apart from the stupendous landscape, were Robert Mitchum as the village schoolteacher, and Sarah Miles as the wife who has an affair with a shell-shocked English officer. But their thunder was stolen by an Oscar-winning performance from John Mills as the amiable, slack-jawed village idiot, who limps and grins and slobbers his way through the film in one of the finest roles of his career.

And that's who's sitting on the windowsill. John Mills, as he was in *Ryan's Daughter*. The dead spit. Except that this fella's singing, and the Mills character was mute. Still, it's been thirty years since they made it, plenty of time for him to learn to sing. And he looks like he's still wearing the same scruffy old clothes he wore in the movie. It must be him. Perhaps the local shopkeepers had a whip-round to keep him on as a tourist attraction. Strange that he knows my granddad's song though. Perhaps all these years in the wilds of west Kerry have given him some kind of psychic Celtic vibe that enables him to tune in to my innermost thoughts, and my granddad's favourite song.

This is the kind of worrying stuff that goes through your head when you're travelling on your own. I head off down a side street towards the harbour. To ward off the crazy thoughts, I talk aloud to myself as I go, and this makes me feel much saner.

The bicycle shop that is a pub also sells vegetable seeds and items of hardware. I go inside for an inner tube and some cabbage seeds, but I don't really need them, so I have a pint instead.

I take a seat at the tiny bar, on a stool next to two conspicuously-veined old Kerrymen.

'How are ye enjoying yer holiday?' one of them asks me.

'It's grand, thanks. I'd say the town's changed since I was last here though.'

'Sure, it has.' He takes a sip of his whiskey. 'I blame that feckin' dolphin.'

A hundred yards away is Dick Mack's, Dingle's most famous shop/pub – half cobbler's, half bar. The right-hand wall is lined with alcohol, the left-hand one with repaired shoes awaiting collection. At night, the shoe worker's wooden counter doubles as extra drinking space. The taste of stout filtered through the smell of leather is a wonderful thing; but I get the feeling that tonight I'm at least five or six pints, or a bottle of wine, behind everyone else in here. There's a manic energy to the two or three conversations into which I'm hoisted, then discarded. Suddenly a young woman bursts through a door from an adjoining room. From inside, I can hear the sound of the kind of uninhibited drunken revelry I've always imagined went on at public executions. She lurches up to me, tries to focus, and says, 'Jeezus Christ, first-class honours, would ya believe that? I got first-class feckin' honours.'

Naturally I congratulate her, because it's always heartwarming to see young people taking their education seriously. It seems polite to ask her what her career plans are.

'So, what are you planning to do now?'

'Have ten more triple vodkas,' she says, lurching violently against a shelf and dislodging a pair of Hush Puppies.

On the street outside, gold stars with names on them are set in the pavement, honouring famous drinkers who have visited the pub. Robert Mitchum, Julia Roberts, Hothouse Flowers and Charles Haughey are all there. Pol Pot, Ian Paisley and Lee Harvey Oswald are expected any day now.

All that Celtic food has made me sleepy, and an early night beckons. I'm almost back at De Valera's when I see a sign: MacCartai's Bar. I drop all plans for bed, apply the rule, and enter.

It's clear that nothing's been changed for years. The ceiling is that nicotine colour that used to be cream. The floor is bare. There are old photos on the wall, not for that fashionable, old-world effect, but because no one's ever taken them down. On the downside, there are no other customers, and the TV and stereo are on simultaneously. No matter. This pub has my name on it, and I will stay for a drink and wait for something to happen.

The woman behind the bar doesn't give me a glance, let alone a word, as she serves me. She seems grumpy, but I expect she's just shy. She's sure to loosen up when she finds out we may be related. It's difficult to strike up a conversation, though, with the last known copy of Santana's *Greatest Hits* booming out of big speakers on the wall, *Coronation Street* on the telly, and her reading the *Daily Mirror* with her back to me. She bursts momentarily into life when two local lads come into the bar for some lager and swearing, but I'm left in the corner like the Invisible Man. I say goodbye as I leave, but no one seems to notice. I trudge back to De Valera's with my tail between my legs, but, really, what was I expecting? That it would be the landlady's birthday and I'd be invited to an all-night party?

That's the trouble with Ireland. It can give you unrealistic expectations.

Dingle and Dunquin were the first places I ever heard Irish spoken as a first language. In 1972 it still felt extremely remote. Word was that many local people had been scandalised by the immoral carryings-on of the *Ryan's Daughter* crowd – women and tequila being airlifted in for the weekend, that sort of caper. Change was in the air, but this still felt like an outpost of the old Ireland. There were tourists of course, but they were hikers, anglers, cyclists, archaeology boffins, all come for brutal red-cheeked watery-eyed outdoor pleasures.

Walking the streets the next morning, it's clear that things have changed. The town itself – a few streets of traditional houses, shops and pubs, clustered around a lovely harbour – still looks the dream Irish town that visitors hope to discover. And increasingly, more and more of them are doing just that. The anglers and outdoor fanatics are now outnumbered by gaggles of affluent, retired European couples in mint-condition leisure-wear, wandering the streets and looking for something to do. They seem to quite like it here, but they're a bit tentative, as if they were expecting something bigger, with more facilities, and aren't quite sure why they've come.

There's a highly visible tourist infrastructure now, which isn't something you could have accused the place of in the past, and a sense that where things used to be random, they're now far more calculated. The town seems to be on the cusp of a change, midway between its former status as a remote, backward fishing port and its future destiny as a chi-chi Celtic holiday resort. New restaurants, new paint, new windows abound. Long-standing establishments like the cap shop I was looking in last night are beginning to look like anachronisms, surrounded by restaurants called La Bohème, clothes shops called Tír na nÓg, and a plethora of places to satisfy all your candle, crystal and druidic jewellery requirements. There's also a worrying number of shops displaying kitsch souvenirs – leprechaunalia, shamrockovia and other assorted paddywhackery.

It's like the man said last night. I blame that feckin' dolphin.

Some time in 1984 a young dolphin began to appear in Dingle harbour. Unusually for such sociable mammals, he was always alone. He started visiting every day and was soon christened Fungie. Word was out among the New Age and hippy communities, who came down to bond with him. It wasn't long before he was marketed to the mainstream, and a raft of Fungie-related cottage industries grew up around him – boat trips and swimming sessions and wet-suit hire and books and photos and hostels. Suddenly Dingle was no longer remote. It became a Destination, recommended by all the *Rough* and *Lonely Guides*, with a marketing strategy, and an increasing sense of organised craic.

When you think about it, it's remarkable how reliable Fungie has been, turning up on cue every day for fifteen years for people to photograph and swim with him. For a wild dolphin, this is exceptional behaviour, and also very good for business. I can't quite banish the lingering suspicion that there's a guy who dresses up in the dolphin suit every day. The bottom will fall out of the tourist boom once he decides he's too knackered to do it any more. If they've any sense, they'll already be training up a replacement. There was a Dutch guy with very muscular arms in De Valera's this morning, who wanted to know if he could have fish for breakfast. Maybe it's him.

I spend an hour browsing in an inviting little bookshop. There's a display of works on local history and archaeology and culture, but no local blockbusters or high-profile fiction set in the area. It can only be a matter of time before towns in the tourism business start realising that literature, like cinema, has huge marketing potential, and start offering inducements to authors to use them as a setting. *Harry Potter and the Dolphin of Dingle. Hannibal Lecter – Silence of the Dolphins. Angela's Dolphin.* That'll pull the crowds in.

I pick an Irish novel called *Father's Music* by Dermot Bolger, which is partly set in Donegal, where I'm headed. As I go to pay, a teenage German boy and his mother are being served. She is buying him a large hardback omnibus of Sherlock Holmes stories.

'I am already reading these stories in German,' says the kid proudly. He seems to be addressing his mother, the bookshop owner and me as a group. At the Stuttgart Akademie for Gifted Adolescents, I'd say he'd be the one with the flushed neck who always had his hand up first. The bookseller has one of those rip-the-date-off calendars with a little motto for each day of the year. The German prodigy is staring at it.

'This date is wrong.'

'What?' says the bookseller. He blinks once, as a subliminal vision of him battering the kid with the Sherlock Holmes book and cracking his skull like an egg flashes before his eyes.

'The date is wrong. It is still yesterday.' The prodigy gives an incredulous chuckle that anyone could be so disorganised, while the bookseller fixes him with a psychopathic glare. Instead of kicking her son on the shins with her hand-made orthopaedic shoes, Frau Prodigy is grinning with pride and encouragement.

'Look, I will change it for you.'

The kid rips off yesterday's date and throws it to his would-be killer, like a fish to a seal, or a dolphin. As he and his mother leave, I'm reminded of Hans, the Beara taxi driver, and the mutual incompatibility of the Irish and Teutonic attitudes to time. I decide to show the bookseller that I understand this and I'm on his side.

'Shall I rip this page off too, so you won't be having to worry about it tomorrow?'

Nothing. Not a flicker. He hates me as much as he hates the kid. He was probably a mellow, happy-go-lucky soul once. Tourism can do terrible things to the human soul, especially once dolphins get involved.

Back on his pitch outside the post office, John Mills is doing a little dance for two Italian couples in overpriced anoraks. He greets me as I pass by. 'Welcome to Dingle. Are ya enjoying yer holiday?' Clearly he has no recollection of me, or of the fact that just a few hours ago he was possessed by the spirit of my grandfather, but I suppose that's the paranormal for you.

I buy a smoked salmon sandwich and a bottle of mineral water which, astonishingly, has been imported from Canada. Clearly corruption on a massive scale must be involved if someone is flying bottles of water from Canada to the wettest country in the world and still making a profit. I drive a little way out of town and have lunch looking out over the ocean, in gentle sunshine. There's a report on the radio about ex-Taoiseach Charlie Haughey and the mounting allegations against him of outrageous scams, disappearing cheques, and unexplained property acquisitions, including his own island off the Kerry coast. Despite all this, says the reporter, the town of Dingle has granted him free mooring rights for life, because he starts their regatta each year. I drain the bottle of water. Maybe Charlie had something to do with importing it. Perhaps he's mixed up with Singapore noodles, too.

After a read and a doze and a stroll up a hill to a lichen-covered stone with mysterious markings on it, I figure it's late enough in the day to take a drive around the coast to Slea Head and the Blasket Sound. I'm guessing that the coach trips, family outings and *Ryan's Daughter* anoraks 'do' the peninsula earlier in the day; and it turns out I'm right. It's turning into a lovely evening, and I have the western edge of Europe completely to myself.

The short journey from Dingle via Ventry Harbour to Slea Head and Dunquin is the most affecting landscape I have ever seen in my life. I remember being awestruck on my first visit all those years ago; and though the road has been widened in places since then, and new houses built, it still touches me in the same way. It's like a mythological place. Tiny enclosed fields run down dramatic mountainsides and are farmed to the cliff's edge, before giving way to a dazzlingly multi-hued Atlantic. Hedges are scarlet with fuchsia. In several places, just above the road, are the beehive huts – the remains of the stone shelters occupied by monks and hermits in the early days of Christianity. You used to be able just to wander into them, but now there's a weird jerry-built shed in which a woman and a sinister dog are lurking to sell you tickets. I've become so used to Ireland's random scattering of antiquities that a ticket would spoil the magic, so I pass by.

On a sharp bend in the road looking out to the Blasket Islands is a life-sized tableau of the crucifixion. As the sun disappears briefly behind cloud, then reappears, there is a dazzling display of light on water. Great Blasket Island seems to come in and out of focus, as twinkling sunbeams bounce off the waves, surrounding it with shimmering haloes. It's so clear that, way off to the south, the Skelligs are visible, shimmering on the horizon like an illusion. As I stand at the cliff's edge, a spontaneous, non-specific wave of emotion surges up inside me. I don't know where it's directed or why it's happening, only that it feels unconditional. A tear wells up in my eye.

I try to understand why this is happening, because much as I love West Cork and the fields where I played as a child, it doesn't have such a physical effect on me. Perhaps it's because Dingle was the place I visited the first time I came to Ireland alone, without my mother and father. Maybe it's conjuring up a lost and carefree youth. I don't believe it made me cry then, though. It's probably more likely that I'm just having an everyday mystical experience; so why not relax and get on with it? After all, how often in your life are you confronted by a landscape whose beauty makes you weep?

Suddenly there's the sound of a car approaching. It's a hire car, one of those ugly, grey, rounded Mercedes mini people-carriers that appear to have been squashed at both ends. It slows down to second, so that the couple in it can take a quick squint at the view; and then . . . the window opens, the woman throws a crisp packet out, and they drive off.

I feel violated. The moment has gone. A once-in-a-lifetime experience, the moment of mystical union with nature – the moment that Wordsworth spent so many years and so many stanzas banging on about – has been destroyed in a flurry of prawn cocktail-flavoured debris. The bastards. Perhaps, like Wordsworth, I will be able to recall the moment in tranquillity and solitude, and gain insight and solace from it; but right now, my instinct is to chase them, force them off the road, and stuff the bag back through the window. There. Now look what's happened to my tranquillity.

I drive on, weighing up the feasibility of ramming them over the edge, but they've disappeared into the distance, and I convince myself it would be a good idea to calm down. I drive past an old cottage. The door is open and through it, on the wall, I can see a picture of the Sacred Heart; on a bench outside, in wellies and cap, clutching a walking-stick, is the old boy who's probably lived there all his life. Twenty yards away, outside the next cottage, a couple are unloading suitcases and wine from a car with French number plates. The next time I'm here, the old man will be gone and there'll be another holiday home to rent.

I pull over a little further along and take a walk on the cliff top to the *Ryan's Daughter* commemorative stone. You'll know you've found it, because it says 'Ryan's Daughter Commemorative Stone', and nothing else. The beach immediately below was the setting for the famous gun-running scene in the movie. After its release, there was a rush of tourists wanting to see the houses, the main street, and the schoolroom. In fact, a replica village had been specially built a mile or two away to serve as the set, but I don't think they told the tourists that.

When I was first here, Dunquin was a handful of old unadorned cottages and farmhouses. Today it's grown into a village of modern bungalows, sprinkled up the hills and along the roadside. I find myself regretting its modernisation, so I stop and try and make myself see sense. I have a compelling argument to put to myself. I listen to it carefully.

Twenty-five years ago there was no sign of this new prosperity. The young people were still leaving, and though the old houses might have been picturesque to an over-romantic outsider, they can't have been much fun to live in. Now, it's grown into a community, with new buildings, new people and new initiatives. Why shouldn't they enjoy the comforts of synthetic modern building materials if they're going to live perched on the windswept cliffs of the most westerly village in Europe? If in the process a sense of the ancient, the timeless and the mysterious is lost, then it's a price worth paying.

By the time I set off to drive back to Dingle, I'm half convinced.

It's late when I get back to town and I'm worried I won't find anywhere to eat. I park by the harbour front and go into the nearest pub.

It's been newly renovated, and shows all the signs of being a deep-fried-in-the-basket job, but at least the kitchen's still open. Expectations are low, so I'm delighted when a smiling girl brings me an excellent meal of crispy fresh squid. I know the fishing boats are only thirty yards away, but it's reassuring that places like this are still using them rather than importing big boxes of frozen breadcrumbed goujons of processed Indonesian ratfish. The Nineteenth Rule of Travel, by the way, states: *When Perusing a Menu, Never Consider Anything Containing the Words Goujon, Platter, or Cheesy.*

As I take my first forkful, I'm aware that the couple at the next table are staring at me. I've just begun to chew when he leans across and starts speaking furtively from the corner of his mouth, like a comedian's manager.

'Wassa squid like?'

'It's great, thanks.'

'We 'ad the burger with cheesy chips.'

'How was it?'

'It was crap.'

'Weren't very nice,' confirms his girlfriend, shaking her head.

Darren and Mandy are about thirty, very English, very friendly, and very out of place. They're dressed for an over-25s smart-but-casual night at a disco called Memories or Rumours. It's their first time in Ireland.

'Me? 'Adn't a clue what to expect. It was her idea. She wanted to see the bleedin' dolphin.'

'Yeah, I read about Dingle and the dolphin, and I thought, I'll go there.'

'I never even knew you needed foreign money. Bleedin' palaver that is.'

'So we've hired a car and he's had me driving round for four days. Eight hundred miles we done. Dublin, Cork, Waterford, Galway, Killarney. 'E just won't stay in one place.'

'What were them cliffs though?'

'Cliffs of Moher?'

'Yeah. They were good. Roads are so bleedin' slow though. You been 'ere before? Where do you think we should go next?'

'I wanna stay here a couple of days, see the dolphin, but 'e just wants to drive somewhere else all the time.'

'We can see the bleedin' dolphin in the morning, then go.'

'I'd rather get to know a place, but 'e won't 'ave it.'

'You've got to see the sights, 'aven't you? I mean, you've paid for the car. 'Ey, there's no trouble round this bit, is there? No mad Paddies with bombs? That's all up north, ain't it?'

' 'Onest, he don't know nothing about the place; 'e didn't even know they 'ad their own money.'

'I can't see the point. I mean, it's all British really, ain't it?'

' 'Scuse me a minute.'

Mandy goes off to powder her nose, leaving me alone with Darren. I take a furtive look around, in case any mad Paddies with bombs have been listening and want to rearrange his grasp of history, but there are just tourists, and a musician in the corner setting up a guitar, keyboards and PA. Darren leans across conspiratorially.

'Fackin' funny old place, innit? We're in this pub the other night, in Galway, right – you been there? Yeah, well, we're right in that main street bit, the pedestrian doodah; any'ow, she goes up to the bar to get a round in. There's this old bloke sat on a stool, Irish geezer like. Only grabs 'old of her tit. I never saw it, but she comes back over and says, " 'Ere, Da, you'll never guess what, dirty old sod grabbed hold of me boob."

'So I'm like, right, he needs a slap and she's all, no, no, leave it there, we're on 'oliday, but I'm thinking no way does he do that to me and get away with it. By now he's gone to the toilet so I follow him in and say, "Oi, you, did you grab my girlfriend's tit?"

'And 'e says, "I didn't mean any 'arm."

' "Didn't mean no 'arm, you dirty ol' bastard?" So I grabs him and bangs him up against the wall – not too 'ard 'cos he's an old geezer, like – and I'm like, well, you go and apologise to the lady. Yes, sir, he says. Back out in the pub though, he's only gone straight over to this big 'airy-arsed geezer . . . Oy, Mand, I'm just telling this bloke – what's your name?'

'Paddy.'

'Just telling Paddy about that fella touching your breast.'

'Awful it was.'

'Get the drinks in, would ya, Mand. And a pint for Paddy. So this big bloke comes over, only turns out to be the old git's son.

'He's like, "Did you assault my father?"

'And I'm saying, "Look, mate, no offence, but he's a dirty old sod, he's groped my girlfriend, someone needs to sort 'im out."

'And he's like, "No one touches my father, understand? I don't care what he's done. Now, get out, now, on to the street, or you're a dead man."

'Well, I wasn't looking for a ruck; you know, second day of the holiday, wouldn't be very nice for Mand, so we just drank up and facked off.' He downs his pint.

'Other than that, though, Galway seemed a really friendly place.'

Mandy's back with the drinks – a pint of lager for Darren, white wine and soda for her, a pint of stout for me. The musician finishes tuning up, sets the drum machine a-clicking, and launches into 'The Streets of London'. A Swedish couple start taping him. I want to be somewhere else, but there's no escape now. I'm Darren's mate. I think he trusts me. At any rate, he senses I know more about the country than he does, and, fair play to him, he's eager to learn.

'So what are they all fightin' about in Belfast, anyway? They're all fackin' mad if you ask me.'

I'm faced with the alarming prospect of discussing the Troubles, in a public place, in Ireland, with a loud ignorant Cockney. Mind you, no one has hit him with a chair yet, so I can only presume his voice has been drowned out by the eternal verities of Ralph McTell's lyrics. So far, so good. I decide to try and divert Darren's attention by telling him a true story.

Last time I was in England I had to stay a night at a hotel in Kensington, and get up very early to go to work. The alarm went at quarter to seven, and by ten past I was leaving my seventh-floor room, grumpy, sleepy and not yet blessed with the power of speech. I had the lift to myself. It stopped at the fourth floor. The doors opened, and in got the Reverend Ian Paisley, on his own, no security, carrying two suitcases. Nothing in life had prepared me for such a surreal moment, and I found it difficult to cope. Should I smile, speak, or assault him? In fact, I just stood there with my jaw hanging open like a loon, toothpaste caked in the corner of my mouth. To be fair to Paisley, he did nod and give a tight smile in acknowledgement. I couldn't bring myself to say 'Good morning', though, in case he disagreed and shouted 'No!' in such a confined space.

So I tell this to Darren, but he and Mand don't seem that amused. Darren looks thoughtful for a moment, then asks, 'Paisley? 'E's that fat kant with the funny teeth, in't he? Is he IRA then? Or is he with them other nutters?'

The musician is singing 'Ruby Don't Take Your Love to Town'. Darren and Mand are joining in the chorus, and it's my round. It's shaping up to be a long night.

A little while later something unexpected happens.

The landlord closes the pub at closing time and makes all the customers go home.

This is the sort of disastrous innovation that comes when tourism reaches critical mass. I'm sure that in back-street pubs the locals will continue drinking as usual until natural wastage takes its toll; but the big, brash, newly painted places – all advertising themselves as 'traditional', and so proving they're not – disgorge their mildly intoxicated multinational clientèle on to the pavements bang on the dot.

Mand has agreed to drive Dar back to the hotel because she's only had six spritzers. I shake his hand and give her a hug, taking care not to grab her breast. Then they get into their car – one of those ugly grey squashed-looking Mercedes mini people-carriers – and drive off.

Chapter Ten

Storming the Castle

It's late morning by the time I've had breakfast, packed my bag, paid De Valera and loaded the Tank. I head up the street to buy a newspaper and a fresh bottle of low-fat water for the journey. Outside the post office, John Mills greets me for the first time. That makes it three times he's done that.

'Welcome to Dingle, sir. How are ye today? Are ye enjoying your holiday?'

'I am thank you, yes.'

'Could you spare the price of a cup of coffee on such a cold morning?'

It's so mild I'm wearing a T-shirt, but that's not the point. Coffee? What happened to a few pence for a cup of tea, then? Tea not good enough any more, I suppose? That's progress for you. One person buys a cafetière or espresso machine, and within weeks an entire way of life has disappeared.

'Would that be instant or espresso?'

'What?'

'The coffee. Would you be wanting instant or espresso?'

He's smiling now, perhaps enjoying the fact that I'm playing along. He has a half-smoked fag behind one ear. I also notice he smells faintly of last night's drink, but then he's probably noticed that about me, so I suppose neither of us is better than we ought to be.

'Espresso would be grand, sir.'

I give him £1.20, enough for a single espresso but not a double, because I wouldn't want him getting too speedy. If he asks for the price of a double decaff latte and an almond croissant next time I'm here, I'll know Dingle has finally passed the point of no return, and all it took was one feckin' dolphin.

There's an article in the paper querying the value of the exam results that students have been celebrating all over the country this week with ten triple vodkas. 'The experts tell us the two growth industries in Ireland are Information Technology and Tourism, but how many tourist information kiosks can they hope to build without flooding the market?' I start up the Tank, and heads turn as the shock waves from the thunderous exhaust echo through the narrow streets.

My last sight in my rear-view mirror as I leave town is of John Mills sloping into Joe Long's bar to kick-start the day. Isn't there a scene in *Ryan's Daughter* where he cons the price of a pint off the Englishman? Nice to see that thirty years down the line he hasn't lost the plot. Hayley must be proud of him.

Looking at the map, I realise that if I go up through Tralee and Listowel to Tarbert I can cross the River Shannon by car ferry, and so avoid Limerick completely. A couple of hours later I'm sitting on deck in the sunshine, marvelling at the Shannon's broad expanse, and at the forthright Dutch lesbian couple locked in an embrace against the lifeboat next to me. The ferry lands in Killimer in County Clare and I head out across deserted country lanes in the general direction of Ennis, where I can pick up the road to Galway. I should make it by early evening.

Unless I get lost, which I do almost immediately. Irish road signs are idiosyncratic in the extreme. Major routes have great big signs, with place names and distances, frequently accurate, in the popular style favoured by many other countries. The hinterland, though, is a masterpiece of disinformation. A sign is used to lure you towards a place that you'll never see mentioned again, unless it's marked in two separate directions at once on a post that's fallen down at a five-way crossroads. Within half an hour

I'm so hopelessly lost I'm afraid I'll round the next corner and bump into the Michael Collins Geordie again.

So when the tyre bursts, I haven't a clue where I am. I pull over and gaze gloomily at the flat rear nearside and the gleaming nail that's embedded in it. What the hell are people doing messing about with nails out here anyway? We're in the middle of nowhere. There's nothing to nail.

I haven't changed a wheel for about fifteen years, but there's no one else to do it, so I haven't much choice. It takes less than half an hour to decipher how the scissor-jack works, and soon the immense weight of the Tank's rear end is rising slowly into the air. I'm so engrossed in the simple manly pleasure of it all that at first I don't notice the cows that have come across to see what's going on. One of them sniffs, and I turn and catch sight of them leering over the wall just a foot or two away from me. I lurch back in terror and nearly knock the Tank off the jack. Christ, cows are horrible up close, aren't they? With those misty, mad, glued-up eyes, and their vile dribbly lips drooling mucus the consistency of batter. And it's very unsettling having them watching you work. My concentration's all shot. A postman got killed by cows in England this year, and a woman out walking her dog. Apparently there are ten or twelve cow-related deaths every year. What if they vault over the wall and crush me? It would only take one of the bastards to flatten me like a veal escalope.

My lapse of concentration – or fear, if you prefer to call it that – means I'm still struggling to loosen the wheel nuts when I hear the voice.

'Why don't ya hit it with a rock?'

A tiny little lady has suddenly materialised at my side. She's wearing an apron, and tartan mules, and is about sixty years old. Perhaps she's crossed over from the spirit world. I can't see where else she could have appeared from.

'Nervous of the cows, are ya? Ah, they're just interested. They don't have a vertical take-off capability so you should be safe enough. I live in the bungalow there above, and I saw you struggling and I wondered if you were needing any help. You need to hit them nuts with a rock, or will I get ye a hammer?'

I tell her I'm sure I'll have it free in a minute.

'Didn't I have a puncture myself only last week in my son's car? He's gone to America. Philadelphia first, then New York, then just travelling around. He loves it over there. But wasn't his spare punctured as well? Isn't that a terrible trick to play on your own mother? Eighty pounds I had to spend. He's hoping to get a green card so he can work over there. I'll be sorry to see him go, but you can't hold the young people back, can you? Are ye sure I can't get you a hammer? Would you like to use the telephone? Will I make you a cup of tea? Come over and wash your hands when you've finished.'

I give a yank on the wheel brace, which frees the stubborn nut. When I look again there's no sign of her anywhere. Strangely, the cows are all 100 yards away too, and I didn't see them go either. There's clearly some kind of mystical faerie Tír-na-nÓggish vibe going on between them and her. I tighten the nuts and lower the Tank to the ground in a flurry of self-congratulatory testosterone. I've got oil on my hands now, and dirty fingernails, just like men with proper jobs. I go up the lane to the Enchanted Bungalow to wash my hands.

There's no doubt that, in general, people are much less guarded in Ireland than in England, especially in the west. Rather than putting on a polite front, they don't mind you seeing and hearing the stuff that goes on, so in my experience an ordinary day usually turns out to be more colourful than an ordinary day back home. Little things happen to mark moments out from the humdrum.

I'm thinking this as I walk out of the bathroom to find the tiny lady pointing a banana at me. There's a moment of uneasy silence, then she says, 'Would you like a banana?'

'Er, no thanks, I'm fine.'

'A biscuit then? You'll have a biscuit? And a cup of tea?'

While the tea brews, she takes out the biscuits, and apologises for the fact they're in an old tin. Then she points out some other old tins on the shelves and apologises for them as well.

'So is it England you're from? I was there twice. I didn't like it much.'

I tell her my family are from Cork.

'Didn't I meet a woman from Cork in the town this morning? Loaded with shopping she was and she'd lost her car, well, not lost really so much as couldn't remember where she'd put it, and there are five car parks in the town now. So we retraced her steps and we found it eventually. I'm told Cork is very nice. Cars can be a problem though, can't they? I was driving my daughter's boy home at about eleven o'clock at night once, in the dark, and there was a car just sitting right close behind us with the headlights full on, so when it passed at a roundabout my grandson shook his fist at them and didn't they go berserk? Pulled alongside shouting at us, and tried to force us off the road and chased us and tried to trap us down a narrow lane. Sure, we were terrified, so when I got home I went to the garda because he's a friend of mine, or of my husband's at any rate, but I know him, and he traced the car number. Turned out it was a local fella and there's me thinking it must be, y'know, itinerants. This fella comes from a lovely family but that's how he's turned out anyway. And a few weeks later didn't his brother fall off a balcony in the Canary Islands and kill himself? It's the poor parents I feel sorry for, and her with brittle bones. Will ya have milk and sugar?'

It's no coincidence that the style of writing known as stream of consciousness was pioneered by Irish authors. Critics have missed the point, however, in regarding it as a radical, experimental reaction against literary convention. For many Irish people, the avant-garde monologue is the most commonplace form of everyday speech; and a very liberating thing it is too. Like the best kind of journey, it's always liable to veer off in entirely unexpected directions and lead you to destinations you might never otherwise have considered.

So by the time I've finished my tea she's gone off on sustained, inventive riffs about Kosovo, and why she doesn't like anchovies, and the theological ramifications of Sinead O'Connor being ordained a priest – 'When Bono becomes Pope, he can make her a bishop' – before explaining the entire history of the County Clare hurling team. Apparently they had decades of failure, followed by a small amount of recent success. Remarkable, really. By the time we've finished the second pot, I've already mentally postponed the drive to Galway to another day. It's no surprise that the Spanish concept of *mañana* is said to be too urgent-sounding to be satisfactorily translated into Irish.

I thank her profusely for the tea and hospitality, which isn't really what you expect when you get a puncture. As we stand at the gate she turns to me.

'I'd say you feel very relaxed in this country. It suits you. Are ye perhaps thinking of coming to live over here?'

'Maybe.'

'There's plenty who do, you know. Plenty of Germans. Now, I've got nothing against them, but the first thing they do is put great big fences up everywhere, then two years later they sell up and go back home, because no one's hurrying except them, and it seems to get on their nerves. Well, good luck to you now. I've enjoyed our conversation. No one ever had time for a chat when I was in England. Mind you, I was in Epsom. Dreadful place. Were you ever there . . .'

Her anti-Epsom diatribe gradually fades out as I edge towards the car. When I turn to wave, she's disappeared; the cows too are nowhere to be seen.

'Well, we played a reggae record the other day, and as it was sunny for a while earlier today, I think I'll play another one.'

The perpetual radio phone-in has been interrupted without warning by a music programme. My attention, though, is on the road signs, on the off-chance that they'll give some indication of where I am. At the moment, that doesn't seem likely. 'Tom Duffy's Irish Circus', they say. 'Fourteen-foot snakes.' 'Crocodiles.' Then suddenly, without warning, I'm at a junction with the main Limerick–Galway road. To my left, the sign assures me, is Galway, but it's a very long way; but to the right, it teases, is Bunratty, and that's no distance at all. I turn towards Bunratty to get my tyre fixed and have a late lunch. Since refusing one in the bathroom doorway, I've been craving bananas.

It's not until I've bought a bunch and dropped off the tyre and taken a walk that I recall Bunratty is one of the top tourist destinations in the country. It's just a few miles from Shannon airport, which means that coachloads of people who were in the Scottish Highlands yesterday, and have to be in a Belgian chocolate factory tomorrow, can come and experience the real Ireland for a day, without having to waste time driving around looking for it. There's a castle and a Folk Park, and an old thatched pub called Durty Nellie's. I have a dim recollection of coming here as a teenager when we were visiting my aunt and uncle and cousins in Limerick, though there was no Folk Park then. The whole country shared that job in those days, but no one had thought to sell tickets.

It's almost four o'clock, the deadline for admission; but I have an irrational hatred of guided tours, historical re-enactments and anything themed. I can't stand cruises either, but that isn't relevant at the moment. Still, the guy said to come back for the tyre around five; so why not confront my prejudices for an hour? If I'm on the road by six I can get halfway to Galway, then stop somewhere for the night. I park among the coaches and family cars and join the nearest queue.

Bunratty Castle is a well-preserved, crenellated stone hulk on a creek of the Shannon estuary just a few miles north of Limerick. Though it featured in the Anglo-Norman troubles of the thirteenth century, most of the structure that survives dates from the fifteenth. I push my way through a coachload of amorous teenagers from Limoges and make my way into an impressive baronial hall. A guided tour is just beginning, so I latch on. The guide, a flame-haired young Irish woman, is extremely animated, but it's hard to catch her accent. She's been talking for the best part of two minutes before it dawns on me that she's speaking French. I'm deeply embarrassed. In France I usually recognise it almost immediately. I try to cover up my mistake by adopting the patronising smile of someone who already knows this bit, and slope off. But the stairwells and passageways are a congested collision of multilingual day-trippers. I haven't been processed through an Attraction like this since Graceland, but at least Graceland was funny. You're expecting a mansion, but you get an early Barrett executive home with zebra-print lino.

Outside in the Folk Park there's a collection of traditional thatched stone-floored cottages, showing the way of life of the small farmer, the blacksmith, and so on. They're kitted out with old beds and cupboards, and a collection of holy pictures that range in tone from the fairly gloomy to the deeply scary. These would have hung in almost every Irish home until 1961, when the Vatican had them replaced by pictures of President Kennedy. Despite myself, I find the cottages quite atmospheric; they're intended to be nineteenth century, but they're not far removed from my recollections of Auntie Annie's house in Dunmanway. The smell of smouldering turf compounds the effect. At any moment a wizened little lady dressed in black could leap out and start force-feeding me ham and potatoes.

Suddenly, a woman does appear in the doorway, but she's unencumbered by cold meats or spuds, so she can't be a relative. She has a friend who's smoking a cigarette. They're smartly turned out and in their fifties. I'm lurking in the shadows in the corner where they can't see me, fascinated to find out what they'll make of it.

They gaze fixedly in silence for what seems like an eternity. Then she takes a long, luxuriant, career-smoker's draw on her cigarette and says, '*Ce n'est pas grand.*'

'*Non. C'est petit.*'

And that's it. They turn and go.

There's laughter coming from the cottage opposite. A small knot of people are gathered in the doorway, and there's the sound of raised voices from inside. I push my way through and find three actors sitting round a kitchen table drinking and conducting a lively discussion, or possibly a violent argument, in the Irish language. The assembled Euro-trippers are gazing at them with the same benign fascination they bestow on traditional musicians in pubs. The performers are good; young men in their twenties, there's a real commitment about what they're doing, even if none of us can understand it. They're dressed simply, in dark suits and ties, as if in the scenario they're enacting they've just come back from church. Hang on, though. They're wearing watches, and one of them's just lit up a filter-tip with a Zippo lighter.

'Ah, come on, lads, give me a break. I've asked you once already.'

There's a security man standing in the doorway. He has an easy, non-confrontational manner not usually associated with policemen who've taken early retirement.

'We'll be closing soon anyway. Come on now, the pub's open above if you're still wanting a drink.'

The baffled tourists part and let the lads through. Suddenly, it's a theatre without a show. So who were they?

'I'd say they're down from Connemara. Course they speak beautiful Irish up there.'

'Do they work here then?'

'Ah no, they're just down for a wedding at the hotel opposite the castle there. Had a few drinks, then came over here for the craic. Pretending to be exhibits, like. Just having a bit of a laugh with the tourists. I'd say they meant no harm.'

Beyond the cottages sits a reconstruction of a traditional Irish main street, which seems a bit pointless when the country's stuffed with the real thing. There are a few shops, a schoolroom, and just the one pub, which seems hopelessly inauthentic. All around me people are taking photographs of each other outside the kind of shopfronts you'll find in any small town in Ireland. I stroll up the street, a blur in the back of all their holiday snaps, and head for the school.

There are separate entrances for boys and girls. Inside the classroom, rows of traditional desks are packed with tourists pretending to be school kids. In front of them, a severe-looking sixty-year-old teacher is pointing at Irish words, chalked on a board. As I walk in I realise too late there's nowhere for me to sit. He spots me, and is on to me quicker than a Christian Brother's blackboard duster.

'You, boy. Where have you been?'

There's a ripple of laughter, then all eyes are on me, glad it's not them. I know it's silly, but I'm embarrassed. This is exactly how the Brothers made me feel on more occasions than I care to remember.

'Er . . . nowhere, sir.'

'Nowhere? Nowhere?'

'Yes, sir.'

'Take your hands out of your pockets in class.'

The rest of the class is cracking up now.

'What's your name?'

'McCarthy, sir.'

'McCarthy? A Cork man, is it? The rebel county, eh? We'll see about that. Well, McCarthy, stand up straight. That's better. Now, repeat after me . . .'

He enunciates some Irish words and I do my best to copy him.

'*Cá . . . bhfuil . . . an . . . pub.*'

'Not bad. Now, the whole class.'

Sixty voices join in this time.

'Well done. Now, McCarthy, do you know what that means?'

All eyes are on me. They're a hard audience to gauge. If I say 'God save the Queen' will it get a laugh? Possibly not. 'Stuff the Pope' could be risky too.

'No, sir.'

'*Cá bhfuil an pub.* It means 'Where is the pub?' Well, it's just up there at the top of the street. You've been an excellent class. Good afternoon to you now, and God bless.'

I head for the door as quick as I can, as keen to avoid eye contact with my smirking classmates as I used to be after some ritual humiliation at the age of fourteen. I walk up to Mac's pub. It's actually a very welcoming traditional interior, but the stigma of drinking in a fake pub in a theme park is more than my soul can bear. Suddenly, reality intrudes and I look at my watch. Twenty-five to six. I've been having so much fun in theme-park hell that I'm too late to pick up my tyre. Damn. I'm going to have to find somewhere to stay. As I head for the car the school master is in the street, heckling passers-by.

'You there, wake up! No holding hands! No eating sweets! Stop that smiling . . .'

I give an involuntary shudder. If a fake situation like this has the ability to churn up real emotions then what, precisely, is my objection to theme parks?

'Organised fun, that's what.'

I'm talking to myself in the shower. It's not a problem, provided you keep things in perspective. When I was a student, I shared a house for a year with a guy who used to talk out loud late at night in his room so the rest of us would think he had a woman in there. He used to come in the kitchen and make two cups of coffee, then wink and go back upstairs to continue the monologue. He's something big in personnel now, but they call it Human Resources.

Half a mile up the road from Bunratty are five enormous American-style houses, all clearly purpose-built as homes with a large B&B capacity. I pick the one that offers 'TV *and* Radio!' and, crucially, 'Hairdryers!'. Everything – floors, walls, beds, wardrobes, ceilings, tables – is made from varnished pine, so that the sound of someone placing a book on a bedside locker seventeen rooms away echoes down the hallway like a truck delivering rubble.

When I arrived a couple from Ohio were in the hallway, about to head off to the medieval banquet. They clearly didn't fancy the few hundred yards of pretty country lane that stood between them and the castle, so they were trying to get the owner, a farmer recently turned hotelier, to sort things out for them.

'Say, could you call us a cab?'

'A taxi? To go to the castle?'

'That's right.'

'But it's only along the road there. Sure, you'll walk there in ten minutes.'

'Yeah, well we'd like a cab.'

'See, I don't think they'll come now for such a short journey.'

'Hey, I'm paying them, aren't I? Guess I can ask them to go wherever I like.'

'I'm telling you, sir, they won't come. Sure, it's only a few hundred yards. Less than ten minutes I'd say.'

'So you're saying they don't want the business?'

'I'm saying it's a very short distance, sir.'

'I don't believe this country.'

His wife intervened before things turned ugly. 'Come on, hon, I guess we can walk. We can take a look at some nature.'

It wasn't as if they were a pair of lard-arses, like the Tweedles in Killarney. They looked in reasonable shape; yet the blanket refusal of most Americans to walk anywhere that has a purpose, like a shop or a bar or a castle, remains one of life's enduring mysteries. Put them in expensive jogging clothes, though, with headphones on and silly little weights in their hands, and they're happy to strut up and down main roads in toxic fumes for hours without going anywhere, because it's Exercise. But walk to the shop? 'No way. Not me. Guess I'll just sit here and silt up.'

I shower and change and head downstairs to see if they can arrange a chauffeur-driven stretch limo with opaque windows to take me to the pub. My footsteps echo off the woodwork like Harry Lime's in the sewers of Vienna. The Reluctant Taximan is in the hall, polishing what appears to be a sacred barometer.

'Will you be going to the banquet tonight, sir?'

'I don't think so, no.'

'They usually have a second sitting later.'

'I'll just be having a couple of quiet drinks, I think.'

'Let me give you a tip. Don't be going to Durty Nellie's. It's just a tourist trap these days. If you want to meet some locals, go to Mac's pub instead. That's where they all go.'

'The pub in the theme park?'

'In the Folk Park. That's right. The park is closed but the pub stays open till late. 'Tis very popular.'

I'm struggling to take this on board, and have to seek clarification.

'So what you're saying is the tourists go to the real pub, but the real people go to the fake pub in the theme park.'

'That's it.'

This is possibly the weirdest thing I've heard so far. I make a mental note to include it in the movie screenplay I've been working on at night after the pubs have shut. It's set in an Irish fishing village that becomes rich from tourism when the local priest secretly dresses up as a dolphin and swims round the bay. There's a sub-plot involving a nationwide noodles conspiracy, some humorous Germans and a bogus stone circle. I'm hoping Hollywood might be interested. They could cast Keanu Reeves as the priest, with Hugh Grant co-starring as a rough and ready Irish fisherman. I've got a good feeling about this. I think it could be a goer.

Sitting right next to the castle on what must be one of the prime pieces of retail real estate in the country, Durty Nellie's is a simple thatch and sawdust pub that must turn over millions each year. There's only a handful of people in when I arrive, all of them eating. I get a pint, and sit on a bench by the window. I've brought *Father's Music*, the Dermot Bolger novel, with me, but I quickly realise that the first page is far too raunchy to read in a public place, so I order some smoked salmon and soda bread instead, and try and calm down. I'm in a small bar between the two main rooms, and for the moment I have it to myself. I've just started eating when the door opens and two short but substantial women walk in. They're in their thirties, wearing nylon windcheaters and baseball caps, and one of them is chewing gum. I know it's wrong to deal in stereotypes, and everyone deserves to be treated as an individual, but I can't banish a nagging suspicion that they might be from the United States.

'Oh, wow,' says one of them. Perhaps she's never seen anyone eating smoked fish before. She goes to the door and shouts outside.

'Hey, Clyde, check this out!'

Clyde comes bounding in like an enthusiastic wolfhound. Boy, is he tall. If one of the women stood on the other woman's shoulders, and then they dressed up in a long coat and went out on a date with Clyde, people would still point at them in the street and chortle at the remarkable height disparity.

'Wow,' says Clyde. 'Okay.'

You can see he's impressed. He whips out a top-of-the-range digital stills camera, and the women instinctively fall into one of those good-time-on-holiday poses you see on photos pinned to bar walls all round the world. Click, and they're outta here. I have the place to myself again. What will they say when they're showing their holiday photos to the folks back home?

'And here's one of us in some place we don't know what it's called where we didn't have a drink.'

'You look like you're having a good time.'

'Oh, we were, we were. There was a guy like, eating fish?'

'Excellent.'

At bang on seven o'clock I've just finished eating and I'm standing at the bar, when the door opens again and two men in their sixties stride purposefully into the room. One of them walks straight to the upright piano against the wall, the other straps on the piano accordion he's been carrying and, without any further ceremony, they launch straight into a rather down-beat lament. People immediately appear in both doorways and gaze in admiration. People behind them push through and take seats in the room, like extras drifting on from the wings to fill the stage in a big musical. It's extraordinary. The tune that had begun to an empty room finishes to tumultuous applause. My pint's still only half poured.

A flurry of skilled professional banter from the accordionist quickly establishes that everyone, and I mean every single person in the room, bar me, is American; yet this afternoon at the castle everyone seemed to be French. Perhaps there's some vampire-type thing going on, where the French all turn American at nightfall. Back at the bench there's only a discarded paperback novel to mark where my seat used to be. I squeeze back in between Kirsty and her cousin Raymond from Philadelphia. Their mothers are sisters and the four of them have spent the last ten days touring Ireland in a tiny car, sleeping four to a room, which I suppose is a kind of fun. Their mothers are on the other side of the room, clapping and singing along to 'The Black Velvet Band,' which is quickly followed by 'Wild Rover'. Everybody seems to know the words, and somehow the American accents don't seem incongruous. I just pretend that I'm in an Irish theme bar in New York, and immediately start to get powerful feelings of nostalgia for Ireland, which seems a perfectly valid way of getting something positive out of the situation.

It's not long before everyone is singing along to old Celtic favourites like 'Pack Up Your Troubles in Your Old Kit Bag' and 'It's a Long Way to Tipperary'. By the time we hit 'My Way' and 'Yellow Submarine', it's mayhem, and still only half past seven.

Suddenly, amid the popping flashbulbs, a middle-aged woman takes the floor. She is holding a camcorder to her eye, delivering a faltering commentary as she goes panning round the room, lurching forward for big close-ups of her family, who are cheering her on. Clearly, she's not used to doing this, but the crowd are playing along, waving and grinning for the camera in an amiable game-show kind of way. Then her son steps forward, puts his hand on her shoulder and stops her.

'Mom, Mom.'

He is embarrassed as you can only be when you're embarrassed for your mother.

'Mom, it's the wrong way round. You're looking through the wrong end.'

Mom removes the lens from her eye and stares at it in puzzlement.

'So that's why I can't see anything.'

She turns the camera round so that it's pointing towards the crowd, and then she's off again.

'Mom, Mom.'

'What now?'

'You have to press like, the little red button?'

'Oh. Okay.'

And that's how they make TV holiday programmes these days.

At the end of the song, the musicians take a short break to regroup and discuss whether they know all the chords to other old Irish favourites, like 'Uptown Girl', and 'Copacabana'. Kirsty and Raymond take me across the room to introduce me to their mothers. We chat while Kirsty gets the drinks.

'Say, Peedurh, can you tell us something? We've been driving all week and we still don't know if the signs are in miles or kilometres.'

'They're in both. Either. It varies.'

'Isn't that kind of confusing?'

'Yes.'

'So, how do you know which is which?'

I explain that you have to try and guess the age of the signpost and the graphics, but they're struggling to keep up. Suddenly the room darkens as an enormous man enters. He's in his fifties, wearing a striped businessman's shirt open at the collar, and pants you could camp in, even if there were a few of you. He places a large cup on top of the piano, and starts to click his fingers. Everything goes quiet. A deep, soulful R and B voice rumbles up from some hidden place inside him.

'Swing low, sweet chariot . . . ugh!'

On the 'ugh' he raises both his arms above his head, jerks his huge bottom to one side, and holds the pose for a moment. The crowd go ape. Then he's strutting and pouting and working the room like Chef from *South Park*, an Irish soul brother, bumping and grinding, spinning on the spot and finally dropping to his knees in ecstasy. I'm waiting for someone to run on with a towel and a gold lamé bathrobe. He clambers to his feet, his shirt soaking, his face red. It's twenty to eight. The audience of Americans cheers and whoops like an audience of Americans. He takes the cup from the piano and drinks.

'Say, I'll take some of whatever he's on,' calls out a voice from the crowd.

'Sure it's just a cup of tea,' says the big man, showing the dregs to the crowd, and it is. 'Well, I'll be going home. Me dinner'll be waiting. Enjoy your evening.' And with that, he's through the door. From the window, I watch him get into a blue BMW and drive off. I haven't a clue who he could be. Possibly some kind of roving social secretary – a craic dealer, paid by government to drop in unannounced at tourist venues all over the country and do whatever it takes to give people a good time. He'll be off to Killarney now, to walk up the high street on a tightrope, in a leotard, with his pole on fire.

Kirsty, Raymond and their moms are going to the second sitting of the medieval banquet at the castle. It's their last night in Ireland, and they want me to come too. I find myself walking down the lane with them to the castle entrance, even though offhand I can't think of anything in the world on which I'd less like to spend £32. Fortunately, it's sold out, so I can shrug and feign disappointment and slope off back to Durty Nellie's with dignity intact. I can save the money and spend it on another tourist attraction. A ticket for *Cats*, maybe: £32 should get me a seat. Restricted view, with any luck.

But Durty Nellie's has lost its magic. It was all over when the Fat Man sang. The raucous, ebullient Americans, high on life and Diet Coke, have all decamped to the banquet, and the musicians have packed up and gone. The mood is downbeat. Four people eating dinner at the next table are sharing a half-bottle of red wine, diluted with water, which can only mean they're French. It'll be all downhill from here.

I sit at the bar with a pint and realise that I'd actually been enjoying tourist hell with the Americans. I miss them. While I'm sitting here counting the white lines on the side of my glass as the pint goes down, they are at the very epicentre of the Celtic tourism conspiracy, smiling good-naturedly as comely colleens in wimples and camp ex-altar boys in tights subject them to unspeakable indignities in the name of Heritage. I have to be there with them. There must be a way of bunking in.

The box-office is closed when I go back. I know the banquet's happening in the baronial hall though, so if I can just get as far as the door, and size up the situation, perhaps I can talk my way in. There's a service gate in the castle wall but it's locked, so there's nothing else for it.

I'll have to break into the castle.

The drink-fresh air-drink-fresh air rotation system of the last two hours helps convince me it's a sensible idea. The outer wall's only about eight feet. That'd be a good place – just there, where that tree overhangs. Perhaps there'll be a break in the barbed-wire. I grip the tree. It feels quite sturdy. All right then, go for it.

Suddenly the service door opens and the security man from this afternoon is standing there. We stare at each other for a moment.

'I was watching you on the video. Were you wanting to get in?'

Quick. Come up with a good story.

'Er, yes. I was just wanting to get to the banqueting room . . .'

Why? Tell him something. Come on, all you need is a convincing story and you're in.

Sorry. No good. Can't think of one.

'. . . you know, for the banquet. I wanted to see if, er . . .'

'No problem. Come on in. We can phone through to the manager.'

We go into a little control booth. There's a black and white closed-circuit security screen on which he's just been watching me case the joint. He dials an internal number on the phone.

'Hello, Brendan. There's a fella here needs to speak to you. Will I put him on?'

He hands me the phone.

'It's the banqueting manager.'

Christ. What shall I say? That I've lost my ticket? That I'm looking for some friends? Perhaps I should pretend to be American, but what if the lie fails? Perhaps I'll be arrested. I can't bear the humiliation.

'Hello, Brendan O'Neill speaking. Can I help you?'

'Oh, hello, Brendan. Look, you don't know me. My name's Peter. I'm over from England. I'm on my way to Lough Derg actually . . .'

'How can I help, Peter?'

'Well, I was wondering could I come up to the banquet . . . ?'

But why? Give him a reason. Any reason.

No, still can't think of one.

'Of course you can.'

What's he saying?

'Just come along to the door at the top of the stairs and someone'll meet you.'

'Oh great. It's just that I, er . . .'

'Look, I have to go now. See you in a moment.'

My mind is in turmoil as the security man walks me across. I have no cover story for gatecrashing this event. In a moment I will meet Brendan and gape at him open-mouthed as he demands to know the nature of my business.

A teenage girl in a McCarry On medieval costume is waiting at the door.

'Peter?'

'Yes?'

'Come this way. Brendan has a seat for you over here.'

The room is packed with 200 or more diners, at half a dozen long trestle tables. Miss McCarry On takes me to an end seat in a corner. A dapper little man in a suit comes across, smiling.

'Peter. Brendan. Pleased to meet you.'

'Brendan. Look, thanks a lot. The thing is I'm travelling round . . .'

'Now you have a great time, d'you hear? Kathleen here will look after you.'

And that's it. That's how to gatecrash an expensive all-ticket event in one of Ireland's most famous fortified buildings. You just turn up, slightly inebriated, try to climb the wall, and then they let you in. In retrospect, I can see that a convincing cover story would have looked too formal and organised, and might have got me thrown out.

'There are jugs of wine,' says Kathleen, indicating several large pitchers on the table. 'Or there's juice or Coke.'

Don't be bloody ridiculous, Kathleen, I think, knocking her gently aside as I lunge for the wine with all the dignity I can muster. It's one of those cloying blends whose colour you couldn't identify in the dark, but perfectly drinkable in an emergency. A dozen young women in pointy hats are singing and playing harps and violins, while in front of them a narcissistic young man with a quavering tenor is smiling and preening, as if he were looking at himself in the mirror first thing in the morning. Kathleen plonks a plate of chicken down in front of me, but I've already eaten, and Clyde has the pictures to prove it. I turn my attention to the couple next to me.

'So what part of the States are you from?'

The woman gives me a big smile. The bloke looks as if he doesn't understand the question.

'Oh, we're not from America.' She grins. 'I'm from Limerick. I'm just showing him the sights. He's from Australia.'

'Oh really? What part?'

He perks up.

'The only part.'

He grins inanely, like a game-show host who's just taken a nasty bang on the head.

'He means Sydney. We'll be living there after we're married.'

'Fuckin' A,' smirks her fiancé, through a partially masticated drumstick.

I'm afraid there's no nice way of saying this. She's highly intelligent, but pug-ugly. He's strikingly handsome, but thicker than most footballers. Sometimes that's the way it has to be. I try to make a go of it. I tell him I wanted to go and live in Melbourne once.

'Fuckin' dump,' he opines.

'Why's that?' I wonder.

'I dunno. Never been there. Don't need to. Hey, darlin', ask that waitress if she's got any more Sprite.'

Christ almighty. A moron Aussie, who doesn't even have the redeeming feature of an interest in alcohol. I don't know how long I can bear this.

'Hey, mate. How do you tell an Abo from an orang-utan?'

Till just about now, I reckon. I refill my goblet and trawl the room for my new friends. They're in the far corner. I'm greeted like a long-lost member of the family. A place is made for me on the bench.

'Do you want some wine? We're the only ones drinking it.'

They're right. All around us are the Americans who were in the pub earlier and they're drinking juice and Coke *even though the wine is included in the price*. If this crowd were English, or

Scottish, or, God forbid, Russian, rather than God-fearing Americans who know every glass is a killer, they'd have to triple the price just to break even. All the wine you can drink, all night. There's a devastating idea for the British catering industry, and emergency services, to consider.

One of the women does a harp solo, then another plays the violin. The Michael Flatley of the medieval banquet world then steps forward one more time for 'Danny Boy'. Then there's some jiggin' and some reelin', and the crowd are a-hollerin' and a-videoin', and a-sneezin', because snuff has been brought round. Kirsty goes at it like Al Pacino in *Scarface* and collapses in convulsions. And then Brendan turns the lights on, and everyone gets on coaches and goes back to their hotels for a nice sensible cup of decaff, except for the five of us, who bowl along the deserted main street of the Folk Park to Mac's Pub.

And astonishingly, my landlord was right. The pub is the only fake building I've been in this evening, but it's the only one that feels real. Little groups of Irish people are drinking here, having ingeniously escaped the all-embracing grasp of the Bunratty tourist industry by hiding in the last place anyone would think of looking for them.

'Ah shit,' you can see them thinking as we tumble through the door. 'They've found us. I hope they don't tell us their ancestors were Irish. That may be more than we can stand.'

Once I've managed to convince Kirsty it would be a bad idea to video the locals, she puts the camcorder away and we install ourselves in a corner for a few nightcaps while they tell me about their holiday. Sitting up at the bar I notice a big lad in a black leather jacket talking with a punky-looking woman, older than him, with bleached blonde hair. When she goes off to the loo, he comes and stands near our table, staring at Kirsty, waiting for a lull in conversation.

'Do you have a tattoo on your butt-tocks?'

He pronounces 'butt-tocks' like it's two words, possibly so that the Americans can understand where the word 'butt' comes from.

'No, I sure don't,' says Kirsty.

'Show us then.'

'How can I show you, if I don't have one?'

'To prove it. Go on, show us your butt-tocks.'

'Get oudda here.'

She's laughing. There's nothing threatening about him. He's just a bit vague-looking, a bit slow-motion. Perhaps he's been mixing his drinks. He takes off his jacket and rolls up the sleeves of his black T-shirt.

'Look, I'll show you my tattoos. Odin, see? And Thor, the God of War. You want to see Merlin the Magician?'

'Sure.'

Suddenly, he's unzipping his jeans.

'Whoa, let's leave it there.'

'It's okay. He's on my butt-tocks.'

'For God's sake, Davey, are you bothering the customers again?'

He's backed off, and is looking a bit scared as the barmaid comes over. He protests his innocence, and we all agree it was nothing, and let's forget about it. But we are tourists, who, in the interests of the national economy, must be protected from this sort of carry-on, so it cuts no ice.

'Davey, this is once too often. You're barred.'

He tries to argue, but the words won't come.

'Let that be an end to it. Drink up and don't let me see you in here again.'

She picks up the empties and turns on her heel. The whole room falls silent. A big tear forms in the corner of Davey's eye and starts running down his cheek. The door from the loo opens and his punk friend, who's missed all the action, reappears.

'Ah, Mary,' he wails, 'I'm barred.'

'Ah Jeezus.' She puts an arm round his shoulder.

'Where will I go now, Mary? I have nowhere to go.'

The mood's gone very sour, but Kirsty's mom does her best.

'Look, it's okay. No one here was offended. Maybe the waitress doesn't mean it. He's just a little bit drunk. I guess we all are.'

'Davey's not drunk,' says Mary. 'He had a motorcycle

accident when he was eighteen, was in a coma for eight months. He's getting better, but these things still happen. Sorry if he bothered you. Come on, Davey, let's get you home.'

Next morning, there's yoghurt and prunes for breakfast. I think the prunes have been soaked with stick cinnamon. Whatever it is, they're very good. There are rollmop herrings on the buffet table too, but I think that's taking the whole European thing a bit far.

Butt-tocks!

Coma!

God in heaven. I'm squirming so much at the thought of it I think I've curdled the yoghurt.

I have a sudden vision of Davey at this moment, curled up in a threadbare armchair, inconsolable, gazing into the cinders of a long-dead fire. Thirty-six thousand feet above the Atlantic, Kirsty is biting her thumb and weeping on her mother's shoulder, while one of those terrifying American air-hostesses tries to take her lunch order.

'Fish or chicken?'

I once made the mistake of asking how the chicken was done.

'Hey, it's airline food, okay?'

I can't sit here feeling guilty for ever. I have to go to Galway to see a priest.

I wonder how he's been coping since the twins were born?

Chapter Eleven

Rooted in the Celtic

'I've met the most dedicated, wonderful Christian Brothers. I also feel that it was an aspect of cleverness to be able to avoid falling into the clutches of the more wicked Brothers. Only the dopes got caught.'

Since I've been on the road to Galway, some of the dopes have been phoning up the radio station. They seem a bit miffed that a former civil servant is suggesting it was their own fault they were sexually abused, because they were thick, and their teachers were horny.

'There were a couple of bad eggs among the Brothers: wicked, cruel devils, and I'm pretty certain there was a bit of sexual carry-on, but what would you expect from young, celibate men? Where is he to turn, the poor fellow?'

He's meant to turn to holy thoughts, isn't he? And if that doesn't work, he should hit it with a steel ruler. That's what we were taught, and it never did us any harm. But he isn't going to go quietly on this one, and it seems he's not just talking about boys' schools.

'I remember we had one young Brother who was a very handsome twenty-year-old. Half the girls were in love with him.'

This stands out as a rare mention of girls in the national debate about abuse by the clergy. A caller goes on to suggest that girls were less likely to fall foul of dog-collared deviants as, unlike boys, they'd been trained in the art of resistance. They certainly had in our neck of the woods. The girls of Notre Dame High School, St Helens – separated from our all-boys regime only by a stream, and a frantically humming hormonal force-field – were warned not to wear patent leather or highly polished shoes, as men would look at the reflection of their underwear in them. When the miniskirt was the height of fashion, girls deemed indecently dressed had brown paper pelmets pinned to the hem of their gymslips, despite the clear risk of attack by sex-crazed Christian Brothers armed with Zippo lighters.

The debate continues for most of the otherwise dull two-hour drive to Galway. This seems to be the defining issue of the moment for the Irish, superseding even the North, Europe, and the economic boom in the popular consciousness. When a country has invested total trust and authority in the Church, as they did as recently as a generation ago, the trauma when the hidden truth emerges can only be guessed at by outsiders.

A former politician calls to suggest an annual day of remembrance for all victims; this is followed by a report that a bishop plans to walk the entire breadth of his county as an act of atonement. This seems a good idea. Perhaps it will catch on worldwide. You could see its attraction; especially in big places, like Texas, or the Northern Territory of Australia.

There's a roundabout of such consummate ugliness on the Galway ring road that it would have been refused planning permission in New Jersey. You'd never dream you were within a mile of one of the loveliest city centres in the country. A tawdry mall of video boutiques and foam-backed carpet emporia festers beneath the golden arch of the giant 'M'. Christ, you think, get me out of this place before I see the cut-price exhaust centre, or World of Leather.

But the most astonishing feature of this depressing landscape is the fact that by the side of the road, in every direction, women in tracksuits – stiff-backed, high-elbowed, bums out, in twos or threes or by themselves, in headphones or neck towels or smoking fags – are power walking. Perhaps it's a virus that's drifted across on a freakishly warm breeze from America. I wonder if the Unionists know about it? They wouldn't want this sort of caper catching on in Portadown or Ballymena as a result of some subversive cross-border initiative. Imagine if the Orangemen all started walking like that. They'd look ridiculous.

It's unseasonably hot as I drive into the city, and the place is seething with people. I head straight for the B&B I've booked in advance on the strength of the street name: Nuns' Island. It turns out to be a splendid old house built in the 1730s with stone walls two feet thick. The river flows past the end of the back garden on its way to the salmon weir, and the sea is just a few hundred yards away. There's a sign in my bathroom that says: 'No Smoking (on Sundays and Holy Days)'.

Like every B&B landlady I have encountered so far, Mrs O'Flaherty is an honours graduate of a course in Celtic Hospitality Studies entitled 'Be True To Your Most Eccentric Instincts'. She's a big woman in a tweed skirt and what I eventually conclude, having eliminated all other possibilities, must be a turquoise mohair cape. A small jowly dog, coughing and wheezing like a Romanian asbestos miner who's taken early retirement, peeps out from beneath a prodigious armpit. She never puts it down, and I have to concede the possibility it may be surgically attached.

'I've lived all my life here,' she tells me. 'The city has a wonderful history. Did you know there was once a sign over the west gate of the town? It said "From the Ferocious O'Flahertys, Good Lord, Deliver Us".'

She raises her eyebrows as if to say, 'Well there you are then', and gives me a potty but endearing smile.

'The city was once ruled by fourteen English families called the Tribes of Galway. Did you know that? And do you know about the Lynch Stone?'

'No,' I say, but I bet I soon will.

In 1493 James Lynch FitzStephen, the mayor of Galway, went on a business trip to Spain. To thank his hosts for their hospitality, he took their only son back to Galway for a holiday. But FitzStephen had an only son of his own, who was involved in a passionate love affair. Fearing the Spaniard might be a rival, he accused him of trying to steal his girlfriend. The Spaniard, baffled, insisted he was only here for the oysters and the stout. This cut no ice with young Lynch, who stabbed him dead, then confessed to his father.

The mayor did what any father in his position would have done: he arrested and tried his son, found him guilty, and sentenced him to death. When an executioner couldn't be found because the lad was so popular, he strung him up himself from an upstairs window of his house, in front of a fascinated but unenthusiastic crowd.

'So is that where the expression "to lynch someone" comes from?' I ask.

'Do you know,' says Mrs O'Flaherty, 'I haven't a bleddy clue.'

Outside in the street there's a Poor Clare convent on one side, and the Samaritans on the other, making it one of the world's top destinations for suicidal nuns. The Poor Clares are a silent order, so the counselling sessions could drag on a bit.

As I approach the centre of town there's a definite hint of music in the air. When I was last in Alice Springs they were trying to throw off its long-standing image as a violent outback hell-hole by piping muzak into the streets. You would walk along in 110 degrees of heat, past poverty-stricken Aborigines, tattooed amputee bikers, and malevolent pit bulls, your face covered in enormous flies, to the reassuring sound of the James Last orchestra playing 'Wichita Lineman'. Hey, you were meant to think, it's completely normal here. Everything's just fine.

I only mention this because Galway has made a giant leap forward with the concept of outdoor muzak: there is live music everywhere. In the street where all the shops are, which I'm pleased to discover is called Shop Street, a Basque woman is singing unaccompanied ballads. A few yards away a gossamer-winged fairy of indeterminate sex is standing on a metal post playing the flute. Just up the street a glamorous young Breton with a fiddle is jamming with a fat hippy on uilleann pipes. I pause for a moment at the foot of the stairs leading up to the restaurant where the freckly girls in Suzie Wong dresses charged me £9 for noodles. They're gone up to £12. Galway must be doing well.

I elbow my way through the throng of musicians and install myself on the first floor of an old-style coffee house with wood panelling and big fireplaces, looking out over Shop Street. I use the pay phone to call my friend Noel. The last time I was here he took me up a mountainside in Connemara with a seventy-eight-year-old poteen-maker who'd learned his craft as a teenager from his father. We spent the day watching him double-distill brown bog water in two oil drums over a turf fire into something that tasted like the finest malt. Noel acted as interpreter, as the old man spoke no English. Perhaps he'll have another adventure in store for me this time.

A lady in what sounds like a sensible blouse answers the phone at the place where he works.

'Noel? Oh, I'm afraid he's on holidays. I'd say he'll be away another week. I think he's gone to London.'

I don't know anyone else in Galway.

Shirt-sleeved crowds are enjoying a drink in the sunshine outside the bars on Quay Street. There are lots of Spanish people, apparently undeterred by the 1493 stabbing; but as I settle at a table on the corner outside O'Neachtains, I'm struck by how many visitors seem to come from Northern Ireland. There's a group of five women across the street, drinking in loud voices; a family with hyperactive hungry children, arguing about burgers; and two tough-looking men in their thirties, lurking behind pints at the table next to me. All have Belfast accents. One of the guys notices me listening to his conversation and catches my eye.

'How are ya?'

Half an hour later we've had two drinks, and they've explained to me why there are so many Ulster accents on the streets of Galway. It's marching season in the North, and

lots of people like to get away from the mood of confrontation.
I'm presuming they're from one of the nationalist areas, but how
can I find out without sounding too obvious? I'll have to be
tactful.

'So . . . er . . . you must be Catholic then?'

Now why on earth did I say that?

'Am I fuck!'

Oh God. This is where they take me off to a piece of
wasteland and put a bullet through my head.

'I am,' says his friend, laughing, 'but he's a fecking Prod. We
come down here together every year. Make a weekend of it.'

'Aye,' says his friend, 'or a week.'

Three bars later I realise it's that uncomfortable time of day
when you either have to decide to go for a meal, and I mean
right now, or accept that you've renounced solids for the rest of
the day in the interests of research. What about the place with
the twelve-quid noodles? Perhaps we could go there now, and
eat some?

'Don't be so fecking daft. You're on holiday. You can eat
when you're at home. Have a bag of nuts, why don't ya? Same
again, is it?'

Later we go down to the docks to what they promise is one of
the roughest pubs in town.

'You'll be all right with us, mind.'

Course I will. A pair of pugnacious Ulstermen with ten pints
inside them is a virtual guarantee of a quiet night. The pub's
clientèle are ravaged-looking, but friendly, and the landlady
couldn't be nicer. Two old guys have just started playing flute
and mandolin, when a young man in his twenties walks in
carrying a violin case. His long black hair is in a ponytail, and a
straggly moustache and goatee beard complete the bohemian
credentials. He hovers near the musos for a while, then begins to
play. Heads turn. I move closer to watch. His fingers are long
and slender and seem unnaturally flexible. He's playing the
traditional tunes with a rare delicacy.

The thing is, he's Chinese. I wait till he takes a break, then
collar him.

'I grew up in Seattle, but mom and dad both came over from China.'

His voice is tinged with incongruous elements of a Galway accent. He says he's classically trained, but just wanted to come to Ireland 'to learn a few tunes'. He's been in Galway five months, drifting round the bars, playing with whoever happens to be there.

'The musicians in this town,' he says, 'are the best I ever played with.' He writes his e-mail address in my notebook – even though I haven't got a computer, which strikes him as a very amusing concept – and invites me to stay next time I'm in Galway. Now I know two people here; four if you count Billy and Pat from Belfast, who've moved on to Southern Comfort and red lemonade, a terrifying-looking drink that tastes even scarier.

'Hey,' says Pat when I join them at the bar. 'Is that the Chinese fella out of the Chieftains?'

'No,' says Billy. 'That's a different Chinese fella you're thinking of. So shall we drink up, or will we stay for one?'

Some time after dark, but before morning, we find ourselves in the upstairs room of a back-street pub that I couldn't find again if my life depended on it. A semicircle of men who look like history teachers and professors of linguistics are playing a traditional session. As we arrive, they're joined by a guy who's so fat he can't breathe properly, yet still manages to sing an exquisitely beautiful ballad in Irish. The crowd is the usual mix of solemn Scandinavians, Teutons and Mediterranean types at the front, and Irish at the back. The German couple at the table next to us – a heavily made-up woman in fur-fabric animal prints, and a man with a serial killer haircut and a Tom Selleck moustache – look like low-budget Hamburg porno stars whose best years are behind them. He keeps throwing us withering looks of disapproval for making a noise, but this doesn't stop Billy and Pat talking nineteen, possibly more, to the dozen.

'Ssh!'

The sour-faced German ex-stud is looking daggers as an enormous blond man in an interesting variation on the shell suit goes up and stands next to the musicians.

'Good efening. I am from Copenhagen, and I would like to sing for you a song.'

Suddenly he launches into 'The Leafing off Lifferpool'. The musicians sit holding their instruments. A couple of them seem to be chuckling. The Irish people at the back have stopped talking now, and are watching with keen anthropological interest. When he gets to the chorus, Sven conducts the crowd with his enormous arms, urging them to sing along. The international contingent tentatively join in with an extraordinary ragbag of accents.

> So vear ye vell, my own true loff
> Ven I return united ve vill be
> It's not the leafing off Liffapool that leefs me
> But my darlink when I finger thee.

There's a big cheer when he finishes, but not, I fear, for the reasons he thinks. The musicians get stuck into something downbeat and melancholy. Billy looks across at the tables of benign, well-behaved, affluent European tourists.

'That's the great thing about the Troubles. Keeps all these stupid bastards away from the North. Right. Who's round is it then?'

I wake up in Nuns' Island feeling as if I've lost a day of my life, like an alien abductee. There's a guy at breakfast, from San Francisco, who's bought a farm in Kerry. I ask what he does, and he says he designs museums. He doesn't ask what I do.

To clear my head I take a stroll round the shore. It's a warm sunny morning, and three boys are splashing about in the water with their dad, a thickset man with a vest-shaped suntan. Two men in old-fashioned swimsuits have climbed high up on to a disused railway bridge, and are daring each other to dive in. It's like a black and white snapshot of the past.

Back in Nuns' Island I fire up the thunderously revving Tank and rattle off past the Poor Clare convent.

'Jesus Christ!' says the Mother Superior, speaking aloud for the first time in seventeen years. 'What the hell was that?'

I drive west out of town, past the new seafront developments at Salthill, and into Connemara. The road hugs the coast, so for the next half-hour I've got Galway Bay on my left, with the Burren and the mountains of County Clare in the distance beyond. It's a glorious day, and the incongruous mix of brand-new houses and ancient stone walls is bathed in languid early morning sunshine. Soon the houses thin out, the countryside gets wilder, and the road swings north with the coastline. The Benna Beola and Maumturk Mountains are glowing an un-earthly pink ahead of me as I turn left, for Rossaveal and the ferry to the Aran Islands.

I never used to be sure where the sweaters came from, because I never really knew if Aran was off Scotland, Northern Ireland, or the west of Ireland. In fact there are Aran Islands in all three places, including a cluster off Galway: Inishmaan, Inisheer, and the largest of the three, Inishmore, site of many early Christian and pre-Christian antiquities, which is where I'm heading. I leave the Tank in a car park and buy a ticket from a hut. I'm the last person to board the small ferry before it leaves its mooring next to a trawler and a muddle of lobster huts at the end of the jetty.

The boat isn't full, but that may be because earlier embarkees have already thrown themselves overboard to escape the pene-trating buzz-saw drone that envelops the whole passenger lounge. Its source is a student from Chicago sitting several rows away from me, though mere distance can do nothing to deaden the impact of her relentless nasal monologue. She has a voice that could bone herring at twenty fathoms. As she bores her travelling companion into submission, the rest of us, cowed into silence, sink deeper into our seats, our books, or the trough of despond. When we dock at the end of the fifty-minute ear-bashing, we are familiar with every detail of the semi-formal ball she attended recently, the Chateaubriand – 'it's like, really good beef' – on which she gorged herself, and the new boyfriend she met. He, like her, is a student of literature, though she confesses to being intimidated by his passion for the subject.

'He's gotta buncha books.'

'Really? Omygahd!'

'Yeah. He likes having discussions about, like, literature and stuff? Weird.'

As we queue to disembark she's ahead of me, debating, at the approximate volume of a medieval town crier, whether to accompany her parents on a skiing trip to Colorado. A grinning islander reverses a pick-up truck straight into the gangplank in a spontaneous assassination attempt, but it's too late. She's already escaped into the huddle of pony-and-traps, minibuses and cyclists on the busy quayside.

I walk round the small harbour to the cluster of houses that make up the capital village of Kilronan, and book myself into the first B&B I see. It's perfect. I've a comfortable bed, and a view of the harbour, and there's a sparrow flying round inside the hall. The clip-clop of horses' hooves going past my window sounds so impossibly idyllic that I have to lean out to check my landlady isn't down there banging two coconut shells together.

I've made the detour to Inishmore to visit Father Dara Molloy, who came here in 1985 to assist one of the island's parish priests. The elemental nature of the place, and its history as one of the major cradles of early Celtic Christianity, quickly led him to a radical reappraisal of his beliefs; he rejected the Roman Church and began to practise his own brand of Celtic spirituality, which I don't think was what the bishop had in mind when he sent him. When I came here in 1995, he was operating in an interesting area where Paganism and Christianity meet and decide to try and get along. I phoned a few weeks ago to see if it was okay to visit, but he wasn't there.

'I'm afraid he's over in Galway.'

'Do you know when he'll be back?'

'Not really, no. His partner has gone into labour early. She's expecting twins.'

After a splendid lunch of chocolate and tap water, I set off for Dara's place. Across the lane an old man is working on his beachside vegetable plot in the garden of a weather-beaten house. His potato and cabbage beds have been heavily layered with seaweed. Inishmore has no native soil to speak of; what you see is a vintage blend of sand and seaweed, created by the islanders themselves over countless generations. Inches, or feet, below the topsoil, depending on the age of the garden, lie virgin sand and stone.

Rows of identical bikes are parked in racks outside the post office, so I decide to go in and hire one for a couple of days. The girl behind the counter seems puzzled.

'I'm sorry. We don't hire bicycles.'

Maybe I imagined the bikes. I turn round to check if they're still there, moving slowly so as not to startle them.

'It's the fella a few doors down you want to see. They're his bikes.'

I wander along to find him, but he's gone for lunch, or he's out fishing, or maybe he's emigrated. At any rate, he's not there. It's only a couple of miles to where Dara lives, so I decide to walk.

Inishmore has a population of around 800. It's only about nine miles long by two miles across at its widest point, so it's a great place to walk or cycle, if you can find the guy who hires the bikes. There's a brief flurry of traffic whenever a ferry is coming in or leaving, but today the narrow lanes are pleasantly deserted apart from the occasional minibus, and a few tourists on bikes. I wonder where they got them? I suppose I could hide behind a big stone. I could wait until someone from Barcelona or Stuttgart dismounts to take a picture of a cow, then steal their bike. Even if I got caught they'd never convict me. The bikes are all painted yellow, so the identity parade would be a fiasco.

It's a terrific walk. Leaving the village I pass a pub painted a voluptuous shade of red, with dozens of hyperactive chickens and cockerels swarming about outside, like bewitched drinkers who are paying the price for offending the local sorcerer last night. Several cottages have lobster pots in the garden, and in one a Celtic cross from a graveyard is leaning against a shed. Everyone who passes – pedestrians, farmers in tractors, pony and trap drivers – says hello, as they have on every lane and track and path I've travelled so far on this trip. Like the mundane shopping transaction that becomes a social occasion, this makes a refreshing change from the south of England.

I go walking a lot on the South Downs Way, a wonderful neolithic pathway across the chalklands that look down on the English Channel. Once you get away from the car parks where dog owners take their half-mad pets, deranged from incarceration in suburbia, to shit and attack sheep and horseback riders, the path is surprisingly empty, even in the height of summer. On top of the Downs you can see for hundreds of yards ahead so you always know when someone else is approaching. For several minutes you watch each other getting closer; and then, as you're about to pass, the other person suddenly develops a deep interest in something in a hedge or on their boot, and tries to pretend they haven't seen you, because they don't want any human contact with you.

'*Hello!*' I bellow with the most aggressive smile I can muster.

'Oh,' they fluster, feigning surprise. 'Er, yes. Hello.' Occasionally, the posher, older hikers will simply grunt and stare, as if you've come up the drive to the front door when you should have used the tradesmen's entrance. What do you mean, hello? they're thinking. I refuse to acknowledge the existence of someone who may not be my social equal.

Perhaps I'm being hard on the English. They, or we, are a very private race, which isn't something of which you could ever accuse the Irish. I think it'd be impossible for one stranger to pass another in rural Ireland and not acknowledge the moment, and this is one of the defining differences between our two nations.

The dogs are different, too. I've passed several on this afternoon's walk, and not one of them has even bothered to bark. One actually walked with me for half a mile to keep me company. They don't seem to have caught on to the notion that prevails among dogs in the rest of Europe – that they're meant to be defending stuff from you. They will, however, chase any car that passes, though I suspect this may be a legal requirement enforceable by the gardai.

'Ah, good evening Mrs O'Riordan. Sorry to be bothering you, but I hear a Toyota Corrola went past earlier today, and Boru just lay there like a plank.'

'I'm sorry about that now, Sergeant. Next time I'll smack him on the nuts with a hurley.'

'Good luck now.'

'Good luck.'

Dara's not in. He's gone out for a meeting, so in a way Inishmore is just like Soho. Tess invites me in to meet the twins, who are girls, smiling and gorgeous. I'm surprised to find there's a two-year-old boy as well. I have some tea and watch *Teletubbies* in Irish, which is a steep learning curve. I agree to come back and spend the day with Dara tomorrow. In the meantime I take a couple of copies of the magazine they publish, the *Aisling Quarterly* – its motto 'Rooted in the Celtic, Living in right relationship, Working for transformation' – borrow a bike and head off for Dun Aengus.

The bike has a penitentially hard seat. I head west along the northern shore of the island, the mountains of Connemara still pink on the other side of the bay. Seabirds and seals are sunning themselves at the water's edge. There are no people. On either side of the narrow road, tiny postage-stamp fields stretch off into the distance, divided up by more dry-stone walls than I've ever seen in my life. At some point in the past, these stones were picked from the ground to create the fields. The plots are so small, and the walls so numerous, because of the poverty, and also because there were so many bloody stones that you didn't want to be carrying them far. If you'd made big fields, the walls would have been about forty feet high.

Large parts of the fields are simply giant slabs of grey limestone. Occasional cows graze in the tiny green patches that are peppered between the rocks. The ruins of thousand-year-old churches, built from the same rock, dot the gently sloping hillside. The entire landscape is a breathtaking study in elemental grey and green. After half an hour of brutal impalement on the unyielding, anthracite-hard saddle, I see Dun Aengus silhouetted

on the hilltop ahead of me. Bikes and vehicles have to be left
behind. If you want to continue, you have to go on foot.

Thank God for that.

Dun Aengus is a ring fort dating from about 1100 BC. Once
described as 'the most magnificent barbaric monument extant in
Europe', it sits on the summit of a cliff that falls 300 feet sheer
into the sea. Its massive, horseshoe-shaped stone walls, enclosing
a central living area, terminate on either side at the cliff's edge.
You wouldn't want to sleepwalk.

As I climb the hillside a steady trickle of visitors, many of
whom I recognise from this morning's boat, are on their way
down. I'm flanked on either side by enormous slabs of stone,
stretching off as far as the eye can see. Whoever built it must
have carved the blocks straight out of the ground. However they
achieved it, the whole enterprise suggests a high level of social
cohesion and organisation. Two further outer walls were added
many hundreds of years after the original was built. As you go
through the second of these, you pass the spot where the
headless skeletons of a man and a boy were found during
excavations in the 1990s. The remains dated from the Viking
period. Vikings versus the guys who lived here; that must have
been some match.

It's one of those places that send a frisson of electricity
coursing through you. The water pounding the rocks below
sounds like explosions in a distant quarry. I'd been told in
Galway that the thing to do is lie on your stomach, edge
forward, and peer down over the drop, but I'd rather crawl
five miles naked over broken glass with Gary Glitter on my back.

Perhaps I'm a bit dim, but I hadn't expected the view. From
this point, looking back in the direction I've come, you see both
sides of the island, and the ocean on either side. To my left is
Galway and Connemara, which I was prepared for; but to my
right are the Cliffs of Moher, twenty miles away on mainland
County Clare. To the south of them, far, far to the south, is
more coastline, and mountains, and finally, on the distant,
crystal-clear horizon, one massive mountain. The next day a
guy in a shop tells me it was Mount Brandon, seventy-five miles

away in the Dingle Peninsula, but he might have said that to make me happy.

There are only a handful of other people up here, and I'm tuning into the mood of the place, wondering who the builders were, when I hear a rumbling sound in the distance, like a low-level aircraft approaching at speed. Suddenly the sound bursts through the stone archway into the inner sanctum. It's the student from the ferry, this time elaborating on her plans for Thanksgiving. As I turn to leave, she and her friend are approaching the edge, where she's about to attempt the first direct communication with the United States using human voice alone.

Or perhaps her friend, patient, long-suffering, but devious, is about to nudge her to her death on the rocks below. I don't hang around to find out.

In a little hut near the foot of the hill I buy a hand-knit sweater from a lady who tells me she makes them for Sharon Stone.

Back in Kilronan at the end of the day I sit outside Joe Mac's pub looking over the harbour. The water turns purple and green as I watch the sun go down on Galway Bay, which seems suitably kitsch. Over a couple of languid pints I browse through the *Aisling Quarterly*. It opens with an article by Dara Molloy about the imposition of uniformity of worship once Christianity became the religion of the Roman Empire. By the twelfth century Celtic Christianity had been all but obliterated.

> Christianity had now created the first multinational product. Religious expression had been stripped of its diversity, its cultural and geographical connections, its integration with seasons, climate and local festivals . . . just as McDonalds is recognisable for its premises and its food no matter where it is situated in the world, so Christianity had done the same. It was Christianity that gave McDonalds the idea.

I wonder if the local priest had him tarred and feathered when he turned up here saying things like that? I must remember to ask. In the absence of McDonald's I take myself off to a little seafood and pizza place. Unfortunately, the waitress says the seafood platter's off, the crab claws are off, and the mozzarella and pepperoni are off. Such are the rigours of island life. I settle for a salad, a steak, and an early night.

Back in my room there's a note saying someone's been in to mend the window. Unfortunately they've applied a potentially lethal cocktail of solvents and gloss paint to the offending area. It's a warm evening, and the heating's been left on, so it's like being in a bodywork and paint spray shop in Mexico City. In fumes like this you'd need a protective mask to check your car oil, let alone sleep. My eyes are watering, and there must be less than a fifty-fifty chance of my surviving the night.

I pull the sheets over my head and slip off into a deep and toxic slumber. I'm woken just the once, by my own cries, from a nightmare in which I'm trapped on a cliff edge in a car whose lethal exhaust fumes are changing into poisonous birds.

'In 1985, when I came here, the island had ten thousand tourists. This year it'll be two hundred thousand.'

It's mid-morning, and I'm examining a standing stone with Dara. It's marked with primitive Celtic crosses, carved perhaps a thousand years ago on a monument that even then had already been here for a very long time. The walk over after breakfast served as an excellent solvent-abuse detox session. In defiance of all known precedent, it's another lovely day. So has tourism ruined the islanders' way of life?

'Not at all. There used to be just fishing or emigration. Now there's a choice. People can choose to stay. Some are even coming back from America.'

He's in his forties, with thick dark greying hair and beard, and exudes a gentle charisma. The house they've built overlooking the shore, where volunteers come and live while helping produce the magazine or working on the organic garden, is just above us, but hidden by a rocky outcrop. This tiny piece of land between the house and the beach is rich in ancient sites: there are several standing stones and Celtic crosses, a holy well, a salmon pool that features in Irish mythology, a Viking burial, a ruined early Christian church, and an unconsecrated children's cemetery. On Sundays Dara says his own version of mass out here in the open air. At other times he leads pilgrims in the rounds – a traditional Celtic spiritual practice, believed to have originated in pre-Christian times, but practised by the early monks who populated Inishmore from the fifth century onwards. The pilgrims walk clockwise round the holy well, praying as they go, counting out the seven rounds with pebbles.

Most of the standing stones are taller than we are. A couple of them are carved with designs that have been found nowhere else. The one next to the church is drilled with a circular hole, through which lovers have traditionally threaded a handkerchief while making a wish. Isn't this the kind of practice, I wonder, that gained the Irish a reputation for superstition rather than religion?

'That's a very fine distinction. After all, what's a prayer if it isn't a wish?'

The children's graveyard, close to the water's edge, is a deeply atmospheric place. Children who died before being baptised were laid here, in unconsecrated ground. A jumble of uninscribed stones marks the confusion of graves.

'There's a woman in her seventies, still living here, who remembers when she was a child a baby being buried here, at midnight with no priest present. There was a lot of shame. It was a terrible thing.'

After lunch of bread and cheese, we walk to the highest point of the island where there's another fort. On the way up, I ask him about his abandonment of his vow of chastity.

'Fatherhood really suits me. It's made me complete.'

Parenthood, I say, opens up a part of us men that we never knew existed.

'I know. And it's a very big part.'

I wonder whether he's ahead of the game; will the Church one day abandon celibacy? He doesn't think so.

'The post-Celtic Church has been organised on the model of the Roman Empire, with a single patriarch at the top from whom all authority flows. It's structured like an army, so that everyone will obey without question. Celibacy is a method of control. A passionate devotion outside the job might subvert the structure.'

The fort of Dun Eochia is smaller and less frequently visited than Dun Aengus, and we have the place to ourselves. From up here the island looks like a block of sheer stone, the patches of grass just lichen on a rock. A goat is bleating in the distance.

'This is one of my favourite places on the island. The Celts believed that our world and the spirit world are very close, and that there are particular places of energy where the divide is very thin, and it's possible to step across to the other side. I think this is one of those places.'

It seems like a good place to ask the renegade priest the million-dollar question.

'So do you believe in God?'

A pause.

'Do you believe in a life after death where we'll be aware of ourselves as individuals, where we'll be able to say, "Oh, hi, Mike, nice to see you again"?'

He smiles. 'I'd have to say my beliefs have changed in the fifteen years I've been here. I absolutely believe in a spirit world. I believe we're close to it here.'

He looks around.

'And I believe religion should serve the people from the ground up, not from the top down. It must nurture their souls, or it is nothing. But as to whether, once my body's in the ground, I'll be conscious of myself as a separate entity – I'm not sure I will. I suppose . . .' He chuckles. 'Perhaps you'd have to say I was an agnostic.'

I've never met an agnostic priest before, so I feel I should tell him what the country and western detective novelist Kinky Friedman has to say on the subject of belief. 'I'm a Jehovah's Bystander. We believe in a supreme being, but we just don't want to get involved.'

There's a beautifully carved Celtic cross in the centre of Kilronan, if a place so small can have a centre. It was carved by James Pearse of Dublin, father of Patrick Pearse, a leader of the 1916 Easter Rising. In the evening teenage kids hang around it, smoking and flirting like they do in bus shelters and shopping precincts in busier parts of the world. Behind it, there's a pub called the American Bar. I don't know why it's called that. Dara said this afternoon that the islanders have always looked to the west: emigration usually meant Boston or Chicago or San Francisco, rarely Dublin or London. To my ear, there's a strong touch of American in the local accent, but whether that's an accent they sent to the States, or one that's been brought here by returning emigrants, I couldn't say, and nor could anyone I asked.

But that's the accent I hear when they're speaking English, which in most cases is a second language. In the American Bar tonight everyone seems to be speaking Irish but me. It could be Hungarian or Basque for all I can understand. Out here the language defines who you are, as does the gene pool, which has remained relatively undisturbed over the centuries. It's a magical place, but I'm not naïve enough to imagine myself living here, as I usually do in places I really like. My landlady's sitting over there in the corner, but the place is packed and I don't think she's noticed me. Four men are playing fiddle, accordion, flute and guitar, and a drunken old boy with overgrown hair and big clumpy boots is dancing up a storm in front of them.

'Wow! It's like a Guinness ad or a scene from that Tom Cruise movie,' says a loud and familiar voice behind me.

'Gahd! Imagine if you could, like, live here?'

Her friend didn't chuck her off the cliff, then.

Feels like bedtime to me.

The paint and glue fumes had pretty much dissipated when I got back, and I enjoyed a relatively hallucination-free night. I think Mammy may have stayed out late, because at breakfast this morning I was served by her eight-year-old daughter. She said, 'You're welcome,' and 'Have a nice day,' which was a bit of a worry.

I've spent the day walking and reading and digesting what I've heard. I bought an excellent *Pocket Guide to Árainn*, by Dara O'Maoildhia, which I later found out translates as Dara Molloy. I'd recommend it if you're ever out this way. Don't borrow his bike though. My arse is destroyed.

I've just boarded the afternoon ferry. About twenty minutes ago I was browsing without intent to purchase in the biggest and most expensive sweater shop in town, when suddenly the door flew open and in poured two dozen Japanese people in designer clothes, some of them running. One woman started shouting. 'Best stock!' she shrilled. 'Best stock! Best stock!' A smiling assistant pointed her in the direction of the most ruinously expensive handknits, and I headed for the boat.

They've just turned up in their bus. They can't have been in there ten minutes, but judging by the carrier bags they've pumped enough cash into the local economy to pay someone to clear the island of stones. I've got a seat on the open deck. As we pull away from the jetty, I can see Dun Eochia silhouetted on the skyline on top of the island. It sets me thinking about something Dara said as we were on our way down. I think he may have made sense of my Anglo-Irish identity crisis.

Chapter Twelve

Cross in Cong

I'm in a restaurant in Cong, in County Mayo, waiting for my main course to arrive. The omens aren't good. Vegetable of the Day is Mexican Potatoes; and when I went upstairs to the loo a few minutes ago, two hysterical teenage girls burst out of the living-room with lollipops stuck up their noses, sticky end first. The couple at the next table to me are listening to the conversation of the people at the table next to them, and openly discussing it. I'm listening to all four of them, but mostly I'm reading the newspaper.

'He was walking down the middle of Washington Street. He was as totally naked as the day he was born.'

These were the words spoken by Garda Rice as he gave evidence in court. The report continues: 'The two gardai were on a midnight patrol in the city centre when they came upon the two nude doctors, a court sitting was told.

'Two British doctors – a cardiologist and a psychiatrist, both of whom are due to sit examinations to be consultants – were in Cork on one of their stag weekends, when they walked about naked in the city centre just after midnight.'

In fairness to the Scots and Welsh, I should point out that the paralytic quacks weren't British, so much as English. It's an Irish paper, so I suppose the confusion is fair enough. The English press, of course, have got this nationality business down to a fine art. If you win an Olympic medal, an Oscar, or the George Cross, then you're British; unless you're involved in a sex scandal, a drugs deal, or a court case, in which case you're once again Scottish, Welsh, Northern Irish, or black.

The report is worrying on two counts. It reminds us once again how naïve we are to entrust our health and well-being to ex-medical students. Why on earth do doctors drink so much? I suppose it gives them something to do while they're smoking. But more troubling than the profession of the inebriated nudes is their location, and the fact that they weren't the only ones at it. 'Three other English' – there you are, they got it right that time – 'visitors for stag parties that weekend,' concludes the report, 'were arrested for being nude, in public, in Cork.' It brings to mind the South Uist hedgehog catastrophe.

There were no hedgehogs on the island of South Uist in the Outer Hebrides until 1974, when some bright spark imported seven of them in a disastrous attempt to control the slug population in his garden. Today, there are an estimated 6,000, advancing ever northwards in a relentless, spiky tide that cannot be resisted. And as they progress, they're devouring the eggs of rare birds, and so inflicting dramatic and permanent upheaval on the fragile eco-balance.

The unsettling case of the nude English doctors suggests to me that something akin to the South Uist rogue hedgehog scenario is happening with English stag parties in Ireland. Not so long ago, English bridegrooms and their flabby, bevvied-up en-tourages wouldn't have considered Ireland a suitable venue for their desperate rituals. Then, as air fares began to drop, and word got out that Ireland was a very cool place, a few ground-breaking best men organised the first wave of pre-nuptial weekends on the booze. They might have eaten birds' eggs too. It's plausible, given their subsequent track record.

Anyway, some years down the line, Dublin is now saturated. It can take no more Londoners in false rubber breasts, no more comatose Liverpudlians chained to lamp posts with boot polish on their genitals, no more nude doctors. So now they have spread, like egg-slurping hedgehogs, to Cork. Waterford will be next. There have already been sightings in Galway. Politicians of all parties must mobilise resistance. The EC should give Ireland massive amounts of money, no questions asked, one more time. As flights get even cheaper, and new airports open in the far west and north, nowhere is safe. The Irish way of life is under threat as never before. Unless a nation is prepared to make a stand, hopelessly drunken doctors may achieve what a thousand years of English landowners, politicians and soldiers could not.

Trust me, I know what I'm talking about. I've been to South Uist. I've met the guy who fastens the little flashing lights on the hedgehogs and follows them at night, and he's not as mad as he sounds. I've seen what the prickly little bastards can do.

Mind you, I wouldn't mind the stag nights coming here, to Cong. That might wipe the smile off a few of the smug faces I've seen tonight. This place has put me in a bad mood. It deserves all the nude doctors Britain can send.

Cong sits on a spur of land between Lough Corrib to the south, and Lough Mask to the north, with the Joyce Country and spectacular rivers and mountains of Connemara to the west. I remembered it as a delightful little place with an almost fairytale feel about it. It's famous for its splendid twelfth-century ruined abbey, and also for the Cross of Cong: a richly-jewelled processional cross from the same period, regarded as one of the finest European works of art of the era, that is now in the National Museum in Dublin. *The Quiet Man*, the John Ford movie starring John Wayne, was also filmed in Cong. Among the village's many engagingly non-mainstream attractions is the Dry Canal, a doomed nineteenth-century attempt to link the two loughs. After five years' digging, water was released into the canal, and immediately disappeared, because it had been dug on porous limestone. What a hilarious Irish joke this would be, were it not for the fact that the engineer in charge of the project was British. Sorry, English.

And I suppose he may have moved by now, but last time I was here, the Edge, the guitarist from U2, was living here, in the house where Oscar Wilde grew up. It was meant to be a big secret. But as soon as you arrived in town and went to the pub, the barman would say, 'What'll it be? By the way, do you know the Edge lives here?' It was the same in the shop. 'That'll be £4.90. And the Edge lives here. Straight out that road. You can't miss it.'

So, yesterday evening, on the ferry ride back from Inishmore, I decided I'd stop off in Cong. From there I could meander through Connemara up to Westport, then on to Sligo, and Donegal at last, for the penitential barefoot fasting and application of the red-hot holy leeches.

But it was an overcast evening as I came ashore, and I didn't feel inclined to make the spectacular journey up to Cong in the gloom. As I was manoeuvring the Tank out of the car park, a fella I'd seen on the boat came across.

'You're not heading for Galway, are ya?'

'I don't know where I'm heading, but it won't be Galway. I think I need to find somewhere to stay.'

'Sure, your best bet would be Spiddal, there's loads of places there.'

'Where's Spiddal?'

'It's on the road to Galway.'

So I was heading to Galway after all.

He was a young man with dark hair, brown eyes and a tartan holdall. He said he goes out to the islands whenever he can because he works for an estate agent in Galway, and he hates it. So, I wonder, are there still property bargains to be had?

'You'd still find places up in Connemara, but you might find it hard not speaking Irish. The Germans buy lots of places, but they sell them again soon enough.'

He told me about some clients of his, two gay German guys, who spent two years doing up a little cottage outside Galway, until it was just perfect. Then they decided Ireland wasn't really for them after all, and put it on the market. One of them was a photographer, and he presented the agent with a handsome portfolio of pictures of the property, and a video.

'We've a lady on our books who's been working as a

housekeeper for a priest, but the priest's died. She's looking for somewhere small, and she's very house-proud, you know, very fastidious. So I figure maybe this place could be right for her. So, I give her the details, and the video, and tell her to get in touch if she wants to go and take a look. Drop me anywhere here now. This is Spiddal.'

I pulled over to the side of the road and turned the engine off while he finished his story.

'Next day, she's back, and she's angry. Won't even talk to me. She'll only talk to the auld woman who does the photocopying. Turns out that the video' – he was laughing now – 'the video had been used before.'

Oh no.

'So there's the video of the house like, all nice, and when that ends it's, you know, fuzzy white snow, so she gets up to turn it off . . .'

Dear God, no. And her a priest's housekeeper too.

'. . . and this porno film comes on. Gay stuff. The real thing, like. And it's halfway through so it's really into the action. She went mental.'

He opened the door and climbed out.

'Thanks for the ride. There are places to stay all along here and some more B&Bs up that road on the left by the pub. She's decided she'd prefer a flat now. Good luck.'

I'd been through Spiddal before on the way out to the ferry from Galway. It's a pretty little village on the shore of Galway Bay, with just a couple of 'Cambio' and 'Wechsel' signs to indicate it's now an international hot spot. I found a B&B that, disappointingly, had no colourful landlady with multiple eccentricities. There was just a quiet young man who showed me out to a comfortable room in a bland annex and gave me a key without asking my name.

I soon found an old pub that smelled of new wood. It had just been renovated and enlarged and fitted with new plasterboard ceilings with those inset fish-eye lights. On a night like this, in high season, it looked like a licence to print money. In one corner ten, and I counted 'em, ten musicians sat in a circle playing two flutes, two fiddles, a harmonica, a bodhran, a guitar, a mandolin, a squeeze-box and a tin whistle. When a traditional session is good, it swings, like jazz. These people were good.

I stood at the bar and watched the usual round-up of nationalities revelling in the atmosphere. The bar staff, dressed in matching polo shirts bearing the place's name, were speaking English to customers, but Irish among themselves. I tried to pick out local people in the crowd, and soon realised that they were doing the same. It struck me as the perfect way of reaping the benefits that tourism can bring, while retaining a local culture, a scene, a network of friendships and gossip on which outsiders cannot impinge, even when they're in the same room. It was like watching two parallel universes, both happy with their lot.

A woman came up to the bar to buy a big round. She was wearing a T-shirt that said: 'Connor O'Neill's Traditional Irish Pub. Ann Arbor. Michigan'. Next to her, a big ruddy-cheeked guy with hairy ears, who I took to be the owner, was rabbiting away to an old couple who were wearing too many coats for the time of year. When he paused to take a drink, Ann Arbor touched him on the arm.

'Excuse me? I really find your accent very interesting, but it's kinda difficult for me to understand. Which part of Ireland are you from?'

'I was speaking Irish, love.'

Back in my room I decided to watch a bit of TV, but there wasn't one, so I listened to the radio instead.

'Hi, I'm Boy George. If, like me, you're slightly over thirty . . .'

You what?

'So were the eighties a glamorous period, or just a load of people messing around with their mum's mascara?'

No one cares, George. We're in Connemara.

'So remember, Premier Direct, cheaper car insurance for the over thirties.'

It's true. I heard it. Celebs do these ads if they think they can get away with it and no one they know will hear it. A little while later, Bryan Ferry came on advertising Athlete's Foot Powder, but I was fast asleep by then, so I missed it.

Next morning I drove west along Galway Bay, then north into Connemara. Outside Casla, I stopped to pick up a hitch-hiker, a New Zealand woman with a sunny disposition and more freckles than I've ever seen.

'Great kaah,' she said. 'My dad had one of these. A but noisy though, usn't ut?'

Statistics show that New Zealanders are the most travelled nation on the planet, as no one else is that keen to go 13,000 miles for a bar job. Vicki was travelling on her own and sleeping in a tent. She'd been away from New Zealand for five years, but this was her first time in Ireland. I asked her where she was going next.

'I dunno. What I really need is a laundromat, and access to the unternet. You don't know if there are any cyber cafés out here, do you?'

We drove through some of the most wonderful scenery in Ireland, following silver streams through wild and deserted mountain valleys. Stems of fluffy white bog cotton sprouted from the peat on either side of the road. The sun flitted in and out of high cloud, creating the constant interplay of light and shadow on hillside that is one of the delights of the landscape of the west of Ireland, when it isn't lashing it down. I dropped her outside the Sheep and Wool Museum in Leenane. Maybe they'd have a cyber café. On the laundromat front though, I was completely stumped.

As you enter Cong from the Leenane road, you encounter one of the many bizarre features that give the area a rather spooky quality. You'd have no way of knowing this, though. You'd think you were just crossing a bridge over a pretty little pool next to the petrol station and the supermarket. In fact, this is the Rising of the Waters, a unique natural phenomenon in which the waters of Lough Mask disappear into underground streams for three miles before bursting out here, where they sometimes overflow and transform the main road into a duck pond. A few yards further on, the flow of water disappears once more into Poll Tuaithfil – the Pool of the Turning Waters – to emerge miles away in the vast expanse of Lough Corrib. These weird underground aqueducts provide poetic, if not scientific, corroboration for the many local legends with subterranean connections.

All of which is a great reason for visiting the village, as I suppose is the fact that *The Quiet Man* was filmed here. In case you didn't know this, there's a *Quiet Man* pub as you approach the village, and a *Quiet Man* coffee shop, and a *Quiet Man* hostel in the centre. Murphy's Store played the part of Pat Cohan's bar in the film and, though it's still a shop, the recently painted sign now says; 'Pat Cohan – Bar'. A card advertises: 'Boat Trips arranged from Steven who was in the film *The Quiet Man*'. You'd want to wear a lifejacket, as the film was shot in 1951.

I arrived late in the afternoon and set about finding somewhere to stay. And this is what has put me in such a bad mood, as I sit here waiting for my main course to arrive. Hang on, here it is. So that's what Mexican Potatoes are like. Christ, there are chunks of watermelon in it. And three grapes. You can see why tortillas would be so popular over there.

First, I went to two B&Bs with 'Vacancy' signs in the window. 'A single? Sorry, we're full.' I decided to treat myself to the hotel on the main street, and in return got a big smile from the man at reception.

'Do you have any rooms?'

'Indeed, we do. How many of you are there?'

'Just me.'

'Ah no, sorry. Full.'

The ageing English hippy behind the counter at the hostel interrupted me before I could finish my sentence with, 'Nothing at all' and looked pleased about it. He had a supercilious smirk that said, 'I've got a thriving business and you haven't even got a bed for the night, you loser'; or perhaps I was becoming paranoid by then. If so, it was with some justification. At a two-star hotel, at six in the evening, the proprietor stared at me through narrowed eyes.

'I have a room but I'd have to charge you a lot of money.'
'Okay. How much?'
'It's a big double room, see.'
'How much?'
There was a pause, while he weighed me up.
'Sixty pounds.'
As I went through the door he was shouting after me, 'It's big enough for a family, you know.'

I suppose you expect to be Killarnied in Killarney, but not in a little village of 300 people. Mind you, *The Quiet Man* was filmed here. Have I mentioned that?

Just outside town is Ashford Castle, formerly the home of the Guinness family and now a luxury hotel. Believe it or not, bits of *The Quiet Man* were filmed there, so rooms start at £140 a night. There's a uniformed guard, and a Checkpoint Charlie to keep riff-raff out, though they can pay two quid to go in and stare. I headed out of town in the other direction.

'All rooms en-suite' said the sign outside a massive, new, lonely house with some freshly constructed standing stones in the garden. A man took me upstairs to a small cupboard, kitted out with a dwarf's bed and sink.
'Where's the bathroom?'
'Down at the end of the corridor.'
'But the sign says "All rooms en-suite".'
He shrugged his shoulders. 'Yeah, well, it's just a single.'

At last, half a mile down the road, at an even lonelier house, I found a cheerful woman who was delighted to give me a big room and bathroom looking out on to silent fields, woodland and an ivy-covered ruin. Too late to improve my mood, though. By now I was spitting blood. I changed and headed back to town, certain I was going to have a bad time. So naturally, I did.

I wandered round for a while in a red mist, convincing myself that the fairytale town that had so enchanted me just a few years ago had sold its soul to tourism. Even Murphy's Store/Cohan's Bar wasn't selling sweets and tinned food and weird dry goods any more, just souvenirs and memorabilia for the wretched movie. It didn't feel like the friendly place where, just a few years ago, every other person asked me did I know the Edge lived here. Oh sorry, that's meant to be a secret.

Eventually I came into this little place on the main street to try and calm myself down with a meal. The food's not bad so much as unusual. I ordered duck à l'orange, and there's the duck all right, floating in the middle of the grey liquid. It's a bit pale and fatty, but I can live with that. I think it may have been microwaved, or boiled in the bag, or possibly both. As well as the Mexican potatoes, and the watermelon, and the grapes, it comes with Irish potatoes, red, yellow and green peppers, two kinds of lettuce, cauliflower cheese, broccoli, sweetcorn, carrots, red cabbage, parsley and a slice of orange, all on the same massive plate. It's a colourful mixture, possibly put together by someone in the throes of a nervous breakdown who's locked himself in the kitchen and cooked everything he could find. Through the clashing hues and flavours you can almost taste his sobs. The red cabbage is excellent, mind. And at least I won't go hungry. One plate of this between two would be more than even the Tweedles could cope with.

And the staff are delightful. A girl of sixteen and a lady of seventy, for whom nothing is too much trouble. I declined a bread roll before my meal. 'Ah go on, take one,' said the lady, 'they're free, you know.' At one stage, she went running past my table with an extra side order of potatoes in a rigid-looking sauce. They weren't Mexican though. No watermelon. Maybe they were Bolivian. She's talking to the rather lairy couple at the next table now, who look as though they gave the sherry some hammer before they came out tonight.

'The thing is, she's short-staffed, so I had to come in. I shouldn't really be working.'

She lowers her voice and furtively looks round to see if anyone's listening; then realises it's safe to speak, because the other couple are arguing, and I'm just writing things down in a book.

'I've got an infectious disease. Really, I should be at home.'

By ten o'clock I'm back at the B&B. Despite the risk of infection, I've brought back three-quarters of a bottle of Côtes du Rhône from the restaurant. I'm lucky to have eaten at all. Cong seems to be unique among Irish villages in not having a single attractive pub. I looked inside four tonight, and drank in two of them. All had been enlarged or brutalised in some way to cope with greater numbers of visitors. Industrial-looking food was being churned out in depressing surroundings. In all of them the TV was on, in two of them a jukebox as well, and in one there was techno muzak. Dirty plates lay uncollected on tables; no one seemed to care about the customers, because they were tourists, and would come anyway. It was a bit like being in England.

It's clear that a fair number of the hotels, shops and bars are in the hands of the same two or three families, for whom it is boom time. Now the Irish economy is so driven by tourism, will every special little place end up like this, as they see what's to be earned by marketing their idiosyncrasies, leaping aboard the Celtic Tiger, and getting the builders in? A successful tourist industry can quickly turn a place into a parody of itself.

As I fill my tooth mug with the last of the wine, I'm thinking that surely you can only live off *The Quiet Man* for so long. Perhaps it was different twenty or thirty years ago, but I'm sure that most of the visitors coming here now hadn't even heard of the wretched movie until they read about it in the guidebook.

'Oh look, that's where they made that film with John Wayne.'

'Which one?'

'You know.'

'Have we seen it?'

'I'm not sure.'

A shrewd little village that wants to put itself on the tourist map in Ireland should simply invent a film that was supposedly made there decades ago, and create the artefacts to go with it. Humphrey Bogart, say, in *A Drop of the Black Stuff*. Look, here's the bench he sat on. This is the shawl that Lauren Bacall wore. No one would check. They'd turn up in their thousands. A resident but reclusive rock star would be handy too, and a dolphin. Or a whale.

It's ten to eleven, and I'm getting into bed with wine-stained lips, when the sound of a car breaks the silence outside. As the engine continues to rev, the doorbell rings. My room is downstairs right next to the door, so I consider answering it, but as I'm in a bad mood, naked, with purple teeth and lips, I decide to let events take their course.

I hear the landlady open the door. A female American voice shrills through the darkness.

'Excuse me, I know it's late, but do you have a room? I'm afraid we're lost. We just arrived in Dublin today . . .'

Dublin? God in heaven. It's the entire width of the country away. How the hell did they manage to end up here? It'd be hard enough to find this place even if you were looking for it.

'. . . and we really don't know where we are. We're desperate. Do you? Do you have a room?'

'How many are you?'

She sounds as if she's scared it might be a coachful.

'Four. There are four of us.'

'Well, I have just the one room with a double and twins.'

'Is that four?'

'It is.'

'Great. We'll take it. Thank you.'

'It'll be £60.'

'Perfect. Thank you. Oh, and could you tell me, where are we?'

'Mayo.'

'Excuse me?'

'Mayo.'

'Right. I'll go get the bags and the kids.'

When I go along to breakfast next morning they're already there: Mom, her student-age daughter with a girlfriend the same age, and a twelve-year-old son in a baseball cap. It's a huge dining-room, a recently-built annex that wouldn't disgrace a medium-sized hotel. There's a strong whiff of EC subsidy scam.

From their conversation, it's clear that this is the first time the late-night arrivals have been outside the USA, let alone to Ireland, and the multiple confusions over what may or may not be available for breakfast are painful in the extreme. The landlady does her best to cope, but the bafflement engendered by 'over easy' on the one hand, and 'rashers' on the other, wastes a good ten minutes of everybody's life. As I'm savouring the delicious tension in the minutes after they've ordered, but before they've been confronted with black pudding for the first time, the daughter – still clearly rattled by the inexplicable bagel famine – looks up from the tinned grapefruit and addresses her mother.

'Mom, what'll we do today?'

'Find some Guinness, I guess.'

'Is there a town called Guinness?'

'I don't think so, hon, no.'

'Really? I'm surprised.'

The landlady comes back with the full cooked breakfasts. The kids gaze at them in bemusement. Mom looks up and smiles.

'Excuse me? I have to ask you something.'

The landlady smiles in anticipation. 'How can I help?'

'Is this where the sandwich dressing comes from?'

The landlady desperately scans the sauce and mustard cruet for a clue, but Mom's meaning remains tantalisingly elusive.

'I don't understand.'

'Mayo. Is this where mayo comes from? Like, tuna mayo?'

I should know by now that sometimes it's best not to grumble when things go against you, when you're turned away from somewhere you think you want to be, and end up somewhere else. The unexpected destination is invariably the best. It was worth everything the collected hoteliers of Cong could throw at me, and a lot more besides, to be landed here against my will, and so come to a new understanding of the concept of Mayo.

Long before the Celts came to Ireland in the fourth century BC the country was occupied by tribes of obscure origin, who have now taken on near-mythical status. Until about 1000 BC, a small dark race called the Fir Bolg held sway; but then they were swept aside by the Tuatha de Danaan, a fair-skinned people who were also reputed to be powerful magicians. The decisive battle – the first ever recorded in the history of the country – was fought at Moytura, on the edge of the present-day village of Cong.

The whole area has a still and eerie feel to it. As I drive out after breakfast, there isn't a soul about – other than the long-dead Fir Bolg and de Danaan, of course, who I feel are watching me from behind every dry-stone wall. There's a brooding, empty quality to the landscape that is both exciting and un-settling. Just a few minutes' drive from the village I park by the deserted roadside and climb a stile into a field, then carefully pick my way through a threatening flock of potentially badger-skinning sheep to a stone circle.

The stones stand on a ridge, partially sheltered by trees, looking over a patchwork of fields criss-crossed by stone walls. As soon as I'm among them I feel an intense sensation of well-being. It's pleasing to imagine that I'm tapping in to the residual magical energy of the Tuatha de Danaan, though it may be just the relief of escaping from Cong's tiny but ferocious tourist industry. I'm also experiencing once again that thrill of unim-peded and unobserved contact with our ancestors' bits and pieces that the west of Ireland provides in such abundance. Because these places have never been developed, but have just sat there waiting for us, it's possible – if you're blessed with the faintest spark of imagination – to feel a very direct link: those people were here once, and now so am I. Perhaps there's a little bit of the Tuatha de Danaan in all of us.

The archaeologists and mystics who are still arguing over what stone circles were for could perhaps take heed of the explanation given by the ancient bards. The Fir Bolg's star warrior was Balor of the Evil Eye, a three-eyed giant who used his extra one to turn opponents to dust. This is the kind of thing you'd want to take into account when you were working out your game plan the night before the battle. According to the bards, the de Danaan's tactic was to erect these stones and paint warriors on them; so when Balor gave them the evil eye, and they didn't disintegrate but, rock-like, stood their ground, he presumed he'd lost his power, and left the battlefield in disgrace. The Fir Bolg then found themselves on the wrong end of a fearful drubbing.

A little way away outside the village of Cross I park outside a bungalow with a gardenful of plastic slides and swings, and head up an unlikely looking lane to Ballymagibbon Cairn. It's an immense pile of stones, its peak level with the treetops. Once again there's no one about; the only reminder that there are people nearby is the comforting sound of a gunshot as I reach the top of the lane. After just a couple of minutes lying full-length behind a wall in the coward position, as laid out in the Geneva Convention, I get up and climb the stones.

Legend has it that the cairn was erected at the end of the first day of the four-day battle, when each Fir Bolg warrior brought a stone and the head of an enemy in tribute to his king. If true, it makes you wonder how they lost. It's one of five cairns, spread across five miles of the ancient battlefield, that are said to cover a network of passages leading to a central cremation chamber.

It's certainly an appropriate monument for County Mayo. From the top, looking out across miles and miles of stone walls and ruined farm buildings, there are more rocks than you'd see in an average lifetime; and all of them – walls, cairns, farms, barns – shaped by people who are no longer here. The hand of man is visible, but man is nowhere to be seen. You can hear him, though. Bang! Another gunshot. I feel curiously vulnerable silhouetted against the skyline. Suddenly, the trees all round me begin to thrash and shake as a fierce wind blows up from nowhere. I scramble down the rocks, watching for severed heads as I go.

It's a couple of miles' drive to an isolated hamlet called the Neale. In a field, guarded by frisky horses, I find the Gods of the Neale – an ancient stone carved with a man, an animal, a reptile and an inscription no one has been able to decipher. In a field a couple of hundred yards away is a large stone pyramid, grey as today's sky, built as a folly in the nineteenth century. Across the road sits an overgrown graveyard of Celtic crosses and an impossibly romantic ruined church. By a fork in the road, the Long Stone is reputed to mark the grave of Lu of the Long Hand, son of the king of the de Danaan, who was killed at the Battle of Moytura. For a winning side, they really don't seem to have done terribly well.

But a dreadful thing has happened to the Long Stone. On the wall of a ruined building by which it stands is a vivid, yellow, freshly-painted sign advertising accommodation and 'tourist facilities' just down the road. Paint has been splashed all over the stone as well, and they haven't bothered to wipe it off. I suppose it's not quite a case of tourism killing the goose that laid the golden egg, but covering it with yellow gloss is almost as bad.

Rural Ireland wakes up late now all that small-farm egg collecting and milking by hand is a thing of the past. It's mid-morning, and I still haven't seen a soul, but suddenly I hear voices in the distance. A little way up the road a woman cyclist is approaching, pursued by a man in football kit. A local hurler, or Gaelic footballer, training for the big match, I suppose. But then they stop and he poses, panting, near the stone. I notice it's a hired bike. She takes out a camera, snaps him, and whoosh, he's off like a greyhound from a trap back in the direction they came from. They haven't said a word to each other, or me. It's like a silent comedy, only not funny. She studiously ignores me as she packs the camera away, so I say, 'Hello.'

She smiles to placate me, but clearly wants to be gone. He's already 200 yards away.

'Hi.'

She remounts the bike but I have to know.

'So . . . where are you from?'

'From Germany. Excuse me.'

She gives me a quick blast of Balor's evil eye and then she's off in pursuit.

The Tuatha de Danaan may have won the day at Moytura, but they in turn were defeated by the invading Celts. When they knew the game was up, it's said they used their magical powers to turn themselves into the little people of Irish legend, and flee underground. The area around Cong is honeycombed with the caves and underground passages into which they disappeared. On the way back to the village I stop again near the stone circle at a place called Nymphsfield. Over the centuries, groups of faerie children and tiny men and women have been sighted here, dancing and generally enjoying the craic in the moonlight – the de Danaan, celebrating their famous victory over the Fir Bolg, or so the story goes. It's a delightful thought; there's definitely a mysterious and haunting, if not haunted, atmosphere about this whole area that is quite captivating.

I'm beginning to feel foolish for letting a few ruthless room-renters spoil my visit. In future I'll try to remember a room's just somewhere to sleep, and it really doesn't matter. The place is the thing. And as soon as I focus on these positive thoughts it's as if I hear voices. Hang on, I really can hear voices. Faint, sure enough, but there all right. The phantom spirits of Nymphs-field? The long-dead Tuatha de Danaan of Moytura? What's that they're saying?

'*Vier Minuten zwanzig . . . fünf und zwanzig . . . dreissig. Komm! Schnell, schnell . . .*'

The grimacing runner and his cyclist girlfriend thunder past, in pursuit of Ireland's carefree imperfection. I head for the car, and Westport.

Rather than take the direct road north, I decide to veer west through Joyce Country again, and back into Connemara. The sky has cleared, and the wonderful flat valleys, tussocky grass and wild mountainsides look good enough to be in a movie; which they are, as I realise when I stumble across a feature film crew on a back lane just outside Leenane. A mechanic is lying under a vintage Jag while a sound technician adjusts his boom mic. By the way, if you ever see a film crew working, don't go up to the sound guy, point at the boom, and make furry animal jokes. He'll probably smile and pretend no one's said it before, but one day one of these guys is going to snap and massacre someone.

Leenane is a beautiful village ringed by mountains at the end of Killary Harbour. They made a movie here a few years ago too called *The Field*. Now there's a coffee shop called The Field Coffee Shop, so there's a danger the place could get Conged. As I leave town, I find myself wondering what archaeologists will make of it all in a couple of thousand years' time. Will they find evidence amongst the stone ruins of Cong that the legends are true: that people did indeed travel from all over the world to worship, for reasons now lost deep within the mists of time, at the shrine of *The Quiet Man*?

The journey from Leenane to Louisburgh is one of the most dramatic stretches of road in the country. After passing through wild foothills as you skirt the north side of Killary Harbour, by the time you reach Delphi you are surrounded by some of the most spectacular mountains in Connemara. Heading north through the mountain pass that runs along the eastern edge of Doo Lough there's a stone monument at the side of the road. I pull the Tank over on to worryingly boggy ground and walk back to read the inscription. 'To commemorate the Hungry Poor who walked here in 1849 and walk the Third World today,' it says. And suddenly, I know where I am.

It was through this valley that more than 150 famine victims walked in the depths of that winter. In Westport they had been refused sustenance at the poorhouse until they had registered with the Poor Commissioners, who were fourteen miles away at Delphi House. In ferocious conditions they walked to Delphi, only to find that the commissioners were having dinner and would not see them. Dozens died in the snow in this beautiful but desolate place in the shadow of Ireland's holy mountain, Croagh Patrick.

The Reek, as the mountain is also known, dominates the skyline as you approach Louisburgh and Westport. It's a clear day now and I can get a good look at it; but there's no sign of a great big light on top just yet. Maybe Gerry's had problems with the digger. They can be very temperamental bits of machinery.

There's a woman hitching on a lonely stretch of road. I presume she's an Irish student, because she looks like one. She turns out to be a Canadian sculptor from the Yukon, but how was I expected to know that? She's heading for Castlebar, Mayo's county town, which is just seven or eight miles on from Westport. I ask her what takes her there.

'I'm going to the library to listen to a writer.'

'Anyone I might know?'

'Er, the guy who wrote that book? About Ireland? I can't remember his name.'

We spend a while going through all the books about Ireland, until finally we hit on *Angela's Ashes*.

'Frank McCourt? In Castlebar library? Are you sure?'

'I guess so. Look. I have a flier.'

A handwritten photocopy announces that the Pulitzer Prize-winning author will indeed be in Castlebar at six this evening, and now so will I. I've only read the first half of the book, because I keep losing it, but at least I've read it twice. If we're tested on it, I'll just have to bluff like I did at school. At least McCourt won't hit me with a leather strap if he catches me out.

The library's packed with every McCourt fan in Mayo, all clutching copies of the book. I feel vulnerable and conspicuous without one, like the guy in *Invasion of the Body Snatchers*, hoping the others won't realise he's the only one who hasn't been taken over by aliens. As anticipation builds, there's an announcement. 'Mr McCourt will be twenty minutes late as he's been delayed in a hostelry in Leenane while coming from Galway the pretty way.'

He's eventually introduced by the librarian, who then does a curious thing. Instead of relinquishing the podium to McCourt and letting him have the space to himself, he sits on a stool right next to him throughout the performance, like Garfunkel during a very long Paul Simon solo spot. He even interrupts at one point to get the audience to sing 'Happy Birthday,' to McCourt's evident embarrassment. Maybe it isn't his birthday.

He's dressed in a blue jacket and red shirt, and looks considerably younger than his sixty-nine years. Half a century in New York has done little to alter his Irish accent. Yet some people emigrate to America or Australia or wherever it may be, and within eighteen months have taken on the local accent so totally they sound as if they've never been anywhere else in their lives. It must be a conscious act of will, indicating whether you wish to be absorbed, or stand apart in honour of your roots.

'God provided me with a miserable childhood and the words to describe it,' says McCourt. He talks about the librarian at the Carnegie Library in Limerick when he was a child. 'She wanted to be between us and the books, in case we might touch them or read them. She looked like an Iroquois Indian with syphilis.'

After he's read from the book, he takes questions. Someone asks him about the title. What does it mean? 'Angela was my mother and when she died we cremated her, so – *Angela's Ashes.*'

'But critics are saying the ashes are the fire she stared into, or the cigarettes she smoked, or the sons from whom she rises like a phoenix . . .'

'These days they're giving exams on my book that I would fail myself.'

I'm plucking up courage to ask something, but I'm scared he'll catch me out. After all, he's a teacher. He'll know instinctively that I haven't read it all. What the hell. I put my hand up. But what if he asks me about the second half? It's too late now. So I ask him, where does he feel he belongs? He has no hesitation.

'New York.'

And so I'm just going to ask this wise man, this Pulitzer Prize winner, this Prince of the Diaspora, whether he thinks it's possible truly to belong in a land where you've never actually lived, when suddenly the librarian's on his feet, to point out Frank's wife, and get a round of applause for her. Or for Frank, for having such a nice wife. It's not clear which.

So I don't get to ask him.

Afterwards, I'm walking to the Tank when I pass a bar called P. McCarthy. Actually, I don't pass it. I stand outside, look at it, then go in. The barman tells me the P stands for Pete. I've never actually met anyone called Pete McCarthy before. Perhaps we'll look just like each other and form a lifelong friendship. I ask if he's around.

'Ah no, he sold the place on a couple of years ago. I've no idea where he is now.'

There's a little Chinese restaurant across the street. It looks a bit seedy, but it's an awfully long time since I've had any Singapore noodles, so I decide to take a chance. It's a tiny place with about eight tables. I sit in the window, so that if Frank McCourt walks past I can bang on the glass and ask him whether I belong.

A family of fat bastards from Manchester are eating sweet and sour pork and chips at the next table. Like Tweedledee in Killarney, they're washing it down with Diet Coke, in the hope that they'll look like Kate Moss by morning. There's a Chinese lady in charge, but my order's taken by a morose local girl in platform-soled sneakers who seems ill at ease with the whole concept of Chineseness. She looks at me as if I'm a headcase when I ask for chopsticks. At the next table, huge quantities of chicken curry, chop suey, rice and extra chips have now arrived, and the children – two ovoid blimps with bright red sweet and sour chins – are woofing it down with serving spoons, racing against the clock and the adults in a gastronomic equivalent of *Supermarket Sweep*.

I'm waiting for the food to arrive, sipping excellent jasmine tea, when three blokes come in and order a takeaway. One of them turns round and sees me.

'Hiya, how are ya doing?'

He's at the other end of the room, not that far away, but I can't work out quite who he is. It's hard to know what to do in these situations, isn't it? I give him a big smile, and wave.

'Hiya.'

He's walking over now, with a big smile himself, and his hand stretched out in greeting. He's in his thirties, arty-looking, with longish hair and a brown suede jacket. Where do I know him from? Have I worked with him? Or is he someone I've met on this trip? This kind of thing happens all the time these days. Sometimes I can be talking to someone for five minutes before realising who they are. I reckon my brain may have been adversely affected by other people's mobile phones.

He's almost at my table. He's very enthusiastic. The fat Mancs are all watching. I stand up to meet him, smiling in feigned recognition. Then his face drops.

'Oh, sorry. I thought you were someone else.'

I'm left standing there like a lemon, my hand stretched out. He picks his embarrassed way back across the room. The blimp kids are fighting over the rice that's fallen on to the tablecloth, because that's all that's left now that they've finished their banana fritters. The three guys leave with their takeaway. He tries to look straight ahead, but he can't resist a sideways glance as he goes through the door.

I know it's possible with guilt, but can you be racked by curiosity? If you can, I am. Who did he think I was? He was Irish himself, local I expect. What if . . . what if I really do look like the bloke who used to own the pub over the road? *What if he's mistaken me for Pete McCarthy?* The metaphysical implications are mind-boggling. Perhaps I should follow him out of the door and ask him, but then two things happen. Three, really.

The waitress comes across with my meal and begins to unload the tray on to my table, effectively blocking me in. I can see the three men crossing the street and approaching a parked car. I half stand, undecided; the Mancs get up to leave, milling around by the till and filling the doorway. So I sit back down, resigned to the fact that I'll never know.

And then Frank McCourt walks past the window. I'm sure he sees me, but he just walks past, and then he's gone. First the guy in the suede jacket, and now McCourt; two crucial questions, and neither of them answered. Mind you, McCourt's probably just being polite. He must know how members of the public hate being pestered by celebrities when they're out just trying to have a quiet meal.

The noodles are very good. Very spicy. The salt and pepper squid's good too, though fiercely hot. It comes with intriguing garnish: lettuce, cucumber, tomato and a glacé cherry. The bill for everything is only £12, which makes these the cheapest noodles in the country by a long way. The Chinese lady is beaming as I go up to pay.

'I watch you eat with chopsticks, very very good, where you learn? You been in China?

I tell her I've been to Hong Kong and to Guangzhou and she goes ballistic.

'Guangzhou! Guangzhou! I don blieve it. You been in Guangzhou?'

She looks at my credit card as she hands it back. 'Mr McCarthy! Like pub across road! I don blieve it. And you been in Guangzhou! Very good with chopsticks!'

I can still hear her as I walk out into the darkening, McCourtless street.

'Mr McCarthy! In Guangzhou! I don blieve it.'

Chapter Thirteen

Holy Ground

'That conical mountain to the left,' wrote Thackeray, 'is Croagh Patrick.'

The Reek dominates the whole of this corner of Mayo. Its near-symmetrical pyramid form is like the blueprint for an archetypal mountain, the resonant shape of a fairytale peak from a children's story book. It is here that St Patrick is said to have issued the exclusion order banishing all snakes from Ireland when, in 441, he spent forty days and forty nights fasting at the summit. The mountain towers over the islands of Clew Bay, the small but perfectly formed town of Westport, and P. McCarthy's pub, which is where I'm staying.

Just seven or eight miles from its namesake in Castlebar, this is the place where they once laid on the seventeen toasted sandwiches, as noted in Budapest a year last St Patrick's Day. Since then, it's changed hands. The new people aren't called McCarthy, but they've kept the name outside in big red letters.

The landlady shows me to a room clad entirely in varnished pine that appears to have been finished the day before yesterday. I ask about the previous owner.

'He was called Pete McCarthy. He went and opened a place in Castlebar.'

I feel like a particularly incompetent private detective, trying to track down my namesake and continually getting further away. Maybe he's emigrated to England to see if he feels he belongs there.

They say that an hour after eating Chinese food you're hungry; but an hour after eating Singapore noodles you're thirsty, so I wander out into town for a nightcap. Matt Malloy, who plays flute in the Chieftains, has a pub that's famous for traditional music; but it's so full of affluent natives of various Mediterranean countries in posh waterproofs and Aran handknits that I can't get in. Across the street in a room behind a small grocer's shop I find a cunningly concealed one-room bar. It's narrow and cramped, with benches and wooden booths, and is full of locals chattering away over the sound of Man United on the TV. I buy a pint, some razor blades and a Biro and install myself in a corner. Immediately, the man on my left turns to say hello. The Irish are so hospitable, aren't they?

' 'Ello.'

Hold on, he's got a south of England accent.

' 'Ere. Don't I recognise you from Brighton?'

Great.

'You've picked the right place. I love it in 'ere, just locals. You only meet tourists in all the others. Three times a year I come over, for the birds; you know, the feathered variety, heh, heh.'

Oh God, no. A birdwatcher.

'On your own? Yeah, me too.'

A birdwatcher with no mates.

'Yeah, I've seen you around town. And in those TV travel programmes. That must be a cushy job, getting paid to have holidays. I work for Connex South Central meself, on the admin side.'

Connex? The bastards who took over the railways in the south-east when British Rail were taken outside and shot. First thing they did was abolish the buffet car, the bacon sandwiches and the cheese on toast that once made Brighton commuters the happiest in the world. There's a kid in a cap now, with a trolley-load of confectionary and tea-flavoured drinks. I try to pin this disgraceful act of vandalism on my new friend, but he denies all responsibility.

He tells me something about his job that I don't understand and can't remember. Then he drinks up.

'Well, must dash. Can't linger. Up early in the morning. Places to go, birds to see, heh, heh, heh.'

I'm forced to consider the awful possibility that all those blokes you see with binoculars and flasks and ornithological reference books spend their days making dreadful bird-woman puns to each other.

'Nice meeting you. Hope you don't mind me saying so, but you look a bit lonely. Mind how you go.'

That was half an hour ago. No one else has talked to me. Beckham's just scored. I think I'll go to bed now.

I was only going to stay the one night, but the skies are clear next morning and Croagh Patrick looks hard work, but inviting. It was a sacred place long before St Patrick showed up, and it seems a pity to be so close and not give it a go. I've just missed the big annual pilgrimage, when thousands of pilgrims go up together. It used to be the thing to do it barefoot, but the first-aid bills were colossal, so the Church said, 'Get some shoes on!' Perhaps I'll go up on my own this afternoon, or, better still, tomorrow morning. Lough Derg will wait one more day.

Westport is a delightful little planned Georgian town, with what appears to be a little planned Georgian river right in the centre, where people can fish. There's a comforting main street, with shops selling things you actually need, and plenty of wooden window frames and Georgian doors that have somehow survived the renovation boom. It doesn't seem to be the sort of place to cash in on some spurious connection – 'Welcome to wonderful Westport, home of St Patrick and one of the blokes out of the Chieftains' – so it's a bit perturbing to see a bar and restaurant called Thackerays, even if it is in the hotel where he stayed:

> Nature has done much for this pretty town of Westport; and after nature, the traveller ought to be thankful to Lord Sligo who has done a great deal too. In the first place he has established one of the prettiest, comfortableist inns in Ireland in the best part of his little town, stocking the cellars with good wine. Secondly, Lord Sligo has given up for the use of the townspeople a beautiful little pleasure ground about his house.

Sligo was quite a lad. A friend of George IV and De Quincey, a patron of the arts and the turf, he was also a governor of Jamaica who helped free the slaves. He rode mules across Greece with Byron, and won a 1,000 guinea bet by driving his own coach from London to Holyhead in thirty-five hours. He also stole the 3,000-year-old columns from the entrance to the Treasury of Atreus at Mycenae, and bribed the crew of a British warship to help take them home, for which he got four months in Newgate Prison.

It must have been some court case. On the day Sligo was released from jail – in a plot development that would have been rejected by the soaps as too far-fetched – his mother married the judge who sentenced him.

Sligo's home, Westport House, is a splendid Georgian affair in a beautiful setting on the edge of town, facing Clew Bay, its islands, and the Atlantic. As I'm climbing the imposing stone steps to the front door, a family of six are queuing at the admissions desk in front of me. The two girls are very excited.

'Mammie, Mammie, when will we see the rabbit?'

'You'll see him soon enough, now.'

'We want to see Pinky!'

The skull and antlers of a 12,000-year-old elk, preserved through the millennia in an ancient peat bog, hang on the wall of the vaulted entrance hall. A fine collection of paintings of the house, the bay, and Croagh Patrick, by the celebrated Irish landscape artist James O'Connor, flank the splendid staircase that sweeps down into the hall. And descending the stairs, with a jaunty gait and a barmy wave, is a six-foot nylon fur-fabric pink rabbit that's looking a bit frayed round the edges. The kids go potty. Ignoring the obvious risk of electrocution by nylon-generated static, they mob the great big bunny.

'Pinky! Pinky! Pinky!'

The poor sod inside buckles under the onslaught of good-natured blows to the head and kidneys.

'Da! Da! Da! Take a picture! Take a picture!'

I suppose it might be useful as evidence when the case comes up.

The costume is so thick you just know it's still damp with yesterday's sweat. The two boys, rather ominously, are rehearsing some computer game kick-boxing techniques which they are about to apply to Pinky's ribcage. Their father, a nervous and troubled man, who presumably has to spend large parts of his life in a confined space with these tiny hyperactive ninjas, is clearly aware of the urgent need to create a diversion so that the severely fustigated rabbit can retreat to the blood bin. But has Da got what it takes?

'Okay, kids, what's it to be first? The eighteenth-century art collection – or the giant log flume?'

Howling in anticipation, the kids charge outside and down the stone steps, like looters who've forgotten they were meant to steal something.

The house, though grand, has a rough, lived-in feel. The oil-painted faces in the family portraits are vivid and eccentric. The Lord Sligo of Byron's acquaintance hangs next to his mother who married the judge. Given the colourful burlesque of his life, it's perhaps appropriate that he's the dead spit of the comedian Mel Smith; unlike the current owner, his great-great-great-great-grandson, who looks more like Steve Martin.

Within an hour of my arrival, I find myself chugging through lush Irish jungle on a mini-railway, discussing Irish history with Jeremy Ulick Browne, Lord Altamont, and the eleventh Marquess of Sligo, who are all the same person. I've never been on a children's ride with an Anglo-Irish Protestant aristocrat before, so I try and make the most of the opportunity. He is armed with a wealth of historical anecdote about various reprobate ancestors. Ireland, I remark, is a country with so many stories to tell.

'Yes,' he says. 'And some of them are true.'

The grounds in which Thackeray once strolled now house a campsite, holiday cottages, a bar and, of course, a giant log flume. Jeremy looks on in delight as a constant stream of high-spirited children, soaked to the skin, and shouting so their swearwords can be heard above the Verdi opera that's playing on the Tannoy, drift past in plastic logs. I'm trying my best to disapprove of all this vulgar, populist stuff, but I can't. Everyone's clearly having a good time, and the wild and crazy lord's naïve, almost boyish enthusiasm for his toys is rather infectious. Westport House almost proves that fine art and giant pink rabbits can happily coexist.

Before I leave, we discuss nationality and a sense of belonging. Lots of people, he says, don't really understand what a British peer is doing here in Westport. I know what he means, because I'm one of them. So is he Irish, or British, or English, or what?

'We were asked to be in a TV programme a few years back, *Wogan's Ireland*. So Terry Wogan comes along and we do our stuff and then at the end of the morning, he says to me, "So are you Irish then?" '

He grinned and rolled his eyes.

'So what did you say?'

'I said, well, I'm not bloody Chinese now, am I?'

I suppose he could have been, if his ancestors had moved to Hong Kong instead.

'Those unacquainted with the oddities of Irish history are surprised to find the ancestral home of a British peer in such an Irish part of Ireland.'

So wrote Jeremy's father, the tenth Marquess. It's early evening and I'm in a waterfront bar reading his family history. I like reading in a pub rather than a library or study, as it's generally much easier to get a drink.

I'd presumed that the estate had been booty for some aristocratic adventurer or one of Cromwell's men; but it seems Mayo was considered a bleak and worthless place, more usually associated with banishment than reward. Jeremy, according to his dad, is there because, 'in 1580, one John Browne, an adventurous misfit, with little to lose at home, arrived in Mayo.' He settled at the Neale, among the faerie folk and their weird stones. Nearly 100 years later his great-grandson, a barrister, married a descendant of Grania O'Maille, the pirate queen, and moved to her home town of Westport, where the Brownes have remained, continually inter-marrying with the Irish families who were there long before them. This 'Irish dimension', according to the tenth marquess, was crucial.

'It distinguished the integrated Anglo-Irish who stayed from those essentially alien, who left. The latter might keep an estate as a source of rents, or as a pleasant change in the social and sporting calendar. To them, Ireland was an appendage of England, the Irish themselves slightly inferior Englishmen; comic simpletons or dangerous traitors according to taste and to how they were behaving.'

It's a warm evening and light till very late, so I have dinner in the pub garden looking out on the bay. It's terrific: lightly spiced sautéed fresh squid, with Greek salad and soda bread. Mind you, that's two nights running I've had squid. And I had it in Dingle too. Hope I'm not getting into a rut. I always used to think seafood was really light and healthy and good for you, but someone on the telly said that squid and prawns are absolutely chocka with cholesterol. There's something like four times as much cholesterol in squid as there is in lard, I think they said. Or twice as much lard as there is in lard. Something like that, anyway.

Back at McCarthy's, I'm in bed reading the paper when I make a decision: first thing in the morning, I'm going up that holy mountain. That'll work the cholesterol off. It's a worry knowing what food to eat these days, isn't it? For years they've been going on about how wonderful fish is, especially oily fish like herring. Very good for the brain, that's what they used to tell us. And now here's a report in the paper about new research saying that if you eat herring or mackerel more than once a week, then you'll get cancer. Your kids, meanwhile, will be getting cancer from fish fingers. It doesn't say which brand.

I turn the light off.

Lard is probably made out of squid, isn't it?

Next morning, the sky is Corfu-blue as I nip down the street for a paper to read at breakfast. I'm walking back at a brisk stride up the main street when a little old man appears from a doorway and springs out in front of me, like a goblin in a fairy story. He takes me by the arm. Perhaps he's going to tell me I've got three wishes.

'You're going too fast. Slow down. There's no need to hurry.'

I tell him I'm rushing because I'm going up Croagh Patrick and I don't want to leave it too late. His expression darkens.

'Be careful, now. There was a man died up there last Sunday. Fifty-one years old. Brought him down with a helicopter. And a woman before him. A shepherd and his dog found her down a ravine. Four months she'd been there.'

It's half eight in the morning, for God's sake.

'Going up isn't the problem. It's going down you have to be careful. There's a place where it slopes like this – that's where you might go tumbling off. Good luck now.'

I have orange juice, muesli and coffee, with a massive cooked breakfast. In the paper there's a review of the week's news. Apparently, a bloke died on Croagh Patrick last Sunday. Fifty-one, he was. Seems they had to bring him down in a helicopter.

Within two minutes of beginning my ascent, I have severe chest pains. We could be looking at another helicopter job here. It feels as if the sausages, black pudding and hash browns have lodged in some crucial aperture, like a wedge of damp card-board, as they try to penetrate my system. It occurs to me that for days now I have been on a strict diet of fried breakfasts, Guinness and squid. That'll explain the tingling sensation all down my arm, then.

Still, it's a glorious day and there weren't too many cars in the car park when I arrived, so at least there shouldn't be a mob of pilgrims. The man in the refreshment caravan was staring at me as I filled my bottle from the tap. As I walked past, he called out.

'You're not planning to drink that, are ya? Sure, look at the colour of it.'

I suppose there was a slight brownish tinge to it. It would probably have made very tasty poteen.

'I'm not saying it's killed anybody yet, mind.'

So I walked across to his caravan. There was a bundle of flimsy-looking sticks leaning against it. 'Sticks' said the sign, accurately. '£1 each'. I asked if there was anywhere else to get water. He shrugged, and glanced at a big cardboard cash-and-carry box of small, lukewarm mineral water bottles. Fat-free. Just the job. I got two.

'That'll be £2.'

The path rises sharply from the statue of St Patrick at the foot of the mountain. I'm trying to walk off the heart attack, but so far it's not working. It'd be a nightmare doing this barefoot, with all these jagged rocks. I wonder if the pilgrims cheat and go on the grassy bits at the side, or do they stick to the stones and shale, on account of God being omniscient?

I stop for a rest by a large rock, on which there's a child's abandoned Doc Marten. Perhaps it's a sculpture. Suddenly there's a noise, and a sweaty, grey-bearded man in running kit comes charging down the slope past me. Sacred jogging. It could catch on. There's another guy across to my right, way off the track, standing in a ditch. He's wearing shorts, patterned nylon ankle socks, and plastic sandals, and he's filming massive close-ups of heather with a camcorder. So close to the car park, and bonkers already. I'm going to treat this mountain with respect.

In a little while, without really noticing, I've hit a rhythm and the pain is gone. Ahead of me, a man is dragging his two sons towards the still-distant summit, whether they like it or not. They don't seem to. The bigger boy calls out.

'Da, it's a very big mountain.'

'Sure is, son.'

He's about seven, and is walking mostly under his own steam, but keeps tumbling off the path in little mini-landslides. The smaller boy can't be more than five, and Da is holding him firmly by the hand. Every time he falls, he's yanked up, and his feet windmill in mid-air before hitting the holy ground again.

'Please, Daddy, please, Daddy, drink, drink, need a drink, Daddy.'

'Come on now, son.'

But son manages to wriggle free and sits down on a rock near me.

'Please, Daddy, please, drink, drink.'

'All right, Joey, we'll just have to leave you there. Come on, Michael.'

'No, Daddy, no, please, drink.'

It's always risky interfering when someone is torturing their child in public. It's best not to sound censorious, or you could end up maimed before help can arrive, especially if you're halfway up a mountain, holy or not. I cunningly disguise my rebuke as an offer.

'Have you run out of water? Have some of mine.'

'Ah no, it's okay, their mother's got the water but she's away back down the track.'

So he's already abandoned her to her fate, and now the kids are going to die of dehydration. Here's a good man to be in a tight spot with. Maybe he'd like to take me scuba diving later. I throw him one of the bottles.

'Go on, it'll make my bag lighter.'

The little boy drinks greedily. I ask Dad where they're from.

'County Down. Hey, will you look at that?'

Far below us the ocean is completely still, and a dozen shades of blue. A host of islands disappears gently in a fine heat haze. 'Were such beauties lying upon English shores, it would be a world's wonder,' wrote Thackeray of Clew Bay. 'Perhaps if it were on the Mediterranean or the Baltic, English travellers would flock to it by hundreds. Why not come and see it in Ireland . . . a country far more strange to most travellers, than France or Germany can be.'

'Thanks, Mister,' says Michael. Between them, they've finished the bottle. I can see Da isn't really a cruel man. It's just that
he's driven all the way down here from the North to climb the
Reek; his enthusiasm is fighting against the dawning reality that
the boys won't be able to make it. That's how it looks to me
anyway. Either that, or he's hit his wife with a rock and dumped
her in a crevice, and the kids will be next as soon as I'm gone.

'Bye, boys.'

Halfway up, as you reach a ridge, the wind suddenly kicks in.
From here, as well as looking north across the bay, you can also
see south to the mountains of Connemara. For a while, you're
walking along a narrow plateau from which the ascent to the
summit looks difficult and dangerous. Up to my right is the
towering granite of the mountain, lined with what look like
giant fingermarks, as if someone's fallen off, then clung on,
scraping the side as they fell.

A muscular woman in pukka hiking gear falls in next to me
for a while. She's come from Dublin, as she does most weekends
to walk the craggy ridges of the west.

'I hate this feckin' mountain,' she says of her country's most
holy peak. 'Always in the feckin' way.'

'So, how is Dublin these days?'

'Feckin' ruined with phoney Oirishness for tourists.'

'So why not move out here?'

'I have to stay. I'm a feckin' civil servant.'

The final ascent to the summit is a steep one, scrambling over
loose rock and shale that's been badly eroded by the constant
passage of pilgrims. As I'm taking a breather and munching on a
life-enhancing apple, a woman comes bounding down the
precipitous slope at tremendous pace, as if she's wearing seven
league boots. It's Vicki, the Kiwi hitch-hiker I picked up a few
days ago, timing herself in some kind of masochistic speed trial
against the mountain. New Zealanders will never walk up or
down anything if there's a chance it will hurt more to run
instead. Theirs is not a country so much as a fitness camp. Why
look at something, they reason, when it will toughen me up if I
charge at it with my head? This is an entire nation on a self-

imposed commando training course, where no mother of three dare show her face in public unless she can torpedo-pass a rugby ball thirty yards with one arm in plaster.

As if to illustrate the difference between the northern and southern hemisphere approaches to physical conditioning, a grey, poorly-looking man comes crawling up the slope towards us. He appears to be suffering simultaneously from a severe hangover, cold turkey and terminal TB. Perhaps fearing that Vicki may be about to challenge him to a game of one-a-side rugby, using a stone for a ball, he collapses at our feet in a gesture of abject surrender.

'D'ya have a ciggie? I'm gasping.'

Gasping is seriously underestimating the situation. He sounds as if all his internal organs are about to rupture like badly perished rubber bands. As he wheezes and rattles like a consumptive beagle on a tobacco baron's treadmill, his flickering, unfocused eyes suggest he may also be in the advanced stages of myxomatosis. It's a mystery how he's made it this far. Perhaps he had a coughing fit and fell out of a passing helicopter ambulance.

I don't smoke, and now I remember why. But Vicki offers him a roll-up. In his elation, spittle bubbles up in the corner of his mouth, like pancake mix. He recoils in panic when she offers him the Old Holborn and the papers.

'Christ, no. Could you find it in your heart to roll it for me?'

She smiles as she realises this is a fitness opportunity. She rolls the fag, rhythmically and deliberately, using the exercise to improve her upper body strength. TB says he's come from Fermanagh. He's left his smokes in the car because he's on a fitness kick. Vicki passes him the roll-up, and he lights it.

'Would you do me two? I've been asking all the way up and no one bloody smokes.'

She obliges, one-handed this time, to build up stamina levels in her right forearm. I offer him half a bar of chocolate. Pocketing the second cigarette and the Cadbury's, he pulls himself to his feet, takes a long drag, and starts heading back down the slope into the path of the advancing pilgrims.

'Hey, don't give up, you're nearly at the top,' shouts Vicki. 'Fuck that,' replies TB, flicking the butt back over his shoulder on to the holy ground.

Croagh Patrick has been a place of Christian pilgrimage for over 1,500 years, but archaeological evidence shows that the summit was occupied by a ring fort, and at least thirty huts, long before St Patrick's time. The mass pilgrimages that still attract huge numbers in July and August coincide with the ancient festival of Lughnasa (the Irish word for August), when tribute was paid to the pagan god Lugh, once worshipped by our friends the Tuatha de Danaan. Today at the peak there's a small white church, built in 1905, and the ruins of an early Christian oratory, carbon-dated to 430–890 AD. As I hit the summit, forty or fifty people are milling round taking photos, eating picnics or praying in the bright sunshine and fierce wind. A worryingly batty man in his thirties is whacking pebbles a long way up in the air with a hurley stick. On high mountains, as on high buildings and underground railway platforms, it's always best to keep an eye out for the loon who might want to nudge you off. I take refuge in the church.

An intense little man with a white goatee is leading a group of young people in some devotional chanting and singing in the Breton language. I'm reminded of a visit I made to Brittany a few years ago. The head teacher of a Breton language primary school – outlawed for years by the authorities in Paris, but now permitted, though with some reluctance – spoke with passion about the affinity he felt with the Cornish, the Welsh, and especially, he said, the Irish. It must be hard, I suggested, to know who to support when France play Ireland at rugby. He looked at me like I was mad.

'No,' he said. 'It is very simple. Ireland, of course.'

There's a little vestry on one side of the chapel, packed with bottles of mineral water, bags of fruit, muesli and chocolate, and some canvas and oil paints. It all belongs to Chris, the mountain's artist-in-residence. No, honestly. Chris is nearly three-quarters of the way through a forty-day and forty-night stint on top. He says his presence is 'a social sculpture in memory of mystics of the past'. Locals are betting on how long he'll last. While we're talking, someone comes to tell him that a curry is on the way up for him tonight. And yes, there will be poppadoms. Plain or spicy? Probably a selection.

He says he's seen that all sorts of people come up here for very different reasons.

'The travellers come in very big numbers. There were two or three hundred of them on Monday and Tuesday. They have an incredible devotion. They left little gifts and offerings in nooks and crannies everywhere – letters, medals, family photos. A CD of a Spanish rock star. On my first night up here, lying in my tent about a quarter to one, I thought it was the wind at first but it was voices, a traveller woman and her two kids. They'd climbed the Reek in the middle of the night, barefoot.'

He says that the tradition of barefoot pilgrimage isn't penitential but reverential, so as not to despoil the ground with shoes.

'And then, in the evening, the athletes come. There's a whole crowd of them. Run up and down. Every day, some of them. Forty-six minutes is the record.'

I ask him about his paintings, but he's dismissive of them.

'Er, they just give me some exercise, keep me brain alive. It's a social sculpture. The work of art is my presence here.'

I think I understand, but I decide not to pursue it, in case I don't. Instead, I ask for his thoughts on my identity crisis.

'Well, you'll have a cultural inheritance learned from your family, and there's nothing mystical about that. But in the mystical traditions and in early Christianity you have the notion of consciousness continuing from one embodiment to another. I think sometimes when people feel a connection with a place, it's because strands of their consciousness have been there.'

I think he mistakes my wincing into the wind for a smug smile, because then he reminds me of something I know, but sometimes forget, in my eagerness to have more of a claim on this country than Klaus, the Tweedles, and all the rest of them.

'Just remember, it's an easy place to be at home in, Ireland. I think the people are very skilled at relating. I notice, watching the different nationalities on the mountain, the fluidity of interaction the Irish people have with the visitors, and with each other. It's a skill that's less developed in other nationalities, and it's so instinctive it doesn't even look like a skill.'

On the way down this afternoon, I saw a kid crying because he couldn't go any further; a bloke in a red shirt and black beard way up a hillside playing the harmonica; an Englishman shouting at his children that they'd all bloody well go back down in a minute if they didn't bloody behave; a freckly ginger-haired baldy bloke in purple shell suit bottoms, flip-flops and nothing else; and a woman in a stars and stripes headscarf, sitting in the middle of the trail recounting the embarrassing details of her private life into a yellow cellphone. A breathless fat guy smiled and asked me, 'Do they have a table for four up there?'

My hips and knees are aching from the impact of walking down, which always hurts more than walking up, but I'm feeling good for having done it. And it's not just the physical buzz from working off the squid and black pudding. There's a spiritual element too, and it comes not from any inherent power or magic the mountain possesses, but from what's been bestowed on it by the people who have gone there every hour, every day, for millennia. And for once, my delight in a place has been enhanced by having lots of people around, knowing that they're all still furthering that process.

So now I'm relaxed, well fed and luxuriating in the afterglow, while all around me people are waving stools over their heads. A tall, enormously fat man, in a custard-yellow shirt that would be a floor-length dress on anyone else, is throwing a pear-shaped woman round the room, and a table-load of eighteen-year-olds have moved the birthday cake off the table so they can dance on it. In a minute, they'll dance on the table. Perhaps this is what they mean by craic. At the moment, the craicometer's 98.6 and rising.

A quick hobble around Westport earlier confirmed my suspicion that a musical apartheid system is in operation. A dozen or more bars were playing host to mild-mannered, respectful, predominantly European visitors – many of them openly drinking coffee or fruit juice – listening to introspective diddly-di. But back here in P. McCarthy's, downstairs from my polished pine suite, and just 100 yards but several worlds away from the town's official music pubs, the shocking truth about Irish music lies waiting to be discovered.

I've come in for an eleven o'clock nightcap, and the place is going berserk. Everyone's on their feet, apart from the young guy at the table over there, who's having a haircut while a semicircle of raucous women roar in encouragement. In fact, everyone in the place is roaring, or howling, or whooping. On stage, a man with black nylon hair, matching chin-length sideboards, and Roy Orbison glasses is strumming a guitar in accompaniment to a drum machine that is going through the full repertoire of cymbal crashes, tom-tom rolls and big bass flourishes. It's clear that the traditional music he's playing is touching something genuinely heartfelt in his audience.

The stools, by the way, are above their heads so they can be waved in time as the whole room sways and sings along to 'Daydream Believer'. In the middle of the room, a wee kind of village idiot man is cavorting on his own and playing the spoons badly – mind you, anyone would to 'Daydream Believer' – and mimicking the dancers, but no one seems to mind. 'Waterloo', 'Mama Mia' – half the lad's hair is off, and now he's snogging his hairdresser – and now it's 'Can't Help Falling in Love With You', and everyone's dancing, smooching, embracing in groups of at least three or more, experience having taught them that more legs mean greater stability if balance becomes a problem.

Now, more than ever, I'm on my own. Suddenly I feel vulnerable. Away from the carefully manicured image presented in the town's 'traditional' music pubs, I have stumbled on the reality. I know what's going on. In Matt Malloy's and the rest of them, when the last Italian has left, and the fiddle and bodhran have been put safely away for another night, they'll draw the blinds, breathe a sigh of relief, and crank up Abba and Neil Diamond. Away from the Celtic correctness demanded by the Chieftains' global concert audiences, old Matt himself will probably take the floor and lead the natives of Mayo in the music their fathers loved.

'Sweet Caroline – nah nah nah . . .'

But what if someone spots there's a stranger in the room? And what if they don't want the unpalatable truth to seep out? I feel like the guy in the horror movie who has to hide behind a gravestone when Christopher Lee and all the extras in the long hooded robes file in and start chanting and tying up virgins. If they realise I'm in here, things might turn ugly. Uglier.

Slowly, I edge towards the door through the pulsing crowd. In the film, if there were a spare gown with a hood, I'd be wearing it now. Softly, softly, past the man-mountain in the yellow shirt – doing the hand jive to 'Crocodile Rock' now, while Village Idiot with the spoons tries to copy him – through the door and safely into the street. Outside, it's still Ireland as we know it, or as we've been told it is, with no clues as to what's going on behind closed doors. I edge a few yards along the street to the front door that leads to my pine-clad cell, and safety.

In the small hours of the morning I wake, suddenly, in a sweat, to a moment of blinding revelation, and sit there in the dark, trembling. Maybe the mountain has worked its magic after all. The village idiot with the spoons? Of course. It was Bono! The musician in the nylon wig and shades? Christy Moore. The big fat guy in the yellow shirt? Van Morrison. They don't fool me.

But they needn't worry. The dark secret of Irish music is safe with me.

Chapter Fourteen

Road Movie

It is a truth universally acknowledged that you cannot make a road movie in England. Everywhere is too close to everywhere else. By mid-afternoon on Day One, you'll just run out of road and have to turn back. But in America, spiritual home of the road movie, there is space into infinity, you can drive for a week, and the road just goes on for ever.

At first glance, the distances involved in traversing the west of Ireland might seem small, yet paradoxically this would be prime road movie territory, Kerouacesque or Wenderish in its potential. Here you can drive all day and the road still goes on for ever, because for large parts of it you will be driving at twenty miles an hour behind an agricultural conveyance. You will also have the benefit of a wealth of wrong turnings to choose from, an option not available when you're sitting motionless outside Birmingham in the centre lane of the M6 motorway on a Friday night. Thelma and Louise could have escaped to Connemara instead of Arizona, and had more fun into the bargain, but they wouldn't have got much joy in the West Midlands of England.

So you need to be patient. Although you may have a fixed destination in mind – Lough Derg for example – you must not pursue it with the single-minded fury of a sales rep from Leicester who has an appointment in Newcastle, but wants to be back in Bristol in time for a dinner party with the director of marketing and his over-manicured ex-beautician wife. You must never divide the distance by seventy-five miles an hour, and say that's when you'll be there; that way, madness lies. Dublin, and its ever-increasing sphere of influence, operates increasingly along such alien notions as a full appointment book, designated quality time, and death by stress. But once you cross the Shannon – even though geographically you have only come a short distance – different rules of time apply, and most people still understand the crucial secret of human happiness: that it's better to do a few things slowly, than a lot of things fast.

I find myself contemplating this eternal truth as I sit becalmed behind an impressive quantity of steaming pigshit on the road from Westport to Knock. If this were a road movie, just think of the tension if there were some bad guys chasing me a few miles back down the road. Right now, they'd be leaning on the horn, gunning the engine of their black BMW, and sitting motionless in the middle of a procession to a roadside grotto of Our Lady. The villain – Tim Roth – would lean forward and tap the driver on the shoulder.

'So, how long till Lough Derg?'

The driver – played by that huge, scary ginger guy with the tash, who plays all the psychopaths in anything set in Glasgow – turns round as a priest in a surplice and biretta walks past, followed by an old lady in black, some heifers, and six altar boys carrying a weeping statue of the Virgin.

'Christ only knows.'

The priest hears him and bangs on the window with his holy water brush. Psycho turns off the engine, and another few minutes evaporate into the Celtic ether.

Meanwhile, back in real life, just a few miles up the road, the pigshit consignment has turned off to make its delivery at a chicken feed factory, and I'm tooling along an empty lane at an impressive forty, gripped as ever by the rich pageant of un-expected obsessions unfolding on the radio phone-ins.

'I'd like to draw attention to the disturbing trend of young kids to hang around near the goalposts in park football matches.'

'What are you getting at, Fergus? Do you mean they're not putting enough effort into the game?'

'I mean they're not even in the game! They stand near the goal, and when the ball comes, they run off with it.'

'Well, I agree. If that's true, it definitely is a disturbing trend.'

Strictly speaking, Knock isn't on the direct route from Westport to Sligo; but as there's no way of knowing whether the direct route would get you there any quicker than a random zigzag, there's no reason not to go there. I figure it might be a good place to stop for lunch. In the road movie, I'd be sitting in a café window, eating wild smoked salmon on home-made soda bread, when Tim Roth and Psycho thunder past in the BMW without seeing me, scattering aged nuns and infirm priests in their wake. They have failed to understand that there's no point in rushing when you're out west. In Connaught, as in life, nothing is gained by getting ahead of whatever it is you're chasing.

Since 1879, when a vision of Our Lady is said to have appeared there, Knock has been the Lourdes of Ireland, with a hugely popular annual pilgrimage season. As I arrive, there's a large banner draped across a roundabout in the middle of the road. 'Up Mayo – Good Luck Peter', it says, which by anyone's standards is a marvellous welcome. Either it's a message for the local lad who's playing for Mayo in the big match this weekend, or another miracle, solely for my benefit. I park and start looking for somewhere suitable to have lunch. 'Up Mayo – Come in Peter and Have Your Lunch' – that's the sort of thing I'm hoping for.

Not long ago, Knock was a little village with a little shrine. But then they built a huge modernist basilica complex with eighteen, I counted 'em, eighteen self-service holy water fountains. Thanks to the efforts of a high-energy wheeling and dealing monsignor, there's also a new airport with a runway big enough to take the largest jumbos. Pilgrims can now jet in from Adelaide or Chicago without having to faff around spending money in Dublin or Shannon. One of the consequences of this fly in, pray, buy stuff, fly out conveyor belt is an economy driven by the kitsch souvenir industry.

The shops are all named after saints – St Peter's, St Mark's and so on – presumably to indicate divine endorsement. I remember, years ago, in Skegness, there used to be a shop called His Place, where you could buy balloons that said, 'I am the Way, the Truth and the Life'. Clearly evangelical artefacts have moved on a bit since then. 'Official World Millennium Candle as seen on The Late Late Show', says a sign in the window. 'Kneeling Nun Dolls – Only £14.99.' These come with rosary beads, John Lennon glasses and piercing blue eyes as standard. I'm strangely drawn, though, to the white plaster busts of Jesus's head. They're lightly dusted in glitter, with a dayglo purple crown of thorns, and are guaranteed to change colour according to the weather. You can see how that would come in handy. But my favourite, at a keenly priced £1.59, is a Sacred Tax Disc Holder. This comes complete with Motorist's Prayer, 'May the Lord Grant a Safe Journey to All Who Travel in This Vehicle', and is guaranteed to deter the most devout traffic warden.

I'm aware that pilgrims come here – as they do to Croagh Patrick – with the most sincere of motives, but the gulf between the two places couldn't be greater. I'm hungry, but I don't think I want to eat in a town so dedicated to separating the visitor from his cash. I go back to the car, put my tax disc in the sacred holder, and stick it on the windscreen. It seems like a good time to check my oil and water, which I don't recall doing since the service area at the Severn Bridge on my way to Wales. But the release catch under the dashboard isn't working. Something's jammed, and I can't get it open. I search the main street, but there's no sign of a Sacred Heart Volvo Dealership. I'll just have to drive on in a permanently sealed unit of impenetrable rattling metal. The last of the bird blew out some days ago, but who knows what other horrors lie in store now?

On the edge of town I pass a row of guest-houses: Basilica View, St Brendan's, Divine Mercy B&B; but before divine mercy, I have to face the cleansing fire of purgatory. I'm in the home straight to Donegal and Lough Derg, in a car that could go bang and die in a plume of acrid smoke at any moment. My fate is in the lap of God, or the gods, or my own existentially pure actions, depending on your theological point of view.

After driving for the best part of an hour I see a turn-off for the village of Tubbercurry. Because my brain is addled from travelling on my own for so long, it strikes me that it would be amusing to have lunch in an Indian restaurant here. Unfortunately no one's had the foresight to open one yet, so I have to get a sandwich instead. As I sit in the car eating it, I notice I'm parked outside a florist's called Guns 'n' Roses. which may be the world's first paramilitary flower shop.

On the radio a panel is discussing whether brothels should be legalised, which isn't the kind of thing you'd have heard here a few years ago. The presenter is trying to remain neutral, but one of the panellists, a colourful, loquacious, and possibly intoxicated old journalist, isn't standing for that.

'Ah, you've been too long at RTE. I can remember when you had opinions of your own. Come on, tell us what you think.'

'First you tell us. What do you think about legalised brothels?'

'I think they're unnecessary.'

'Unnecessary?'

'Yes. What's the point of going to a brothel if you can make a phone call and get the girl to come to you?'

There are gasps of disbelief from the other panellists. You can almost hear the chairman's jaw drop open.

'God almighty! You can't say that.'

'I'll say what I like.'

There's shouting in the background now, and a clumsy but unsuccessful attempt to get him off-mic. But the journo won't be stopped. He starts shouting at the presenter.

'Look at him! Look at him! His eyes are rolling back in his face. There's spittle rolling down his chin. He's going all red! He's worried he's going to lose his precious job!'

I drive on, but happily it goes on like this for another half an hour, keeping me smiling all the way to Sligo.

> Sligo's situation is particularly charming. Bold limestone hills dominate it to the North, while on the East side is the picturesque Lough Gill. The port occupies a site which was of first class importance from the earliest days. A great thoroughfare between North and South led to the ford across the Garavogue. Sligo was the birthplace in 1865 of W B Yeats, the famous poet.

The prose isn't up to Thackeray's usual standard, but that's because Thackeray never made it this far, so he didn't write it. I've been keeping an eye out for an alternative source of antiquarian information to illuminate my journey. The *Automobile Association Illustrated Road Book of Ireland* 1963 (including Gazetteer, Itineraries, Maps and Town Plans) fits the bill. It kicks off with 'A dedication to the reader in Ogham, the ancient Irish linear writing'.

'Bendacht For Cech N-Oen Legfas,' it says. 'A blessing on all who shall read this,' a rather beautiful and anachronistic way to begin a guidebook. With its evocative black and white drawings, grid maps, and advice – 'High speeds and comfort do not go together because of the undulating nature of the roads' – the book effortlessly conjures up a past long buried under new tarmac. It brings back the smell of leather seats in the Ford Consul we had when I was a kid. I remember it being hoisted on board the Dun Laoghaire boat in a giant sling at Holyhead Docks, in the days before Drive On, Drink Up, Drive Off ferries. Its registration mark – EHH 604 – is forever printed on my mind, even though I couldn't tell you the Tank's number, or the one on my car in England, if my life depended on it.

The old hardback guide still has its original green and gold paper cover, adorned with an illustration of the AA winged badge. They used to give you a metal one to stick on your radiator grille in the old days, but then the mods and rockers started fighting, the contraceptive pill came in, and England generally went to the dogs, so they decided to stop giving them out.

I found the book in a back-street shop about half an hour ago, just after I reached Sligo and decided to stay here for the night. Flicking through it now, in the beautiful dark-wood stone-flagged interior of Hargadon Brothers' Bar on O'Connell Street, I'm wishing I'd found it earlier. Every place name in the country, alphabetically listed, has the Irish version as well as the English, and its meaning. Garvaghy – Garbhochadh – rough field. Drimoleague – Drom Dha Liag – ridge of the two pillar stones. Sligo – Sligeach – the shelly place. And there's a reminder that the north-south divide used to be more rigidly enforced. 'A motorist crossing the border by roads other than those approved here, is liable to very severe penalties including confiscation of his car.' And I love that description of Yeats – 'the famous poet' – in case you didn't know who he was. Perhaps in the early 1960s drivers and readers were thought to be two distinct social groups.

Sligo is one of those towns where you can see the mountains from the centre, which I've always found an attractive quality. It offers the possibility of escape. Think what it would do for Birmingham. As I was driving in, I was at a red traffic light when a man in a blue suit and blue shirt got out of a blue car and went into an antique shop that was painted bright blue. The feeling that this might be a piece of avant-garde performance art was heightened by the fact that I was the only person in the audience.

I tried a couple of B&Bs advertising Vacancy, but the owners said they were full. In future, I decided, I would only try the ones that said No Vacancy, like that big detached house across the road there. Unfortunately, there was no reply. As I came out of the drive and waited to cross a road that was busier than I'd expected Sligo roads to be, a woman with mad hair, wearing slippers with pom-poms, came rushing out of a phone box and approached me at an urgent canter.

'Did ya just knock on that door?'

Clearly, she was a crazy person. Perhaps she'd just done a

runner from the ward, before Sister could come round with the evening medication. I decided to humour her.

'I did, yeah.'

'Is it a room you're looking for? I have just the one left, but I'm afraid it's not en-suite.'

No private bathroom? In the newly renovated Ireland, this is a shameful thing to admit, like it would have been twenty years ago to say you'd had a child out of wedlock. But where was this room she was referring to? The phone box? But then she produced a front door key, took me back to the house and showed me a comfortable ground floor room with double bed, TV, and a sink. Breakfast, rather alarmingly, would be at eight. I turned on the TV for an update on the latest Christian Brothers scandal but got the latest Charlie Haughey story instead – £16,000 on French shirts – then walked into town for a pint to celebrate the Tank not having exploded.

Here, in Hargadon Brothers, I've quickly realised that an alphabetically-ordered AA gazetteer is something to be dipped into; trying to read it from cover to cover is like pretending the IKEA catalogue is a novel. But I've nothing else to read. Thackeray and Wibberley are in my bag, but I've finished them. I'm only carrying them around because otherwise my bag would be empty, and then there'd be no reason to carry it around. My copy of *Father's Music* is somewhere in the Tank, where there's a risk of it being destroyed in the imminent inferno. So what am I to do? I can't just drink and stare into space. People might think I'm a policeman. I search the bag again, but I've already read the back of the mineral water bottle. Still no fat. But lurking in its exterior document pocket, where the fluff lives, are the leaflets from Lough Derg. So far I've only flicked through them, in case they frighten me. But now it's only about an hour and a half's drive away, pigshit, heifers, and weeping statues permitting. I plan to be there tomorrow. Perhaps I should acquaint myself with what I'm letting myself in for. I remember reading this bit. 'From midnight prior to arriving . . .'

Hang on. That's tonight.

'. . . the pilgrim observes A COMPLETE FAST FROM ALL FOOD AND DRINK, plain water excepted.'

There'll be no bar on the island then.

'The fast continues for three full days and ends at midnight on the third day. The Vigil is the chief penitential exercise of the Pilgrimage and means depriving oneself of sleep completely and continuously for twenty-four hours. It begins at 10 p.m. on the first day and ends at the same time on the second day.'

Yeah, but you'll already have been up all day; so it's more like thirty-six hours. Thirty-eight if I get up for tomorrow morning's breakfast that I'm not allowed to eat.

'Having arrived on the island the pilgrim goes to the hostel' – oh no – 'removes all footwear, and begins the first station.'

There are then three pages detailing the unimaginable quantity of praying, kneeling and sheer physical punishment involved. At the end, just in case anyone's got the wrong end of the pointy stick about the kind of trip they're signing up for, there's a footnote.

'Pilgrims may not bring to the Island cameras, radios, musical instruments or articles to sell, distribute or for games. Also no snogging, lap dancing or bum fun.'

I just added the last sentence myself in felt-tip.

The enormity of the task in hand is only now beginning to dawn. I really don't know whether I can do this. There's an underlying tone of sublimated violence that transports me right back to secondary school. I have a crystal-clear vision of the thick leather strap that the traditionalists preferred to the cissy, half-hearted cane favoured by some of the younger, more progressive teachers. During my first week in the sixth form the headmaster, Brother Cuthbert, gave me six of the strap for being in the sixth-form common room when I wasn't a sixth-former. When I pointed out that, actually, I was, he said I'd probably deserved it anyway for something I hadn't been caught for, so why didn't I stop moaning?

But I've come this far. I have to go through with it. If I can't cope, I'll just have to leave the island early. Kill a priest and steal a boat, perhaps. Dig a tunnel under the lake. Something like that.

What's the time? Ten to ten. My fast begins at midnight, and I have every intention of taking it seriously.

I go up to the bar and order another pint, and a packet of dry roasted peanuts. You can usually count on being able to taste them three days later.

On the way back to my last bed for a couple of days, I pass a seething mass of people queuing to get into a nightclub. Round the corner and up the street I walk past a Chinese takeaway, but only about ten yards past. Here's a chance to take the eating right up to the wire. Sligo Chinese turns out to be an intriguing dialect, and service is impressively quick. For a shade under £5 I can go back to my room and gorge myself on a pre-midnight feast of Singapore noodles.

On the way up the drive I start thinking of those depressing, paranoid restaurants that display signs saying that you may only eat food bought on the premises. What if my landlady objects to my bringing food to my room? She might be lurking in the hallway with a plate of sandwiches as I come in. They usually are. But my room's at the front of the building. Maybe I can get the noodles in through the window, so I'll be empty-handed if she catches me. Thinking about school while taking strong drink is a lethal combination that has dredged up rich deposits of guilt from the depths.

The window's closed tight, but the top vent is cracked open. Even if I climb on to the window ledge, though, I don't think my arm will reach as far as the catch to open the lower window. I suppose I could get up and try and throw the noodles into the room through the vent, but it's a long drop, and anyway I must be drunk to be carrying on like this. Realising this helps me think more clearly. I place the white plastic bag, and its precious cargo of rice vermicelli with mix meats and seasonal veg in curry flavour, carefully into my bag, cover it with Thackeray, and open the front door.

There's no one in the hall, so I duck straight into my room. The digital clock radio by my bed says twenty-three twenty-six. I turn on the TV. They're showing an old episode of *The Sweeney*. Perfect. I remove the insulated lid from the tin-foil carton to reveal a grey, brainlike mass of compacted noodles, dotted with fluorescent pink char sui pork. No chopsticks though. I should have asked. Too late now. Tentatively I look around my bedroom, on the off-chance that some have been provided, but there isn't even a teaspoon. The noodles gaze up at me invitingly. The clock says twenty-three thirty-five. Just twenty-five minutes to go. I'll have to eat the noodles with my bare hands, like a savage, or a student.

It's a messy business, but I stick with it. On the TV an impossibly young-looking Dennis Waterman is doing his best to convey youthful sex interest. I remember I once saw *Minder* dubbed into German. '*Ach, Terry*,' said George Cole to Waterman, '*jetzt gehen wir nach Craven Cottage.*' And *Bonanza* dubbed into Serbo-Croat, but I can't quote any lines.

I've finished eating by ten to, but the programme carries on for a few more minutes. Then the TV station clock comes on screen.

It's half past twelve.

The bedside clock was wrong. Of course it was. They always are. So I've broken my fast half an hour into day one. This is terrible. They'll know! They'll be able to tell! There'll be some sort of special branch priest eyeing the new arrivals as we step off the boat. He'll look at me and nod, and they'll take me off for a urine sample and an internal examination. I'll be banged up for having a twenty-minute noodle advantage over the other contestants.

My room smells like Chinatown on a Sunday lunchtime. I open the window, then clear up the debris as best I can. Even if you've had cutlery to eat it with, the aftermath of a Chinese takeaway is a dreadful business. I gather up the little yellow tubes and fragments of bright pink meat from the MSG-encrusted melamine bedside table, like a forensic scientist at a Triad murder scene, and put them in the box, which goes in the plastic bag, which I wrap in the rubbish bag from my waste basket, which I zip in my own bag for disposal in the morning. God may know what I've done, but there's no reason why the landlady should.

Next morning I have to go into the breakfast room and watch people eating while I pay, so it's a good job I'm still full. A couple who use too much hair gel come in while I'm waiting for a receipt. She's got a love bite on her collarbone, and he is the most hungover man anywhere in the world at this moment. He refuses cereal with a grunt of disgust, and begs for water. Then he sighs, yawns, groans, and bangs his forehead on the table. Outside the rain is coming down in sheets from a very low sky. I can't eat until the day after the day after tomorrow. I've had better starts to the day.

I can usually rely on the car radio to cheer me up. This morning there's a phone-in on Limerick Hospital's no smoking policy.

'My mother was eighty-six years old and suffering from cancer. I had to take her home so she could have her cigarette and die happy.'

'My father was ninety. They refused him the cigarette that would have allowed him to face eternity in a relaxed fashion.'

Just north of Sligo, I stop at Drumcliff church and visit the grave of W. B. Yeats, the famous poet from the *AA Road Book of Ireland* 1963. There's steady drizzle, and swirling mist, and a plume of smoke rising from a beautiful sugar-loaf-shaped mountain to the north. In the car park, there's a log cabin with Irish knitwear for sale, just as Yeats would have wanted.

The rain eases off for a while in the pretty little village of Belleek, so I stop at the supermarket and pick up an assortment of bandages, foot medication and industrial-strength painkillers. Thick wooded lanes begin to open out on beautiful views east across Lough Erne. There's no new development to be seen. A few old-established houses are dotted across the empty country-side. It feels tranquil, remote, more brooding the further north I get. Pettigoe, according to the brochures, is the last stop before embarkation at Lough Derg. There's a woman on the radio, talking about her work signing the Irish language for deaf people.

'I signed for the Spice Girls once. Felt like a pop star, so I did.'

Pettigoe is old and new Ireland together, a mixture of unadorned old terraces and bright new guest-houses catering for the pilgrim trade – B& no B, I suppose. On the way out of town to the lough, there's boggy, reedy land off to the side of the road. Cows are grazing on the few patches of solid ground. And then I round a bend and see it for the first time.

A huge arch bridges the road, spanning two stone gateway pillars. ST PATRICK'S PURGATORY, say the letters, spelled out against the dark, brooding, swirling sky. Across the steely grey water, through the relentless rain, the island and its penitential buildings look like a miniature St Alcatraz.

This really feels like the end of the road. I lock the Tank and walk across to the shore. Somewhere out there, in a hostel dormitory that smells of feet, Tim and Psycho are fitting silencers, and smiling.

Chapter Fifteen

St Patrick's Purgatory

On a map of the world drawn in 1492 the only place named in the whole of Ireland, and the country's most prominent feature, is St Patrick's Purgatory.

Purgatory is located on Station Island, out in the daunting six-mile expanse of Lough Derg, surrounded by the low, partially wooded, heather-clad mountains of mainland Donegal. It is the only one of seven medieval 'purgatories' – places of rigorous and extreme pilgrimage – to survive. Although no one can be certain, the earliest Irish writings and traditions insist that St Patrick came here; what is beyond doubt is that the continuity of pilgrimage remains unbroken for at least 1,000 years. All things considered, there is a burden of history here to make the most devout pilgrim feel a spiritual lightweight. Me? I'm intimidated.

The earliest pilgrims to record their experiences were medieval knights and monks from England, France, Spain, Hungary and other parts of mainland Europe. They wrote of spectacular and miraculous visions experienced in the cave in which pilgrims were then confined. It's easy to see why hallucinations might have been commonplace. In 1353, the cave was recorded as being nine feet long, three feet wide, and high enough for a grown man to kneel, but not stand. The pilgrim was required to carry out a twenty-four-hour waking, praying, non-eating vigil in the cave, having previously existed for fifteen days on bread and water. Medieval texts make no mention of Singapore noodles or Guinness.

From the earliest days until as late as the eighteenth century, the pilgrim, on entering the cave, was laid out as if dead, ready to confront the pains of purgatory and the judgement of the Creator. Although this cheery practice has since been discontinued, and the fifteen-day fast reduced – first, in 1517, to nine days; then, in 1804, to three – the form of prayer and ritual of deprivation to which the present-day pilgrim must submit is the same as it has been for many centuries.

In 1200 Peter of Cornwall, a regular visitor, wrote: 'Beware. No one leaves Lough Derg without some loss of mind.'

I've parked the Tank in a large lakeside car park in which there are already at least 100 vehicles. For a while I've been sitting here watching the rain beat down on the steady stream of new arrivals. As I haven't seen a soul for the last twenty miles, the fact that they're here at all borders on the miraculous. There are young parents, elderly couples, resolute singles, all carrying a solitary item of no-nonsense luggage. They all seem somehow less daunted than I am. I suppose they're in spiritual training for it, while I'm hopelessly out of condition. If all the pilgrims coming here today were to line up against the wall for the priests to choose sides, I'd be the fat kid that no one wanted to pick.

Once the rain has eased, and I can't think of any more reasons for not getting out of the car, I stand in the drizzle by the boot and assemble a modest overnight bag. With a heavy heart the chocolate, the peanuts, and the hip flask of Jameson's are dumped in the boot, along with other prohibited fripperies, like shoes. I pack my copy of *Father's Music*, on the remote off-chance that reading isn't banned, and walk across to the ticket office. Not that I know it's the ticket office; it's just the only building I can see.

The only people in front of me in the queue are a couple in their thirties. The man asks the girl on the desk where the current batch of pilgrims are from.

'Oh,' she says, 'all over. Dublin, Mayo, Galway. We've a lot from Cork.'

'Are there any from England?'

'Yes,' I blurt out from behind him. 'Me.'

Now why did I do that? Why draw attention to myself, especially when I'm meant to be in pursuit of my Irishness? Perhaps because I'm feeling alien here, so far north, so tightly in the Church's grip; or at least I will be in a few minutes. He turns round and looks at me, puzzled, but doesn't say a thing. Anyway, why did he want to know if there was anyone from England? Is he some kind of hit-man working for Tim and Ginger Tash? Whatever his motives, he turns on his heel and walks back out into the weather with his wife. The girl on the desk looks at me.

'Is it just yourself?'

Oh no. She's not going to tell me there are no vacancies for singles, is she?

'That'll be £20.'

Her accent's very different from what I've become used to: northern Irish, though we're still in the Republic. She has very kind eyes, which encourage me to seek reassurance.

'I'm not sure I'm going to be able to take this.'

'Ah, of course you will. You'll see. You'll be like a new man when you get back here. Don't worry. There'll be priests over there if you need any advice. Or first aid.'

She makes it sound surreal and amusing, but to me it just feels threatening. As I walk across to the boat waiting at the jetty, my stomach rumbling alarmingly, it occurs to me that, at this precise moment, no one on earth knows where I am. Suppose, for the sake of argument, I were to disappear out there; no one would know where to begin to look.

As the boatman welcomes me with a steely glare, I feel like Edward Woodward as the doomed policeman heading out to the island at the beginning of the classic human sacrifice movie *The Wicker Man*.

Except, of course, that he didn't know how *The Wicker Man* ended. I do.

20.30 Day One

I never realised there were so many different kinds of feet.

On a beach, which is the only other time you'd see so many of them, there are lots of other bare body parts too, so the feet don't really stand out. But here, where everything else is covered against the elements with waterproofs and wool, and the feet are just poking out, they really draw attention to themselves, like buttocks peeping out of peekaboo leather cowboy chaps. There are gnarled feet, tiny feet, orang-utans' feet, webbed feet; they are calloused, varnished, varicosed, tattooed and mucky. A lady praying near me earlier today had strange knobbles sticking out from the balls of her feet, near the big toe. I thought I was ready for anything, but I hadn't expected feet with antlers.

Seven hours I've been out here, and I feel terrible. Dizzy, woozy. I'm already thinking of packing in and leaving early because a) I feel foreign, b) I feel dishonest, and c) there were other reasons, I know there were, but I'm too spaced out to remember them.

The only glimmer of hope has been the discovery that the fast isn't total. Each day, at a time of your choosing, you're allowed one meal of black tea or coffee, or hot water, with dry toast or dry oatmeal crackers, to be taken in the canteen. I've just had mine. Everyone at my table had been here before. The guy next to me had already done it once this summer, which seems a tad fanatical, even by the standards that prevail here. They know the form. They talk about 'the beds' – the penitential beds, of which more in a moment – with the easy familiarity of backpackers banging on about beaches in Thailand.

Arriving earlier today felt like coming to a prison, or im-migration checkpoint, or refugee camp. As the boat chugged across the ink-black water, the mood was one of silent fore-boding, or at least it was for me. A country bachelor from another era sat next to me on the hard wooden bench, clutching one of those small battered brown suitcases people carried in 1930s films. He had a flat cap, gabardine raincoat, a frayed collar, and a face that had seen off worse weather than this. He nodded to me once, as if to acknowledge that we both trod the same earth, and one day we would die. The happy-go-lucky mood was already proving irresistibly infectious.

We landed in front of grey, austere buildings, like Ireland used to be, but isn't any more. Huddles of barefooted people stood near the jetty, hunched against the grim August climate, smoking and chatting, scanning the new arrivals for friends, relatives, or anyone with a file in a cake. Their cold, wet, grass-soiled feet suggested a depth of devotion and endurance to which I could never aspire; though I suppose there was a chance they were just using their trouser legs to dispose of soil from the escape tunnel.

The new arrivals were then processed through a reception area and given a number. I'm 124D. No one took our names. We also got a slip of paper saying: 'Another Pilgrim is using this cubicle tonight. You may leave your luggage here. Please do not disturb the bed.'

I went up the stairs to the second floor, reminding myself that I am not a free man, I am a number. There was a dormitory with a couple of dozen bunk beds where sturdy farmers were stowing bags and removing shoes. I was starting to feel overwhelmed, a small boy on my first day at big school. The metal-framed beds and spartan religious atmosphere were straight out of early James Joyce, before he started making words up and you had to try and guess what he was on about. I found the bed that will be mine tomorrow, but is someone else's tonight. Seamus, who will be in the bunk above me once he's inherited it from the current incumbent, introduced himself. He'd just driven from Dublin with a hangover. Hope he didn't drink anything after midnight, or I'll have to dob him in to the Fathers. I took my shoes and socks off, put a hat and coat on, and went out to get started.

Here's what we have to do.

As well as the sleepless vigil and the fasting, each pilgrim must make the stations, a station being a daunting list of prescribed prayers. Though some are made communally, at night, in the basilica, the bulk of them are to be executed alone, in silence, as you walk the penitential Beds.

The Beds are the rugged stone foundations and ruins of ancient monastic cells, around, over, and among which one must trample. There are a worrying number of them. There's St Patrick's Bed, and St Brendan's Bed, and St Brigid's, St Katherine's and St Columba's Beds. Sts Davog and Malaise, though, have just the one Bed between two. At each Bed you walk round the outside three times, kneel at the entrance, walk three times round the inside, then kneel at the cross in the centre, all the while saying to yourself the set number of Our Fathers and so on. As if this wasn't enough, you also walk four times round the outside of the basilica, kneeling at various points, embracing various crosses, and also stand, pray, kneel, pray, and pray on the rocks at the water's edge. All barefoot, mind.

And when you've done all that, you've done one station. While you're here, you have to do nine.

A quick calculation suggests that the conscientious pilgrim will rack up a minimum of 2,421 prayers. I'll double-check this figure later, if conscious. Potential cartilage damage, of course, is incalculable.

Walking along the pathway towards the first bed the slap of bare sole on wet concrete was refreshing, though I could see how it might grate after a while. Suddenly two priests walked past me, all in black, smiling.

And wearing shoes.

So we're not in this together, then. They're in charge, and we're in pain. I wonder if they sidle up and give you a sly stamp on the toes if you're not performing up to scratch. Thank God we didn't have to go barefoot at school. There would have been carnage. Teachers would have queued to jump from the tops of cupboards in steelheeled clogs, crushing our little pink toes like jelly babies. Speaking of feet, I remember one freezing and rainy February day being told the weather was too bad for rugby. A sigh of relief went round the changing-room. 'Get changed for a four-mile cross-country run instead,' said the Brother in charge. So Mike O'Neill presented him with a letter from his father, a doctor, saying he had a septic foot.

'Okay, O'Neill,' said the Brother, 'get changed for a four-mile cross-country hop.'

So there I was, standing in light, refreshing drizzle in a queue of a few dozen people, waiting to get on to St Brigid's Bed, when suddenly the woman in front of me collapsed. Bang, just like that, down she went. Everyone crowded round, while I looked up and checked the buildings for snipers. No one knew what to do. She looked very poorly and yellow, the colour of ancient pub piano keys. Four priests were standing not far away, comparing shoes. Two were ginger, one a skinhead, and one had a goatee. The girl at the ticket desk had told me they'd do first-aid, hadn't she?

'Father! Father! Over here!'

Skinhead strolled across and took command, just as three or four people were trying to sit her up.

'No. Stop! Just lie her flat. Leave her to me.'

His authoritative tone was convincing. The crowd backed off as he put an arm behind her back, and a hand behind her head, and began to lower her. Then, when she was just nine inches or so from the ground, he pulled his hands away, and the back of her head hit a stone flag with a sickening crack. Ooh, winced the crowd, and recoiled. Another woman, her friend, or perhaps her lover, pushed through the crowd and stood by the priest.

'Will she be all right, Father?'

'Ah, I'd say she will.'

But she was just lying there, looking like she was about to die, and no one seemed to know the next move. Then Skinhead called over one of the Ginges, who strolled, at a fairly leisurely pace it has to be said, across to a door in the stone wall, marked 'First-Aid'. Obviously this kind of thing must happen all the time, with all the fasting and deprivation involved. There'll be trained paramedics on hand. It's probably a legal requirement.

After a couple of minutes, a prim, middle-aged lady in a navy-blue two-piece, peach sweater, and black shoes with heels and gold buckles, emerged with half a polystyrene cup of water, and tried to feed it to the still-unconscious woman.

'Are ye feeling better?'

Course she isn't. She's yellow and grey.

'Do ye want to sit up?'

Still nothing. So they picked her up and carted her off to First-Aid, followed by her friend, while we carried on queuing for the Bed. I bumped into the friend a couple of hours later and enquired how she was.

'Ah, she's grand. She's lying down.'

'Are they treating her well?'

'They are. They said she can do an extra station tomorrow if she doesn't finish this one today.'

I'd say that's very reasonable of them. Crueller men would have disqualified her.

When I finally got to do my time on the Beds, I was surprised to find that there was something primal about the rhythm of it, and the feel of the rough, wet, slimy stones underfoot, that was quite pleasing. The designated prayers are the ones so familiar to churchgoers that their meaning is less important than their mantra-like effect; but of course no one actually knows whether you're praying, or concentrating on your own thoughts, or hating every minute of it, as it's conducted in silence. I couldn't match the naked passion of the lip-moving, cross-hugging women on either side of me, though. It's the knees that'll be the first to go, I reckon. Kneeling on rock, and rising, kneeling and rising, so that at the end of an hour and a half of this punishment I felt as though I'd been whacked across them by two big lads with a railway sleeper. It felt calm standing down at the water's edge, gazing out at the silent and empty countryside. There were coins, holy medals, and silver crosses lying in the water. I threw in an English 5p to richen the mix, and also for the craic of seeing the Queen's face down there.

After that there was evening mass in the eight-sided stone-built basilica. I got a good balcony seat from where I could admire the building. One of the ginger priests sang beautifully, accompanied by an ecclesiastical Celtic ballad ensemble on organ, guitar and flute. A couple of times I caught myself nodding off. Only twenty-six and a half hours till bed.

My feet are freezing, and my knees hurt a lot. I fear they may have rising damp. It's after nine, but still light. Think I'll go to the dormitory and put some thermals on, which isn't something I've ever had to do in August before.

00.05 Day Two

When I got to the dorm there were two fat guys getting layered up with fat clothes. They were discussing Chinese food with an intensity that bordered on sexual fantasy. They were clearly mad with hunger. The mention of Kung Po Prawns had one of them bent double, grimacing with lust. The sexiest Chinese and Malaysian food on the planet, they reckoned, is to be found in Tullamore. They're making elaborate plans to break their fast with a spectacular blow-out of satay chicken, crispy duck, sweet and sour pork, beef in black bean sauce, and chilli crabs, to be delivered to their front doors at midnight on Sunday. Perhaps they should consider skipping toast for the next couple of days, to make sure they've got an appetite.

I'm sitting in the night shelter at the back of the basilica, where we can come between sessions of prayer if we don't fancying wandering outside barefoot in a pitch-black howling deluge. We're packed together on long benches, some smoking, some chatting, others sipping water. There's a woman over there reading *Hello!* magazine. I'd have thought that was against the rules. Perhaps there's some religious content though: exclusive shots of the ex-Bishop of Galway at home with his family, something like that.

Right opposite me there's a bony woman who looks like she works in a fish shop. She's wearing leg warmers, which she's pulled down so that they cover her feet. That can't be allowed, can it? Surely she's cheating. It's not fair. I find myself wanting a priest to come in and confiscate them. This thing is beginning to take on a momentum of its own. Even if you don't buy into the philosophy, once you're here you find yourself playing it by their rules. Something inside you takes over, and it becomes a matter of pride. You want to succeed, to score the points, to finish the race, to accumulate the prayers. If they can do it, so can I.

I don't want to go on about it. I just think they should

confiscate her leg warmers, that's all. I mean, it's not unreason-able, is it?

It won't be light for another six hours.

I find myself thinking of something I did a couple of years ago in Australia, when I let an ageing hippy called Graham bury me alive in the outback. The idea was that it was a kind of rebirthing, an initiation ceremony in which you'd break through your own barriers of fear and discomfort and be born anew. You spend all day in a remote place in the New South Wales bush, digging what Graham comfortingly calls 'your own grave', then at sunset you get in it, while another hippy, who's just showed up in a van, plays the didgeridoo. Then Graham fills it in up to your neck, leaving just your head sticking out of the ground, like David Bowie in *Merry Christmas, Mr Lawrence*, only not so badly made up. Then you're left to the mercy of the poisonous spiders you've been finding all day, the terrifying sounds of the Aus-tralian night, and the crushing weight of the soil. After covering my face in insect repellent, Graham made a circle of salt on the ground around my neck. I asked him what it was for.

'To keep the leeches off your face.'

Up to this point, I hadn't considered the possibility of leeches on my face, which is what made this the worst moment of all. Anyway, the understanding was that I would stay in the ground as long as I could bear – all night, if possible – but that Graham was my buddy, so that when I asked to be released, he would comply. After a few hours I did ask; and of course he refused, which is when the row began, with me just a ranting head sticking out of the ground, like something from a Sam Beckett play.

But the next day – even though I hated Graham, and never wanted to set eyes on the bastard again – I felt very good, at ease with myself and full of energy, and the feeling persisted for several days. Maybe it was just banging your head on the wall syndrome, and I was glad it had stopped; or maybe the challenge of dealing with something I'd been dreading, and coming out on the other side, had indeed done me some good.

So perhaps being here tonight is like being buried alive in the

Australian outback by a hippy. If I can somehow make myself see it through, maybe I'll reap the benefits of it – even if they're not the ones the priests might be intending. I did go into a kind of contemplative trance earlier, during some rather beautiful chanting in the basilica, and I came to one unexpected realisation. If I were them I'd order another seafood dish, and cancel the beef in black bean sauce.

Skinhead seems to be the Enforcer round here, the bad priest in the old good-priest/bad-priest routine. He's just come in and told us time's up, back to our prayers. How did that old joke about hell go? 'All right, lads, tea break over, back on your heads.'

01.50 Day Two
Another break after completing one of the stations inside the basilica. It's done aloud, communally, but you have to walk around as if you were still outside, so there's hundreds of people milling around, walking up and down aisles and staircases and pews. There are some of those really annoying spiritual clever dicks who jump in early with their responses, before the priest's finished his bit, then gabble through the prayers dead quick to make sure they get to the end before anyone else does. Someone should give them a slap, but if they're not even confiscating illegal leg warmers, then I can't see that happening. It's a strange, chaotic hubbub of a scene, compounded by the fact that some people are praying in English and some in Irish. I'm feeling more alien here than I have anywhere else in the country.

Hunger doesn't seem to be a problem, just a faint background ache you soon take for granted. Not that that stops me fantasising about food. At the moment, I'm lingering on the langoustines with whiskey mayonnaise, and the Thai marinated fillet steak they serve at the Convent in West Cork, which right now is about as far away as anywhere could be and still be in the country. Other than that, I'm feeling pretty good. Some of the others are looking rough, mind. Maybe the church-going classes miss being in bed at this time more than I do. My knees are killing me, though. You can see why that priest would sue the council.

I found myself a nice first-floor landing where I could do my pacing around during the prayers, with occasional jaunts up and down the stairs for a bit of variety. I've always been a pacer. Pacing around the narrow space reminded me of nights spent pacing up and down dressing-rooms before going on stage. Suddenly I found myself vividly remembering a night I'd all but forgotten. I certainly hadn't given it a thought for a decade or more.

I was hosting a show in Woolwich, south-east London. The promoter had booked two clowns from the circus, performing up the road in Lewisham to do a routine. They produced a live chicken from under a silver salver, and one of them tried to hypnotise it. But try as he might, the bird would not go under. They departed the stage together in a flurry of boos and feathers. As they passed me in the wings, the clown said to the chicken, 'You ever do that again, and I'll wring your fucking neck.' Then I had to go on and amuse the audience.

It seems somehow appropriate that this memory should pop into my head in such a penitential setting. Life offers few experiences more humiliating than following a failed chicken hypnotist, and it must have been good for my soul. I wonder where the chicken is now? I'd walk barefoot over molten lava for it to be here, deep-fried, with chips.

Earlier on the Enforcer gave us a little talk from the altar, warning of the danger of giving in to 'the temptation to lie down or stretch out'. On no account must we do this; but nor must we be surprised, he said, if people around us fall asleep standing up. In a carefully calculated piece of psychology, the Enforcer was followed by Kind Priest – warm smile, white robes, guitar – who, after beginning with a bizarre and unsuccessful sermon about *Saving Private Ryan*, got the crowd back on his side by suggesting that the weird green mould and bacteria that were rampant in medieval bread had similar chemical properties to LSD, and would have accounted for the hallucinations experienced by pilgrims in the cave. Present-day pilgrims, he suggested, weren't attracted by the prospect of psychedelia, but by a spiritual experience that's increasingly out of synch with the mood of go-ahead economic-boom-time Ireland. There was a strong murmur of agreement, followed by the distinctive sound of a couple of hundred people crashing down on to damaged kneecaps for another seventy-three prayers.

03.10 Day Two
Another station done.

I nearly fell asleep standing up ten minutes ago, so I've propped myself up in a corner pew in the balcony. All around me people are sitting and nodding and nudging each other awake. There's a woman over there in a 'Lourdes' T-shirt, and I saw a girl earlier in a 'Fatima' baseball cap. I suppose it's like wearing a Glastonbury T-shirt at the Reading Festival. It lets any lightweights in the crowd know you do this kind of thing a lot.

There's no rule against reading, but I find I keep reading the same paragraph of *Father's Music* over and over again, because I can't remember anything about what I just read. Just now I nodded and dropped the book, twice. Cellphones and computer games are banned, though. So there you have it, if you needed proof: books good, computers bad. It's official, from the Church.

04.40 Day Two
Through the doorway of the basilica I can see the silhouettes of people walking around outside in the rain and dark, in anoraks. They look like medieval monks in hooded cowls.

I'm hungry, but even more tired. If I was at home now I'd go straight to bed without bothering making something to eat. I don't think Thackeray could have handled this. Perhaps that's why he didn't come. He liked the Irish people, but he makes it clear he didn't think much of their religion or their priests. What was it he said about them? I must look it up if I make it back to the mainland in one piece. ('If these reverend gentlemen were worshippers of Moloch or Baal, or any deity whose honour demanded bloodshed, and savage rites, and degradation, and torture, one might fancy them encouraging the people to the disgusting penances the poor things here perform. But it's too hard to think that in our days, any priests of any religion should be found superintending such a hideous series of self-sacrifices.')

Damn. That's given the game away. Killed the tension. You'll know I survived now, or I'd never have found the quote. Listen, though. It wasn't easy.

06.00 Day Two

The rain's stopped, and first light's glimmering over a sombre lake. I'm not sure what happens next, but I think it may involve going to church.

In the night shelter I read a newspaper cutting pinned to the wall. 'Fourteen thousand come each year for one of the toughest pilgrimages in Christendom,' it says. Next to me a country bachelor stands combing his hair with a steel comb. He leans across conspiratorially. 'Ah, feck it,' he says. 'You can't pray on an empty stomach, now can ye?'

I've decided that at ten p.m. tonight I'm going to be right next to the door when the last service ends, so I can run to the dorm and be wrapped up and asleep before most of the other sleepy buggers have left the church. I've also begun fantasising about how nice the rest of my life is going to be once this torture stops.

I find a place on a bench and try to continue Bolger's book. There's a description of a music session in a Donegal pub. The musicians have just been brought a plate of sandwiches. I start wondering what kind they were. Beef? Was it rare? With hot mustard? Were they cut in triangles? Had the crusts been removed? Was the butter unsalted? Christ. A complex novel has degenerated into a food fantasy.

Careful. Skinhead the Enforcer's back. He's been missing most of the night. Six hours sleep at least, I reckon he's managed. His shoes are looking well polished and watertight. If there were a spontaneous popular uprising among pilgrims who just couldn't take it any more, he'd be the first up against the wall.

Brawls would break out on the penitential beds as malnourished hallucinating farmers fought over his socks.

'Can I ask you to go back to the basilica now.'

Time for a bracing six thirty a.m. mass to kick-start the day. Everybody immediately starts to move, unquestioning, but this isn't good enough for him.

'Come on! Stand up! Go through!'

As I stand, I find I'm wondering if I'll be able to get an end-of-row wall seat up in the balcony. So this is what life has come down to – plotting to get the best seat in church. Prison must be like this, finding little targets and rewards to give life structure and meaning.

I make a point of standing on his foot as I go past, but through leather that thick, I shouldn't think he noticed.

09.08 Day Two

I've just popped into the shelter to read a bit more of *Father's Music*. It's building to a frightening climax in tiny, remote villages in Donegal, very close to here. Because I'm trapped on the island, I have the distinct feeling that the events he's describing are actually happening, right now, just over there.

I dozed on and off, uncontrollably, for the duration of the service. My knees went twice, very suddenly, like a scrumpy victim, and I nearly fell while standing. Outside now it's light, with lots of troubled cloud. It's wet and cold underfoot, inducing more fantasies, this time of tropical islands, with beds, and restaurants. No doubt about it, if you're going to go to church in your bare feet, Fiji's a much better option than this. Fiji. Now there's a country with a relaxed attitude to time. They make the Irish look like a nation of Bavarian Punctuality Inspectors.

09.20 Day Two

The old boy who sat next to me on the boat just sidled up. This is his fourteenth time, he confided. His feet are all gnarled, like basketwork. We're in the bathroom in the men's dorm, where I've just splashed some token water on my haggard physog and brushed my teeth in eager anticipation of today's toast. I've never liked communal washrooms, with their noisy bowel movements, and blokes in underwear and shaving foam, and enough warm water and dirt underfoot to start a rice paddy. I'd rather stay dirty. So I do.

Back in the basilica a dozen priests in white robes and comfortable-looking shoes are lined up ready to hear confessions, but I'm afraid this is a bridge too far. Isn't it enough that our knees are going to need reconstruction by Donegal's top plastic surgeons, without adding the ordeal of near-public admission of sin? Confession when I was a kid was an altogether cosier affair. I'd go into the box at ten past six – not a moment earlier – on Saturday night, and say, 'Bless me, Father, for I have sinned, it is two weeks since my last confession.'

Father Murphy's voice would then whisper from the other side of the curtain.

'Is that you, Peter?'

'It is, Father.'

'Would you go out and get me a *Football Pink*?'

So I'd go out of the confessional and down to Eyre's the Newsagents, and get the *Liverpool Echo* sports edition. That's why I didn't go to confession till ten past. The papers weren't delivered till then. Father Murphy was a season-ticket holder at Everton – I think all priests had to be in those days – so I'd go to confession fortnightly, when Everton were playing away, so he could read about the match in the *Pink*. He didn't go to away matches. Wouldn't have made it back in time for confessions.

I've got two more stations to pound out today if I'm to keep on schedule, so I may as well get cracking. It's not as crowded as yesterday, on account of most people being inside confessing in front of everybody else, so you don't need as much vicious elbow work to get you into the holy places. But soon the rain's driving down again, my feet are slipping on the stones, and my knees are feeling twenty-five years older than the rest of me. I'm trying to elevate my thoughts to a higher plane, but this really is brutal. The landscape seems to be closing in as the rain drives down, and the whole place is taking on a deeply forbidding air.

Is this just a waste of three days of my life? There are boats over there, waiting to take the people who had bunks last night back to the mainland. I could just sneak on. No one would know. Except me.

I manage to banish thoughts of escape and hit a steady rhythm, taking a frankly perverse pleasure in the physical discomfort. Wow, that one hurt my foot. Good! Here comes that nasty slippy one with the jaggedy edge. Excellent! As I punish myself, I realise that the big thing today will be deciding when to treat myself to the meal. I need the energy it will give, but I also badly need something to look forward to, and it doesn't look like anyone's going to invite me to a party. I'm allowed to eat when I choose, any time in the next eleven hours, but just the once. Already I'm treating it with all the anticipation of a night out at a major restaurant. This will be purgatory with two Michelin stars.

I'm surprised to find I'm not dying for a pint.

10.40 Day Two

Hour and twenty minutes. Done that station then. Agony, but great sense of achievement. And once you go through your pain threshold, you forget you've got no shoes on.

Think I'll do another.

16.30 Day Two

St Patrick's Purgatory is a large, bustling, noisy, canteen-style restaurant, in the Conran mode, but with more interesting furniture. To start, I chose Oatcake Lough Derg – a plain oatcake, served on a plate. My partner – or the bloke next to me, as he would probably prefer to be known – opted for *Oatcake Sucré, Sauce de L'Eau* – an oatcake dipped in a cup of hot water, then smothered in a generous spoonful of sugar. Both were bursting with flavour. To follow, I tried *Les Toasts Bruns, Sans Beurre et Son Garni* – a perfectly conceived and prepared slice of dry brown toast, uncluttered by over-fussy sauces, and once again served in the house style, on a plate. My partner chose from the *Menu Gastronomique: Les Toasts Variés, Rien*

D'Autre – brown and white toast, free of unnecessary embellishment. It was all washed down with copious quantities of Barry's Tea Bag '99, its distinctive bouquet unsullied by milk, and by a non-vintage Nescafé Noir. At £40 for two, inclusive of tip, return boat trip, one night's accommodation, nine stations, four masses, lacerated feet and shattered kneecaps, it was a bargain. No wonder people come back time after time.

Five stars.

17.30 Day Two

The problem is that once you've had your meal for the day, there's nothing else to look forward to. It's all downhill from here. Once again I was the only person at our table who hadn't been here before, and also the only one not from Ireland. I suppose I'd expected the cosmopolitan mixture you'd find in Killarney or Dingle, but from what I've seen so far there's no one here from another country except me, and I don't really count. My fellow diners were startled when I told them I'd come from England.

'Well, fair play to ya.'

'Good man.'

The young fella opposite eyeing up the last oatcake said he'd hated it the first time he came. 'I found it much too authoritarian.'

So why has he been back four times since?

'Do you know, I haven't a clue. I may not be back for a while this time though.'

'I feel I'm drawing a line under things and wiping the slate clean with God,' said a big-boned woman from Cavan who was wearing a dry-cleaning bag as a waterproof. 'It gives me a feeling of personal renewal.'

A man from Belfast with big thick specs was sitting at the end of the table not saying much, so we all quizzed him next.

'I do a very stressful job, and coming here takes me away from all that.'

So what kind of job would that be then?

'A very stressful one.'

It seemed like he'd been coached in anti-interrogation techniques, so we decided to leave it there.

Outside there's the first glimpse of sunshine in two days. There's a queue of people at the holy water trough filling up mineral water and Body Shop bottles. I'm sitting on a bench looking across the water to the mainland, flexing my pulverised knees and reading *Father's Music*. Less than fifty pages to go. Tracy's passed through Killybegs on the way to Glencolumbkille, just the other side of those hills over there, but we know Luke the Dublin Heavy is close behind her. She is torn between her English upbringing and her Irish heritage, and may end up dead in a ditch because of it.

Sometimes you enjoy a book so much that you have to ration the pages to make it last. I make myself stop with twenty-two pages to go, so there's something to look forward to at bedtime other than forty-seven other men snoring.

20.00 Day Two

We've just had sung mass in the basilica, and now I'm starving again. I'm not sure what the medical term is for having two limps at once, but whatever it is, I've got it.

There was a visiting deacon from Ghana who got a round of applause for being from Ghana. Kind Priest did some topnotch singing and chanting, which set a very serene mood, and then the Enforcer came on and spoiled it with another list of dos and don'ts, mainly don'ts.

I've just come up to the dormitory to admire my bed, fondle it, sit on it, though I know I MUST NOT STRETCH OUT ON IT BEFORE TEN OCLOCK! I haven't lived by such rigid rules since I finished my A-levels and escaped from the Brothers. It's like going back in time. If one of them burst through the door right now and accused me of something I hadn't done, I'd be powerless to resist. This time tomorrow I'll have my freedom, but for the moment I can't think what it was I wanted to do with it. I seem to have everything I need right here, and I'm becoming increasingly confident of who I really am.

I'm 124D, aren't I?

I think I may be becoming institutionalised.

22.05 Day Two
Our sleepless vigil is over.

It's an amazing experience to be with scores, hundreds, of people who hurry directly from church straight to bed because a) that's what they've been told to do and b) there's nothing else to do. The last half-hour has been a rather mystical affair, with strange, harmonious, repetitive chanting – Tai Ze, I think he said it was called – reverberating round the basilica. After the physical battering we've inflicted on ourselves, it created a spiritual mood akin to being tucked up in crisp white sheets, with a buxom nurse applying ice-packs. I think I'm getting into this.

No crisp sheets for me tonight, though. I've brought a duck-down army sleeping bag to protect me from the rigours of an Irish summer indoors. Each bunk has been provided with two thin blankets, designed to make you almost, but not quite, warm enough. I've just given my two to the little fourteenth-visit bachelor who was on the boat with me, who's just across the room there, taking faded winceyette pyjamas out of his antique suitcase. He'll never get them on over that mac.

I was in the lead group of thirty or so who were first out of the basilica and scampering up the hostel staircase, raw feet slap-slapping on the cold pre-cast concrete floor. I'm already in bed as some of the guys are still arriving in the door. A tall, beefy sixty-year-old in the bottom bunk, just a couple of feet across from me, has somehow beaten me to it. Has he been cheating? Anyway he's lying there, motionless, completely silent. I reach under my bed for *Father's Music*. For a moment I panic, thinking it's not there, that I've left it in church; but then I feel its reassuring spine under my fingers. Now where was I? Page 365.

'I found my way to the dormitory. It was a spartan room crowded with triple-bunk beds with horsehair mattresses and iron frames.'

This is perfect! What an extraordinary piece of synchronicity. And just enough pages to send me gliding into deep, well-earned sleep. 'I lay on a low bunk and watched the last light drain from the sky. The dormitories of St Raphael's would have been bigger – eighty boys asleep in each room, dreaming of cars, revenge, and women . . .'

Click!

'Goodnight, Peter,' murmurs Seamus from the bunk above. It's gone dark!

My book thuds to the floor. The bastards have turned the lights off; but there's no sign of any priests anywhere. There must be a central switch somewhere, operated by some vindictive cleric. He'll be sitting in that big stone house near the jetty, the lazy sod, lying back in a big leather armchair, with a Cuban cigar and a tumbler of Armagnac, watching reruns of *Baywatch*. The lighting master switch will be down on the skirting board, so he can just stretch out a well-rested leg and plunge us all into darkness with the toe of a hand-tooled Italian brogue. Then he'll give a bronchial chuckle, stroke the Persian cat on his lap, and dial room service for a club sandwich.

I suppose there's a lesson here for me. Where's the incentive to be frugal with life's pleasures, to save up the pages in your book for later, if you're going to be plunged into the darkened abyss at some arbitrary hour? If life is a book, then read it while you can. Don't save up any pages for later, because there might not be one.

Nothing for it then. I'll have to go to sleep.

22.20 Day Two
Can't get to sleep.

22.30 Day Two
Well this is great, isn't it? I'm tired and aching like I've been awake for a month, being dragged face down over cobbled streets behind a turbo-charged Land-Rover driven by Mad Frankie Fraser – but can I get to sleep? No. I'm just lying here, staring at the metal grille underneath Seamus's mattress, or else at the big beefy bloke across to my left, who still hasn't budged or made a sound. Maybe he's playing possum, and taking everything in. He could be an informer, waiting his moment to see if anyone has a sly snack, or goes to sleep with their hands inside

the bedclothes, so he can report them to the Enforcer first thing in the morning. I try counting sheep, but I don't think that's ever worked for anyone, has it?

I'll count Paisleys instead. Little Ian Paisleys, jumping over a stile. Oh, hang on. He's refusing. Won't jump it. Won't even discuss it. Right. Better get the cattle prod then. Whoah, there he goes! And another! Three Paisleys. Four. Christ, you wouldn't want to be stuck in a lift with all of them, would you. Five. Six . . .

06.20 Day Three

Woke just the once in the night, with a start, to a terrifying sound. Took several seconds before I remembered I was in a room full of battered and exhausted religious fanatics. Forty-seven malnour-ished men can make a surprising amount of noise. Never again do I expect to experience Dolby sensurround quadrophonic Nicam digital snoring of such exceptional quality. There was none of that horrid, gruff, pig-like snorting, because no one here was drunk; but all other tones were represented, all pitches, all time signatures and notes – breathy, chesty, nasal, menacing, wheezing, shrill, purring, a great variegated polyrhythmic wall of sound coming out of the all-enveloping darkness. Just a dozen more Paisleys, though, and I was fast asleep again.

We were woken, as promised, by a bell at six, though no one had mentioned the bleeper that went off at ten to, to let us know we'd be woken in ten minutes. If I can find a suggestion box, I'll propose a hooter to give ten minutes warning of the bleeper. A couple of cockerels, and a chained-up dog that's been fasting for three days, should make it almost certain nobody would oversleep.

By the time I made it to the bathroom it was full of the midnight snorers, all in old-fashioned underpants, stripped to the waist, and smelling of toothpaste and non-sissy soap. I padded round for a bit in other people's drips to soothe my aching feet, then joined the wave of humanity rolling towards the basilica under startlingly clear blue skies. The penitential Beds were empty, because NO ONE IS ALLOWED ON THEM TILL AFTER MASS! DYA HEAR? I found myself walking next to Seamus, my bunk mate.

'Morning, Peter. How are you?'

'I'm good, thanks.'

'Tired?'

'Not really, no.'

'Nor me. I reckon that's because we've not been eating.'

He must be close to breaking point. What the hell can he mean?

'How's that then?'

'Well, eating uses up a lot of energy, you know, with all that digesting. So the less we eat, the less tired we become.'

08.10 Day Three

Six thirty mass was more comforting than anticipated. There was more celestial warbling from Kind Priest, which is very soothing when you're feeling like this. There's no denying the tremendous sense of community and shared experience among the pilgrims. They have so many common assumptions, about life, salvation, and everything else, that they're never stuck for anything to talk to each other about. You can see how shared belief can have a positive effect and make a country cohesive. Mind you, that's what Pol Pot thought, too.

As the service ended, those pilgrims who, in the old days, would have been first to put their hands up when they came looking for volunteers to be martyred, were sprinting barefoot out of the door to get to the front of the penitential queue. Everyone's expected to soak up one final drubbing on the beds before leaving. At the moment there's a bit of an undignified scramble to kiss St Patrick's cross. I was just talking to a bright-eyed mother of four from Derry who comes every year, without her family. I asked her what she gets out of it.

'For three days I can just live in the Now.'

I know exactly what she means. When you throw yourself into something like this, your life is so filled by the sheer physical business of it that there's no room left for the worries of everyday life. Other concerns get pushed into the background. You don't even have the stress of going shopping or spending time deciding what to eat, if you're not allowed to eat.

People are peeling off Himalayan headgear and Arctic foundation garments as they move around the stones, because the sun's quite hot now. Sunburned feet must be a real possibility. Good job I haven't washed them then. All that dirt must be at least factor 25. And why would I want to wash it off anyway? These mucky abrasions are a sign to the world that my soul has been cleansed, or at least that I've had a fair old crack at it. Leaving here and going back to the real world will be like coming back from Spain with a suntan. You'll want to leave your shoes off for a couple of weeks so everyone'll know where you've been.

Go on. What are you waiting for? Back on the beds, just one more time.

Noon Day Three

The lake is shimmering like the Mediterranean under a bright sun as we cross back to the mainland. If it were a film, this would be a grotesque cliché, sin and gloom transformed into grace and sunlight by the redemptive magic of the pilgrimage. As it's actually happening, I'm doing my best to ignore its symbolic significance, and just enjoy the weather. I can't deny, though, that I'm feeling good. There's a crispness and clearness to things that has nothing to do with the sunlight. This has been powerful medicine. If it can do this to me, what must the true believers be feeling?

As we got on the boat a few minutes ago, Kind Priest was there to shake each of us by the hand, while the Enforcer harassed those stragglers who were too exhausted to stand, treading on their fingertips where necessary. I'm only guessing here, obviously. Anyway, perhaps Kind Priest had picked up on my accent, because as he shook my hand, he said to me, 'And where are you from?'

I hesitated. I don't know why. 'Er . . . from England.'

He looked quizzical.

'England, and Cork.'

He smiled. 'So where's your home?'

'I'm still trying to work that one out.'

'Good luck to you now. God bless.'

Chapter Sixteen

Bring it on Home

A week has passed since I came ashore in Donegal and devastated my newly-cleansed system by breaking fast in ill-advised style.

For the next few days, as I adjusted to escape from the rigours of Lough Derg, life took on a heightened, dream-like quality. My dislocated consciousness finally seems to have returned to normal; the stories in today's breakfast newspaper, on the other hand, are as spaced out as ever.

> John O'Connor, 65, a farmer, appeared in Killorglin District Court yesterday on a charge of being drunk and disorderly. When asked to plead, he responded that he did not recognise the court. When the presiding magistrate asked him why, O'Connor responded, 'because it has been painted since the last time I was here'. After a few minutes' laughter, O'Connor was sentenced to two months for contempt.

After a few days in Donegal recovering from Lough Derg, I've come back to West Cork to recover from the few days in Donegal. On the long drive down yesterday, I was listening to a radio feature about the boom in country house hotels, both in England and in Ireland. They interviewed a couple who were paying £200 a night for a room in a place with a health spa, where for an extra thirty quid they could have organic algae therapy. When the reporter asked if this wasn't a bit expensive, the woman said no, because they'd leave the algae on all day if you asked them to. Because it was radio, you couldn't tell whether the sleeves on her jacket fastened at the front or the back.

With every country house hotel in the country to choose from, I had no doubt where I wanted to be. The Convent, where my sanity was restored after the night on the ferry, is the place I need to be right now. It is crisp white linen for my aching body, compost for my well-ploughed soul. It has people instead of staff, there's no TV, and a room for the night costs less than half an hour in the algae trough at Conyuppy House.

When I went down to the village before breakfast to get the paper, Mrs Herlihy who owns the shop was in the street, swatting flies on the outside of her front window. In a comedy film, you'd edit it out as over the top. A Dutch woman with a pierced nose was in the shop ahead of me. She asked for tampons. Mrs Herlihy recoiled several feet, like a priest conducting a particularly difficult exorcism.

'I only have the other type.'

She indicated the non-sinful kind, pre-wrapped in brown paper on the shelf.

'Scho do you know where I could get schum?'

'You might try the petrol station.'

I had the dry toast and black tea for breakfast. No, sorry, I'm still getting the flashbacks. Kippers it was, and two poached eggs, while I watched the two couples at the table by the stained-glass window. Everyone knows what happened last night. There are no secrets here. After another great dinner – bouillabaisse with monkfish and langoustines, herb salad from the garden, fresh-caught mackerel fillets in tamarind and chilli – they took a couple of bottles of Aussie Shiraz through to the lounge for a nightcap. Some time in the middle of the night one of the guys got up for a pee, opened his first-floor window, and woke up when he hit the ground below. Luckily, he landed on the lawn, not the stone, the gravel, or the big blue Volvo. He came back in through the front door, went back to his room where his wife was still sleeping, and got back into bed. This morning he couldn't remember whether it had happened or he'd dreamed it, until his wife pointed out the damage to his teeth.

After breakfast I go down to the abbey to dip the peculiar spot on my elbow in the wart-curing well, then drive out to an enormous deserted beach and walk along it. It feels good to be back in Cork. I still have things to do here, but first a spot of lunch might be in order. It's an age since I treated myself to a toasted special. I drive at random round the narrow unmarked lanes that criss-cross the headland, and end up in a village of a dozen or so houses that doesn't seem to be marked on my map.

The pub, which is attached to the shop, is a single basic room with a concrete floor. On stools at the bar a red-faced Irish farmer and a fat German in a yachting cap are deep in bizarre conversation. There's no menu, but of course, says the lady behind the bar, she'll do me a toasted sandwich. While I'm waiting for my pint to settle, I wander round looking at the photos on the wall. There are lots of boats, and people grinning with big dead fish. There's a black and white photo of the SS *Norwegian* sinking in 1917. Next to it is another photo, of Guinness barrels being salvaged from the SS *Norwegian*. Further along the wall is a photo of Jimi Hendrix driving a tractor.

I zoom in for a closer look. It appears to be a 1960s advert for farm equipment. Jimi is grinning, and so are the two guys from his band who are hanging off the tractor with him – Mitch Mitchell, says the caption, and Noel Redding.

'Here's your pint. I'll make your sandwich now so.'

Next to it is a yellowing newspaper cutting, picturing Noel Redding outside his farmhouse in West Cork. So that was why the Woodstock veteran was playing in the pub in Clonakilty all those months ago.

'Ah, you're interested in Jimi Hendrix, are you?'

It's an odd question to be asked by an elderly lady in a deserted pub, but I feel like I lost touch with the humdrum and the predictable a long time ago.

'Not really, no. I always found him a bit too, er . . .'

'I know. I know. Very noisy.'

I remember the pub near the docks the night I got the ferry.

'He's still very big in Wales though.'

'Is that so? I must tell Noel.'

'So does he live round here then?'

'Just across the road.'

She looks at her watch.

'I'd say he'll be in in about ten minutes. Will I introduce you to him?'

'No!' I don't want to bother the man. He probably gets enough grief from Hendrix obsessives in places like Ohio, with their own websites and automatic weapons. 'Please, no thanks. I'm sure he'd prefer to be private.'

She gives me a puzzled look, as if she hasn't come across the concept before. A quarter of an hour later I've just scalded my tongue on the molten cheese, ham, tomato and onion, when the door opens and a slight figure in woolly hat and glasses comes in, followed by a woman in her seventies wearing a neck brace. The lady behind the bar turns to me conspiratorially.

'Ah, here he is now, with his mother.'

I smile weakly, happy to leave it at that.

'Ah, Noel! Would you come over here! There's a fella here dying to meet you!'

So I buy Noel a pint, and chat with him and his mum, a lovely, politely-spoken woman from Kent. She's lived out here with him for many years now, which probably isn't a scenario either of them had in mind around the time of the photo-shoot for the cover of the *Electric Ladyland* album. Noel says he plays at De Barra's every Friday night, unless he's out of the country. He'll be there tomorrow. The symmetry of the journey demands that I go.

It's a wonder I ever made it back to Cork. Donegal was a black hole into which I almost disappeared without trace. I entered a twilight world where breakfast was at half one in the afternoon, and you'd beg to be let out of the pub at four in the morning. Such are the consequences of accepting hospitality from a musician.

Paul is a guitarist and songwriter I knew in England who's been living in Donegal for five years. He earns a living from live work and the royalties from songs he's written for some well-known Irish acts. I decided to call on him the day I left Lough Derg. After stopping to finish *Father's Music* in the square in the middle of Donegal town, where no one could turn the lights off, I reached his place about two in the afternoon, and assumed he was out when I got no answer. It hadn't occurred to me that he'd been performing last night, and hadn't woken up yet.

I was surprised, and rather delighted, to discover that the Lough Derg experience had left me feeling high and light and warm and positive, just as the girl on the ticket desk had promised; though by the time they let us out of Paul's local in the early hours of the following morning, the effect had been somewhat dissipated. I am now in a position to confirm that, after fasting for three days, twelve hours of stout – with only a bowl of seafood chowder to help absorb it – quickly brings on the most violent symptoms of an amoebic and fatal tropical disease. Rising at two to cook bacon on a single man's grillpan does nothing to improve the situation.

I carried on like this for four days, hopelessly jet-lagged from the sleepless night in Purgatory, and a timetable on which only musicians, owls and badgers could survive.

It was marvellous.

In the afternoons we explored the brutal mountains and windswept coastline of Donegal. It's all but cut off from the rest of the Republic by the western end of County Fermanagh, and it felt curious to be this far north of Belfast, yet still in the Republic. Because we were close to the border with the UK, shops and garages were advertising that they were happy to accept British currency; in its soul, though, the place felt about as remote from England as you could get. I hadn't been prepared for the combination of strong Northern Irish accent and wide-spread use of the Irish language, and I felt very foreign, though I couldn't have been made more welcome.

'Hello Peter!' screamed an exuberant eighteen-year-old lad at two in the morning. 'My name's Sean, and I'm a feckin' eejit!' He vaulted the bar he'd been serving behind, punched that tune from *The Full Monty* on to the jukebox, and stripped, while his sister tried to mop the floor around him. I asked some of the other late-night flotsam about the flexible licensing laws.

'There's an ex-gard has opened a bar. They don't bother him, so they can't really mess with anyone else.'

'Hey, it's not just a bar. A social and cultural centre is what it's called, and a hostel. En-suite bedrooms, and all kitted out in pine. Got a grant for the lot, so he did.'

'So how did he manage that?'

'Oh, nothing underhand about it. 'Twas just corruption.'

Earlier in the evening Paul and his drummer had filled me in on who was who.

'That fella there – best session trumpeter in the country. Christ, he could tell you some stories about Van Morrison.

'See him? Played for Omagh in the benefit against Manchester United.

'That guy in the corner. Never tells the truth, as a matter of principle. Why answer a question, he says, if you can tell a story instead?'

Lots of people seemed to have a French parent, or a Scottish grandparent, or a Spanish wife. 'The only true Irish left,' insisted the country's top sound engineer one night, 'are the travellers, and look how we treat them.' Talk turned to religion. All shades of opinion were represented, but the mood was relaxed and uncontentious.

'You know a few years ago, when all the statues of the Virgin up and down the country were moving, and people were turning up and seeing the miracles? Well, Donegal was the only place it never happened. We had a band up here at the time. The Stationary Statues.'

Even the dangerous combination of politics and strong drink couldn't sour the mood.

'See the Brits finally worked out how to sort things out? They heard Adams and Paisley had been having secret meetings. So the SAS send their top sniper along, and he's waiting up on a roof at the back of this hotel. And sure enough, don't Paisley and Adams come walking out the service door together at the appointed time. But walking right between them is Daniel O'Donnell.'

The nation's top country-and-Oirish singer is a Donegal boy, and famously proud of it.

'The thing is, the sniper's only been given two silver-tipped bullets.'

A pause, and a sip of the drink.

'So he shoots Daniel twice.'

The night before I left, Paul's trio was playing. He has different bands for different types of music. The trio's policy is to play no songs written after Elvis joined the army. At the bar I got talking to a guy who'd been married thirty years to a fortune-teller. Afterwards Paul and I sat up late in front of a fire in his ramshackle Georgian house. He said how unregulated life seems in comparison with England. Different rules of time apply. But the biggest change, he said, was people's attitude to musicians.

'In England everyone just thinks you're a waster. Get a proper job, they think, you lazy bastard. Here, you're a respected member of the community. You entertain them, and they honour you for it. Music's at the centre of everything. I even get invited to dinner at the doctor's house. That was never going to happen in Leeds.'

I told him I was going back to Cork while I still had the energy to get out of Donegal.

'I was down in Cork last month. In Clonakilty. I did a gig with Noel Redding.'

I get to De Barra's around eight, even though as far as anyone knows no one's ever picked up an instrument in an Irish pub until at least half nine. On the wall next to my bar stool is a photo of Noel with one arm round Janis Joplin and the other round Bob Dylan, who's wearing a zebra-print shirt, unbuttoned to the waist. Either it's Woodstock, or Noel's mum took the snap one year when Bob and Janis were in Clonakilty on their holidays.

'So did you find your roots?'

The guy at the next bar stool is talking to me, and for a moment I can't place him. Then I see the scar, and remember the rare steak with garlic butter. It's the builder I met the day I arrived on the ferry, the one who sold the wood to Jeremy Irons, and thought the best thing about this feckin' place was the rain. He buys me a drink.

'So did ya get to any festivals? There's a festival somewhere every feckin' day during the summer, ya know.'

I realise I haven't been to a single one. There didn't seem much point. There was plenty going on without them, as far as I could make out.

'The feckin' Rose of Tralee. That was the place to be this year.'

The Rose of Tralee is a beauty contest that's been going for aeons, with music and drinking also laid on to make sure all interests are catered for.

'You know who played there this year?'

I look at the wall and hazard a guess. 'Bob Dylan?'

'No. James Brown! And a thirty-eight-piece feckin' band. For free. In the street. In feckin' Tralee.'

I'm mortified I wasn't there. James Brown, the Godfather of Soul in, as the man said, feckin' Tralee. Ole James was probably checkin' out the family tree. A lot of people don't realise that the Number One Soul Brother is another famous Irish American, but if you look closely, the haircut gives it away. Everyone remembers 'Sex Machine' and 'Papa's Got a Brand New Bag' sure enough, but people seem less familiar with James's pioneering work as a founder member of the Chieftains. Next time you're in Ireland, go into a record shop and ask for the early James Brown and the Chieftains recordings. They'll be delighted. The poetry's good, too; check out 'Get on Up (in the Celtic Twilight)', Brown's celebrated collaboration with W.B. Yeats.

And Noel Redding? He's Otis's cousin, isn't he?

The band go on at ten o'clock in a back room. There are nine people in the crowd, including me, but it fills up as the evening wears on. At one point an inquisitive and hopelessly pissed farmer comes in and takes a look. Suddenly he starts dancing wildly on the spot, then stops and goes out to the toilet. An hour later he comes back, says something to me I don't understand, then lays his head on the bar. The overpowering fragrance of dairy products and dung, with a soundtrack of Noel Redding singing Dylan's 'Love Minus Zero/No Limits', isn't something you could forget in a hurry.

After the gig I ask Noel if he'd like a drink, but he has to be up early in the morning.

'Sorry, man. I'm playing at a convention. Got to fly to San Francisco.'

Sometimes you just can't imagine what other people's lives must be like.

Next morning I drive into Cork city, park the Tank near where I'd parked the wretched repmobile on St Patrick's Day, and take a stroll across the river to the English Market. I'll be going back to England very soon, and it'd be a crime not to stock up with some decent olives. It's not something they tell you about in the tourist guides, but Cork's got the best olive stall this side of Casablanca.

There's nothing English about the market, apart from the fact that it's covered with a roof, which was a radical innovation from across the sea when it was built in the eighteenth century. At one end of the market a first-floor café and restaurant, enclosed by ornate wrought-iron, looks down over the stalls. The olives are on a corner as you go in, enormous barrels of the things, black, green, spiced, herbed, or chillied. A dozen different kinds of olive oil, from places like Sardinia and Kalamata, are for sale in hand-labelled pop bottles sealed with a cork. There's a vat of pickled garlic, for people with damaged palates who'd like to taste again. After I've stocked up I take a stroll past the fantasy fish stalls, piled high with shark and John Dory, and huge scallops in enormous fan-shaped shells. I won't be taking any fish back in case my bag gets lost and turns up five weeks later, but Karen from the Convent has given me her recipe for mackerel, so I head to the Weird Chutney and Bizarre Sauces stall for a cheap jar of tamarind paste. They may have put an end to duty free, but, trust me, English visitors with an eye for a bargain are coming to Ireland in ever-increasing numbers to stock up on tamarind. Pop over to Tralee to catch James Brown, and you'll have had the perfect contemporary heritage weekend.

Outside the market I decline a *Big Issue* from a woman in heavily embroidered clothes whose head and hair are covered with a scarf. A hundred guilt-stricken yards along the street I stop and buy one from a woman in similar clothes, who's also pregnant. I ask where she's from, but she doesn't speak English. I can only presume they're refugees from the Balkans or one of the ex-Soviet republics. The news has been full of reports of the scenes in Dublin, with scores of European and African refugees living and sleeping on the street in the glitzy financial district, after the closure of a hostel. I heard a TD, a member of the Irish parliament, on the radio yesterday. 'Surely this country which has exported countless millions of its people all around the world can welcome these poor people in their hour of need, especially now we're prosperous for the first time in our history. It seems that as we're becoming more racially diverse we're also becoming a more racist society.'

As if to prove his point, a woman with a Dublin accent immediately phoned in. 'It's just an excuse for claiming benefits and for criminal elements to come in here. The other thing is they're all having so many children. What happens when they're all planted here? Are we going to have the same carry-on they have in New York and London? Keep Ireland for the Irish is what I say.'

I was struck by her use of the archaic word 'planted'; that she should choose to discuss contemporary issues in language associated with a perceived wrong carried out hundreds of years ago.

This sort of intolerance isn't something I've ever encountered over here, and I'm hoping it can't be widespread. After all, the British state has done little over the years to commend itself to the Irish people; yet in a lifetime of coming here, I've never had a single ugly moment, nor even an adverse comment, for speaking with an English accent. In fact, a man once approached my father and me in a West Cork pub and apologised for the rebel songs that were being sung 'That's all right,' said my dad. 'They're very popular where we come from too.'

The family tree is spread out in front of us on the coffee table at my uncle's house, just outside the city. So far he's traced it back to 1700. He seems surprised when I ask where he went to access the records.

'This is just from talking to people, and from what I already knew.'

I remember driving through the countryside with him when I was a child. He would point to someone working in a field or walking by the road and say, 'Now you see that fella, you and he are cousins, second cousins, on your grandmother's side. His father and my . . .'

I remember thinking that he made it sound as if everyone was related to everyone else, which I suppose in a way we were. One of the first things to strike me about the family tree is that, as far back as it goes, the name on both sides is McCarthy. My grandfather and grandmother were third cousins. Of course they were. That's how it was in a time when there was a small population base and no one ventured far from where they were born. People were effectively marrying within a tribe. Apart from one ancestor who died with his family on a famine boat – coffin ships, they were called – on the way to America, there seems to have been no emigration. From what I see here, my mother and two of her brothers were the first to leave the country. So we're the first generation to be born abroad.

The close-knit patterns of what I'm looking at draw me in. I feel part of something coherent and tangible. He is able to give me chapter and verse on any name I point to. The depth and breadth of his knowledge is remarkable. Since his generation, as we've all become more mobile and more scattered, the information has become dissipated and lost. Lots of people these days are consulting genealogists to help them understand where they come from, but not many of us can turn to someone who has acquired the information orally and is able to see the bigger pattern of which it's a part.

Happily, there are no ugly surprises in store like there were for that retired trade unionist in England a few years ago, who fulfilled a life-long passion to trace his ancestry, and within half an hour had discovered that he was related to Margaret Thatcher.

It's surprising how gripping it is to see history written as the names of individuals. Some things leap out at you. Irish Christian names – Tadhg, Peig, Cormac, Aindriu – are succeeded by English ones, as the Irish language is suppressed by law. A note by the name of my grandmother's sister – Auntie Annie from Dunmanway, who force-fed us the chicken and ham – shows that for many years she was the teacher at the village school where Dominic's son and the rest of the English travellers' children are now pupils, which has a pleasing synchronicity. There's a macabre Skibbereen connection in the form of a distant relative who walked round the town with a limp, the result, so the story goes, of broken legs sustained through being left for dead in the famine pit I'd stood by at Abbeystrowny. It's a humbling business. The detail of one's own life can begin to seem an inconsequential and colourless thing.

One event in particular catches my eye. At the top of both branches of the tree are two men with the Christian name Tadhg, pronounced in English 'Tague'. It translates as Tim. The name Patrick didn't become widespread in Ireland until the 1800s; so before the Irish were called Paddies, they were known as Tadhgs, or Tims, a pejorative term that survives to this day in parts of Ulster and Scotland. Anyway, some time in the early 1700s one of these Tadhg MacCartais had five sons; according to the document in front of me, they 'all fled to France from pursuit by Redcoats. All trace lost.' As they didn't have Butlins in those days, I take this to be a reference to the English army. My uncle had grown up knowing this story.

'They were chased by soldiers – I don't know why – and took refuge in a thatched house that stood just behind the house in Drimoleague where your mother and I grew up. The soldiers burned it down, but somehow they escaped and took a boat from Glandore harbour to France. Nothing was heard of them after that.'

Well, I'm sorry, but I'm a sucker for this sort of stuff. I find it impossibly romantic. So France must be full of my relatives. There's a famous Château McCarthy, producer of fine clarets, that I've always known was of Irish origins. Perhaps we're related. I'll turn up on the estate and claim my inheritance.

'The people with the vineyards were earls, Peter. We were small farmers. These five fellas probably ended up cannon fodder for Napoleon, dead in the snows of Moscow.'

He's probably right. Still pretty romantic though, isn't it?

Traffic's bad in the city, so I park and go looking for a cash point, because I've spent all my money on olives and tamarind. I find myself walking along the street where the Whiff were playing in the pub on St Patrick's Day all those months ago – An Siol Broin. It was a dingy, atmospheric little place, perfect for taking half an hour out just now to contemplate the implications of my ancestry. I walk past a huddle of Indian men in cheap jackets and grey shoes, who look as if they've just got off the boat. Hang on. I've walked too far. It must be somewhere back up the street. No, it's not here either. Shouldn't it be just past that mini-cab office?

The dingy pub is no more. The Shelbourn, says the upmarket font on the black-tiled façade with, in tiny letters below it, An Siol Broin. The smoky atmospheric boozer has been devoured by a brand-new 'traditional' bar. Two estate agents and a woman from a management consultancy are sitting in the big new clear-glass window, sipping Malibu with Aqua Libra and cranberry juice, or at least that's how it looks from the street. I pop my head through the door. They're still putting the finishing touches to the décor. The new boards that have replaced the old boards are being stained down to look old. The place smells of sawdust and aftershave, instead of old stout and Crusties.

Some people would say this is progress.

On my way to Drimoleague next morning I stop in Dunman-way for a newspaper and a cup of tea. On the front page there's compelling evidence to support my theory about the abundance of foreign cash, and the proliferation of driveways with electric gates and entryphones, in parts of West Cork. The story's underneath a photo of gardai swarming all over a yacht. 'Three Englishmen were arrested yesterday on board a converted trawler off the Cork coast. When the boat was brought ashore at Schull Harbour, it was found to contain 1.2 tonnes of "Moroccan Gold" cannabis with a street value of fifteen million pounds. A further two thousand kilograms have been discovered in the area in the last six years.'

I'm not sure whether it's intentional or not, but there's a neat companion piece on page two. 'Teenagers questioned in a survey published today say that they spend £25 a week on alcohol, £19 on cigarettes, and £23 on drugs.' Sixty-seven pounds a week? Now that's what I call a tiger economy. At that rate, the stuff in the Englishmen's boat might just last the local kids till half-term.

On the outskirts of town there's a big placard saying that there's a Queen tribute band playing this weekend at the Grade B Hotel. I wonder if they'll be staying the night for some old-fashioned rock-and-roll mayhem? The tellies are so far up the wall they'd never get them out the windows without a cherry-picker. I met Freddie Mercury once, when Queen had just started and hadn't made a record. They played at a youth club in St Helens. He walked into a public bar full of miners and glassworkers wearing black nail varnish and a fur coat. Freddie, not the miners and glassworkers. You could tell he'd do well.

The leaflet advertising the Lough Derg Pilgrimage – the one that effectively decided the shape of my year – is no longer on display in the porch of Drimoleague church. I'd suspected as much. Was it pure chance that it just happened to be here when I turned up that day back in March; sheer accident that I should glimpse it, and so be tempted to undertake my journey? Or had a priest with binoculars spotted me turning up, and sent his most trusted nun down to pin the leaflet on the wall? They'd have needed walkie-talkies.

'Down a bit, down a bit. Up a bit. That's it. Right there, where the bastard can't miss it. He'll be powerless to resist. Quick! He's coming! Lie down behind one of the pews. And as soon as he's gone, take it down, iron it, and put it back in the drawer.'

Whatever the forces that led me there – and I couldn't identify them myself, beyond a decision that this would be my destination – I'm glad I went to Lough Derg. Apart from being a bizarre and vivid experience that I'll remember all my life, it's changed things in ways I'm still trying to define. When I was up in Donegal, convalescing from the pilgrimage in the bibulous and opaque parallel universe inhabited by musicians and other creatures of the night, I began to feel I was coming to an understanding, however incomplete, of my relationship with this country. So even though I resented the priests and their perfectly polished shoes, the physical and spiritual drubbing over which they presided seems to be leading to a clarity and sense of purpose that wasn't there before. The fact that I didn't share most of their beliefs, or those of my fellow pilgrims was of surprisingly little consequence. I'm reminded of a line from Joyce's *Portrait of the Artist as a Young Man*. I first read it when I was fifteen, and have remembered it ever since.

"It is a curious thing, do you know," Cranly said dispassionately, "how your mind is supersaturated with the religion in which you say you disbelieve. Did you believe in it when you were at school? I bet you did."

I take a walk up the hill behind the church to look down on the village, and discover the remains of a ruined abbey and an ancient graveyard that I never knew existed. I've probably been in more cemeteries this year than I have in the rest of my life. Does this indicate a healthy awareness of our own mortality, or am I in the grip of a morbid obsession? I look around the faded headstones and decide that, whatever the answer, this will be the last one. Tonight I'll stay here in the village; and tomorrow I'll head back to England.

★　　★　　★

'So do you reckon the outward-going side of the Irish character is down to so many people believing in an after-life? You're relaxed about death, so you can get on with enjoying life.'

'Well, I think – I'm not sure now, but I think – I think you're probably talking bollocks.'

I didn't get the name of the fella I'm talking to, because there's a guy with keyboards, drum machine, and a V-necked jumper conducting a one-man Jim Reeves revival in the corner, and you have to catch what fragments of conversation you can in between the power surges. I'm staying with my cousin Sean, who now has the farm where my mother grew up. He's built a new bungalow almost on the spot where the five brothers' thatched house once stood. I suppose nothing's ever certain in this life, but he seems reasonably confident the British army won't turn up and burn this one down.

It's all a far cry from the kind of farming I remember here as a kid, when eggs were collected each morning, and cows milked by hand, when harvest was a communal activity for friends and neighbours. It may not have been a money-spinner, but there was still an element of self-sufficiency about it, a sense that all these activities were part of a harmonious whole. Today it's all dairy, says Sean, which relies heavily on the intensive rearing of EC paperwork. He doesn't think his son will follow him into it. So, instead of farming the same little patch of land the family have tended for 300 years or more, the next generation will probably be surfing the net and conducting virtual commerce in Dublin, or Dubai. Already there are stories of cheap labour being imported from Wales and England to do the jobs the Irish don't want.

Sean's son is watching Ireland play a football match on TV, but he's wearing a David Beckham shirt. I ask him who matters most, Ireland or Manchester United? He grins.

'United, o' course.'

My aunt, who was away in Dublin last time I called, is away in London this time. Sean and I walk down into the village to see what else is new. Not a lot, as it turns out. There are no fancy restaurants. No restaurants at all, in fact. No Germans or Dutch have built houses with security fences and great big eagles on the gateposts. McCarthy's Bar on the main street is still untouched since the last time it was modernised, with Formica. The fire is still burning hand-cut turf. The owner, a middle-distance relative, introduces me to a couple of long-distance relatives. We cross the road to the scruffiest bar in town, which still has no credible rival for the title. I'm told you can see the river through a hole in the floor of the ladies. The gents, mind you, is in a far worse state, and appears to have been destroyed by Semtex, then left for insurance assessors who never turned up.

I'm talking to a silver-haired man who's nursing a hangover after a four o'clock finish to last night's Pitch-and-Putt dinner – I'm pretty sure that's what he said – when it dawns on me that it's Billy from up the back lane. We used to play together when we were kids. He's stunned that I remember, and can tell him his name.

'Me own life's a complete blank till the age of fourteen.'

The guy sitting at the table next to me turns out to be a second cousin; so does the eighty-year-old drinking whiskey at the bar, who married my mother's best friend. I'm struggling to decode his accent. I suppose I can understand about sixty per cent of what he's saying. The old West Cork accent, from the distant days before satellite TV, is a very musical thing, but once you lose the tune it's hard to pick it up again. I'm doing my best to follow his conversation with Sean.

'Sure, it's close by the wall so we could pour over some readymix.'

'Readymix might not be the right kind of thing, y'know Dan.'

'We should get the clan together,' says old Dan. 'Make a decision. You promised your father, and so did I.'

Sean explains the situation to me, and we agree to go out in the morning and see what's to be done. As we cross the road for just the one nightcap in the place with the Jim Reeves road-show, there's a gardai car parked near the chip van. There's a rumour a particular officer is overusing the breathalyser in revenge for rumours about his private life, but it isn't a rumour you'd want getting round.

Later, on the way home, passing the neat row of houses where the blacksmith's elemental forge once stood, I'm still marvelling at Dan's use of that word.

Clan.

I was wrong yesterday. There's one more graveyard to visit. It's in a spot called Caheragh, three or four miles away off the Skibbereen road. It's a wild place, not neglected, but remote, and guarded by enormous rooks. The grave is in an unmarked plot close to one wall. Dan was right. It'd be easy to pipe some readymix in, but you really wouldn't want to. After all, this is where our grandmother lies, mine and Sean's; she died giving birth to his father. This was back in the 1920s, and for some reason it was never marked. Sean wants to see to it.

'Nothing too fancy,' he says.

The 1920s. It seems an impossible age ago. Yet I'd known her husband. It was him laughing at me when I was chased by the pig. I look up at Sean, framed against a clear blue early morning sky. However different our lives, we're bound together now, across distance and time, by this woman neither of us ever knew. It's a rare moment, and right that we should be here.

On the way back to the house we stop and go through a rickety gate into a field next to Sean's land. We elbow our way through some stroppy heifers to a huge stone I've seen in the guidebook to Neolithic hot spots that's been kicking around in the Tank all this time. It's a boulder burial.

'Two fellas came from the university. Three thousand years they say it's been here.'

Under the circumstances, a small stone in Caheragh seems the least we can do.

For now though, it's time to go. Get back to England. Away from the graves, and the stones, and the ghosts.

Chapter Seventeen

A Place of Resurrection

'Lost Your Cat? Try Looking Under My Tyres.'

It's noon, and the angelus bell is sounding on the radio as I sit reading the sticker in the rear window of the car in front. The traditional call to prayer seems strangely anachronistic in the new Ireland, though I suppose it's possible that the Dublin traffic has come to a standstill because the drivers still feel a spiritual compulsion to observe the holy moment. So perhaps it's prayer, not profanity, making that taxi driver's lips move.

Since reaching the outskirts of the city I've been trying to find the Port of Dun Laoghaire by faithfully following road signs showing a big picture of a boat. I now know that the only longer route to the ferry port would have involved a diversion via Derry and the Blasket Islands. For my last night in the country I treat myself to a room with a sea view in one of the nineteenth-century hotels on the waterfront. My boat sails at ten past eleven in the morning to 'dismal Holyhead' in 'dismal Anglesea', as Thackeray described it. I expect he was thinking of a different Holyhead.

I'd never intended to take the Tank back to England. The plan had always been to get rid of it over here, though there was never much chance of selling it in a nation of actual or newly aspirant BMW drivers. I'd harboured vague notions of donating it to Wild

Mountain or trading it in for a meal at the Convent, or perhaps selling it to someone in the car-hire queue at Cork airport for a fiver, but the simple fact is that I've become too emotionally attached to abandon it; and though a Volvo isn't a naturally demonstrative vehicle, I'm pretty sure it feels the same way.

It's been the only constant in my journey, a steady and supportive travelling companion. It's even got a sense of humour, as the bird up the exhaust so playfully demonstrated. It rattles, it rumbles, and I can't open the bonnet, but I just don't have the heart to ditch it. The landscape of its interior has become as familiar as any in the country, with its giant heated seats, its scattered maps and books, its sleeping bag, sweetie-wrappers, and manure-encrusted floor. I'm resigned to the loss of its wonderful radio phone-ins, and I'll have to get rid of the pile of yellowing newspapers; but the vehicle itself deserves a dignified retirement. I shall buy it a black-market disabled badge in a pub in Brighton, and park it in a no parking zone on Eastbourne seafront. It can look out to sea and listen to old people in beige clothes saying, 'Ooh, look at that! They used to be lovely cars. Built like tanks, they were.'

The rest of the day's my own. I could go into the centre of Dublin for a look round Trinity College, or a stroll on St Stephen's Green and a pint in James Toner's, or tea at the Shelbourne Hotel. To be honest, though, I don't feel terribly motivated to do anything, so I sit with my feet up looking out on the bay. There's a magazine for businessmen on the bedside locker, and I can't resist the guilty frisson of looking through it without being a businessman. There's hardly anything to read, just glossy adverts for conference centres, and club-class airlines, and call girls who'll show up in your hotel room but not on your credit card statement. But one ad catches my eye. THE IRISH PUB, it says. A MAJOR INVESTMENT OPPORTUNITY. 'In more than a hundred cities worldwide, from Madrid to Moscow, Paris to Prague, Helsinki to Hong Kong, Abu Dhabi to Atlanta, a new generation of Irish pubs continues to prosper, with a new one opening almost every day somewhere around the world . . .'

There's a picture of a smiling barman serving a pint, and

people playing flutes and bodhrans in front of a roaring log fire in Bangkok. It reminds me of how I began, in Budapest. There's a phone number, and an address in Dublin 2.

An hour later I'm sitting in a meeting-room with Paul from Marketing, wondering where are the most unlikely places they've opened up recently.

'Uzbekistan. Kazakstan. Siberia. Las Vegas. At the moment it seems unstoppable. We're riding the crest of a wave.'

So what is this Irishness they're selling? Are people buying into James Joyce and Oscar Wilde? Van Morrison and U2? Identifying with the underdog, and the romance of rebellion? Or have they just heard the Irish are good drinkers, and want some glory by association?

'None of these things really, though some of them help. You have to remember that in many of these places they have no idea where Ireland is, and may never have heard of it. Italy was different. Our football fans went there in '92, had a hooley, and the place went mental. We put in seventy pubs in less than a year. And the Italians are like us. They value family and religion, and having a good time because you're a long time dead. But Italy's an exception.'

So what are they selling to the rest of the world then?

'Sociability and warmth. People are buying into the concept of sitting down and talking to someone you haven't met before. We're creating an atmosphere that persuades people to go and frequent a pub in countries where they don't frequent pubs. We're changing habits.'

Irish staff – at the very least, an Irish manager – is crucial to success.

'The Irish are very good at breaking down the programming that different societies have built into them. So instead of asking for something, and getting served, you get human contact from across the counter. The Americans always have problems with this, that there's no corporate formula. We try and de-programme the staff and encourage them to be themselves. If anyone says, "Hi, I'm Dale and I'll be your server tonight," he's fired. We can't tolerate that sort of shite.'

We go out for a pint and something to eat in a mock-traditional pub they've built in a 1960s hotel in suburban Dublin. After all the time I've spent in the real thing recently, it's a rather unsettling experience.

After lunch, as we drive to their showroom, Dublin resident Elvis Costello is on the radio. I wonder if music is important to their operation.

'It's crucial in controlling people's moods through the day. So you'd get, say, Planxty at lunchtime, then Enya in the afternoon so they'll chill out and stay longer. Crank it up a bit in the evening. The Cranberries maybe, or "Brown Eyed Girl".'

But they aren't listening to the same music in Las Vegas and Uzbekistan, are they, in the same order?

'Er, yeah, they are. It's programmed in advance.'

We go to a warehouse full of old bicycles and staircases, agricultural machinery, jars and bottles and fading tobacco ads.

'You have to remember that Irish pubs were originally community centres, and the best ones still are. So in our pubs eighteen-year-olds are happy to sit alongside sixty-five-year-olds. It adds authenticity. Drink was always an element, but it was never the key element. D'you know we're barely midway in the European alcohol consumption league? They may find this amusing in England, but the Irish have never been big drinkers.'

One side of the showroom that fronts the warehouse contains newly made Victorian hardwood bars and cupboards, and repro Guinness ads; the other, though, is unashamedly modernist. There are smoked-glass tables, chrome bar stools, designer chairs, and all manner of avant-garde knick-knackery.

'The old stuff's for overseas. The new stuff's for Ireland. Dublin mostly. Things are changing. Traditional design is synonymous with the past. They want to sit at glass tables now, with weird chairs, and good-looking women.'

I like Paul for his honesty, for not trying to put a phoney gloss on what they're doing. And one of the things they're doing is making a lot of money. Before I get my taxi to Dun Laoghaire he has a final word.

'We're not saying that hospitality is unique to Ireland. Look at Spain or Italy. Even the States. But we're unique in packaging and marketing it.'

In the back of the cab I'm thinking that what Paul's company is doing is, in essence, also the policy of the whole massively successful Irish tourist industry. Literature and history and landscape and fishing are all add-ons; but what the country has been selling itself on is warmth and conviviality. The fear must be that the process will change the reality; that warmth and conviviality, like other resources, may turn out to be finite. Marketing, of course, is eternal.

We're back in Dun Laoghaire in no time. I've been so preoccupied with my thoughts I haven't even had a chance to ask the driver what he thinks. Miserable, unsociable English bastard, I expect.

I'd like to eat at the sexy-looking bistro that's been incorporated into the old Dun Laoghaire railway station; but there's a Chinese restaurant just up the road, and duty, research and a sense of what is appropriate require I go there for my farewell dinner. In this most sociable of countries, where I have spent the afternoon discussing the virtues of talking to strangers, I'm once again dining alone.

The food is excellent, especially the Singapore noodles, and once again grotesquely expensive. I read today that Ireland is now the second most prosperous country in Europe, after Luxembourg. It had always been one of my ambitions to eat Chinese food in Luxembourg, but now I'll be crossing it off the list.

As I collect my key at hotel reception a boob-tubed English woman and her crop-topped daughter, drunk as skunks the pair of them, are asking after the taxi that's meant to be taking them to the nightclub.

'Oh, and here,' says Mum, passing the duty manager a half-empty bottle of vodka, 'can you put that in the little boxy thing with me key.'

'You can tell you're not Irish,' says the manager as a parting shot as they leave.

You know, I haven't a clue what he meant by that.

Up in my room all the English TV channels are on tap, but it would feel a kind of betrayal to watch the BBC on my last night. The programmes on Irish TV are all crap, though, so I don't watch them either. There's a radio implanted in my headboard, so I lie down and listen to that.

As chance would have it, there's a feature about the lax planning regulations of the last twenty years, which are now turning out to be not entirely unconnected with corruption. A posh architectural expert from England is asked for his opinion of the aesthetic damage that's been done by inappropriate styles of building, and the discussion inevitably moves on to the use of UPVC.

'It is a hideous material,' he simpers, 'amoral, and promiscuous in its ubiquity.'

'But these days,' says the interviewer, 'designs have got better. They're making UPVC windows now that look just like wooden sash windows.'

'Even worse. The one indisputable principle of modernism is that a material should be true to itself and never pretend to be something it is not. What will happen in Ireland is what is happening in England now, where the supposedly everlasting windows and doors are looking so shabby they're being replaced with the wooden ones that were ripped out twenty years ago. It really is a del–isshus irony.'

The phone is ringing, but it sounds a long way away, almost as if it's coming from outside. I walk across to the window to look out, only to see a large old-fashioned boat steaming away. The people on board are waving to me. Then something catches my eye. The white plastic window frame is split, and a chunk has fallen to the floor. Behind the façade the insides are revealed. I stoop to examine them.

Noodles.

The UPVC windows all across the country are manufactured from compressed noodles! No wonder they cost an arm and a leg in restaurants. Building contractors and corrupt politicians have cornered the market and forced up the price. I'll ring one of the phone-ins tomorrow. Better answer that phone now though. Where is it?

'Hello?'

'Mr McCarthy? This is your alarm call. It's half seven.'

I'm still dressed. I get up from the bed, pull back the curtains, and glorious sunshine streams in through wooden sash windows.

After breakfast I take a stroll along the waterfront to the martello tower at Sandycove. There's the first chill of autumn in the air, but the sea is eerily still, and the brilliance and clarity of the light make me feel like I've landed in a fictional small-town port that has broken loose from Dylan Thomas's imagination and drifted across the Irish Sea. Elegant fanlights sit above imposing Georgian front doors painted rich hues of red, green, blue, and yellow. Low grassy dunes run down from garden gates, before giving way to the rockpools of the foreshore. A few bright-eyed early risers are out walking or cycling, as if they've been placed in the shot by a director. It feels so perfect, so overtly fictional that at one point I feel slightly dizzy, and stop to sit on a stone bench.

As I round the headland at the foot of the martello tower, people are swimming in the sea, climbing down the rocks on a metal ladder, and diving from higher up. 'Forty Foot Gentlemen's Bathing Place' says a sign. This is where the men of Dublin – and latterly, I'm told, the women, though there are none in evidence today – have traditionally exercised their right to bathe nude. On one of the rocks a naked elderly gentleman is flaunting himself, hands on hips, like a catalogue underwear model without any underwear.

I walk as far as the tower, which is now a James Joyce museum, but I've no mood for museums today. I'm thinking of what Dara Malloy said that day on Inishmore, when we walked down from the fort together. He'd been talking about the magic that some places hold, that special feeling that embraces landscape and history and our personal associations, but somehow goes beyond the sum of them.

'Energy. Spirit. Even faeries – call it what you like. It's just words to describe a real experience we can't explain when we get that shiver or the hairs stand up. The word doesn't matter. The feeling is real, and you cannot deny it.'

So what, I asked him, about my feeling? Was a true sense of belonging here possible for me; or was I just another victim of the ruthless marketing of sentimental Irishness?

'No, I don't think it's that. But nor do I think it's genetic memory. And I wouldn't think it's so simple as happy childhood summers, though that's obviously played a part.'

We stopped at a stone structure, a waist-high flat slab supported by two uprights. In recent times the islanders had used it to butcher sheep, though no one seemed sure how long it had been there.

'I think everyone has an inner voice, and we can all learn to listen to it. You don't need to analyse where it comes from, but you can attune yourself to it. If you can learn to follow it, it will lead to fulfilment. That's why I came here.'

We walked on down the hill to the road above his house, looking across to Connemara.

'The Celtic monks would wander round Europe until they found the place that was calling to them. Then they'd settle and make their community there. They had an expression for it: seeking their place of resurrection. They believed they were beneath that spot in the firmament that would one day lead them to heaven.'

I'm looking out to sea watching a ferry coming in when I realise it's the one that will take me back to England. I look at my watch. Better get a move on.

As I pass the forty-foot pool, a man of sixty or so is sitting on the wall, shirt and trousers on, drying his feet.

'Ah, what's the hurry?'

Just like the old man who stopped me in Westport that morning.

'Have a swim, why don't you? You need no togs, nor even a towel. Go on. It's the best thing in the world. Twenty-five years I've been doing this, and I never felt more alive.'

'I can't. I've a boat to catch.'

'What part of England are you from? I was down near Bristol a little while ago. Beautiful part of the world. My parents always told me the best things in life were free, but of course I had to go the other way before I ended up swimming here and believing them. I tell you though, this is the place to be now.'

'This pool?'

'No! Dun Laoghaire. Dublin. Ireland. There's a buzz in the air, but people still have time for you. Still talk to you.'

I wish I was making him up, but I'm not. He's real. There he stands, large as fiction, as if he's been sent along by an another author to provide my final conversation. He's looking me in the eye, and I know what he's going to say, but he's going to say it anyway.

'This'd be a place for you to live.'

He holds my gaze for a second or two, then goes back to drying his feet.

'Good luck now.'

Yeah. Good luck.

Acknowledgements

I am grateful to many people in Ireland for their help, hospitality, and stories, in particular Adrienne MacCarthy, Dominic Mogridge, Paul Buckley, Con McLoughlin, Karen Austin, Noel Mannion, Sean McCarthy, Con McCarthy, Connie Murphy and Dara Molloy. I am indebted to Sebastian Barfield for research, and to Angela Herlihy and Mary Pachnos for professional wisdom and infectious enthusiasm. I also thank my family for their support, and for keeping straight faces whenever I referred to wandering round the mountains and bars of the west of Ireland as 'going to work'. No job was ever this much fun.

I took some books with me, and picked up others along the way. They include: *The Irish Sketchbook 1842*, W. M Thackeray (Sutton, 1990); *The Trouble with the Irish (or the English Depending on Your Point of View)*, L. P. O'Connor Wibberley (Holt & Co., NY, 1956); *West Cork, A Sort of History, Like,* Tony Brehony (Kestrel, 1997); *Exploring West Cork,* Jack Roberts (Key, 1988); *A Doctor's War*, Aidan MacCarthy (Robson, 1979); *Discover Dursey,* Penelope Durrell (Ballinacarriga, 1996); *Father's Music,* Dermot Bolger (Flamingo, 1998); *Roadkill,* Kinky Friedman (Faber and Faber, 1998); *Pocket Guide to Árainn – Legends in the Landscape,* Dara O'Maoildhia (Aisling Árann, 1998); *Beara – A Journey Through History*, Daniel M. O'Brien (Beara Historical Society, 1991); *Westport House and the Brownes*, the 10th Marquess of Sligo (Westport House, 1998); and *Illustrated Road Book of Ireland* (Automobile Association 1963). In case you're thinking of writing to the Tourist Board for a copy of *100 Best B&Bs Run By Mad Nosey Religious Fanatics*, I made that one up.

I'd also like to thank the late Mike Mann. Not for anything in particular, I'd just like to thank him, that's all. Come to think of it, he did let me write the prologue in his kitchen.

P McC, March 2000